# Step by Step

Microsoft® Office
# Excel 2003

Curtis Frye

PUBLISHED BY
Microsoft Press
A Division of Microsoft Corporation
One Microsoft Way
Redmond, Washington 98052-6399

Library of Congress Cataloging-in-Publication Data
Frye, Curtis, 1968-
        Microsoft Office Excel 2003 Step by Step / Curtis Frye.
            p. cm.
        Includes index.
        ISBN 0-7356-1518-7
        1. Microsoft Excel (Computer file)   2. Business--Computer programs.   3. Electronic
    spreadsheets.   I. Title.

        HF5548.4.M523F8   2003
        005.369-dc21                                              2003052689

Printed and bound in the United States of America.

5 6 7 8 9    QWE    8 7 6 5 4

Distributed in Canada by H.B. Fenn and Company Ltd.

A CIP catalogue record for this book is available from the British Library.

Microsoft Press books are available through booksellers and distributors worldwide. For further information about international editions, contact your local Microsoft Corporation office or contact Microsoft Press International directly at fax (425) 936-7329. Visit our Web site at www.microsoft.com/mspress. Send comments to *mspinput@microsoft.com*.

**Acquisitions Editor:** Alex Blanton
**Project Editor:** Aileen Wrothwell

Body Part No. X09-71434

# Contents

# Contents

# What's New in Microsoft Excel 2003

You'll notice some changes as soon as you start Microsoft Excel 2003. The toolbars and menu bar have a new look, and there are some new task panes available on the right side of your screen. But the features that are new or greatly improved in this version of Excel go beyond just changes in appearance. Some changes won't be apparent to you until you start using the program.

**New in Office 2003**

To help you quickly identify features that are new or greatly enhanced with this version, this book uses the icon in the margin whenever new features are discussed or shown. If you want to learn about only the new features of the program, you can skim through the book, completing only those topics that show this icon.

The following table lists the new features that you might be interested in, as well as the chapters in which those features are discussed.

| To learn how to | Using this new feature | See |
| --- | --- | --- |
| Use online support tools | Research tools | Chapter 1, page 17 |
| Use professional XML data capabilities | XML Source task pane | Chapter 15, page 283 |
| Create a data map | XML Source task pane | Chapter 15, page 284 |
| Define XML elements | XML Source task pane | Chapter 15, page 285 |
| Define XML viewing options | XML Source task pane | Chapter 15, page 286 |

For more information about the Excel product, see *http://www.microsoft.com/office/excel/*.

# Getting Help

Every effort has been made to ensure the accuracy of this book and the contents of its CD-ROM. If you do run into problems, please contact the appropriate source for help and assistance.

## Getting Help with This Book and Its CD-ROM

If your question or issue concerns the content of this book or its companion CD-ROM, please first search the online Microsoft Knowledge Base, which provides support information for known errors in or corrections to this book, at the following Web site:

*http://mspress.microsoft.com/support/search.asp*

If you do not find your answer at the online Knowledge Base, send your comments or questions to Microsoft Press Technical Support at:

*mspinput@microsoft.com*

## Getting Help with Microsoft Excel 2003

If your question is about a Microsoft software product, including Excel, and not about the content of this Microsoft Press book, please search the Microsoft Knowledge Base at:

*http://support.microsoft.com/directory*

In the United States, Microsoft software product support issues not covered by the Microsoft Knowledge Base are addressed by Microsoft Product Support Services. The Microsoft software support options available from Microsoft Product Support Services are listed at:

*http://support.microsoft.com/directory*

Outside the United States, for support information specific to your location, please refer to the Worldwide Support menu on the Microsoft Product Support Services Web site for the site specific to your country:

*http://support.microsoft.com/directory*

# Using the Book's CD-ROM

The CD-ROM inside the back cover of this book contains all the practice files you'll use as you work through the exercises in the book. By using practice files, you won't waste time creating samples and typing spreadsheet data—instead, you can jump right in and concentrate on learning how to use Microsoft Office Excel 2003.

**Important** This book does not contain the Excel 2003 software. You should purchase and install that program before using this book.

## Minimum System Requirements

To use this book, you will need:

- **Computer/Processor**

  Computer with a Pentium 133-megahertz (MHz) or higher processor

- **Operating System**

  Microsoft Windows 2000 with Service Pack 3 (SP3) or Microsoft Windows XP or later operating system

- **Memory**

  64 MB of RAM (128 MB recommended) plus an additional 8 MB of RAM for each program in the Microsoft Office System (such as Word) running simultaneously

- **Hard Disk**

  Hard disk space requirements will vary depending on configuration; custom installation choices may require more or less hard disk space.

  - 245 MB of available hard disk space with 115 MB on the hard disk where the operating system is installed.

  - An additional 4 MB of hard disk space is required for installing the practice files.

- **Drive**

  CD-ROM drive

- **Display**

  Super VGA (800 × 600) or higher-resolution monitor with 256 colors or higher

■ **Peripherals**

Microsoft Mouse, Microsoft IntelliMouse, or compatible pointing device

■ **Applications**

Microsoft Office Excel 2003, Microsoft Office PowerPoint 2003, Microsoft Outlook Express or Microsoft Office Outlook 2003, Internet Explorer version 5 or later

# Installing the Practice Files

You need to install the practice files on your hard disk before you use them in the chapters' exercises. Follow these steps to prepare the CD's files for your use:

**1** Insert the CD-ROM into the CD-ROM drive of your computer.

The Step by Step Companion CD End User License Agreement appears.

**Important** If the license agreement screen does not appear, start Windows Explorer. In the left pane, locate the icon for your CD-ROM drive and click the icon. In the right pane, double-click the file named **StartCD** or **StartCD.exe**.

It is necessary to accept the terms of the license agreement in order to use the practice files. After you accept the license agreement, the Step by Step Companion CD menu appears.

**2** Click **Install Practice Files**.

**3** Click **Next** on the first screen, and then click **Yes** to accept the license agreement on the next screen.

**4** If you want to install the practice files to a location other than the default folder (C:\SBS\Excel), click the **Browse** button, select the new drive and path, and then click **OK**.

**5** Click **Next** on the **Select Features** screen and then click **Next** on the **Start Copying Files** screen to install the selected practice files.

**6** After the practice files have been installed, click **Finish**.

Within the installation folder are subfolders for each chapter in the book.

**7** Remove the CD-ROM from the CD-ROM drive, and return it to the envelope at the back of the book.

# Using the Practice Files

Each topic in the chapter explains how and when to use any practice files. The file or files that you'll need are indicated at the beginning of the procedure in blue type, as shown here:

Open: SampleFile from the *SBS\Excel\SampleFolder* folder.

Usually you will be instructed to open the practice files from within Excel. However, you can also access the files directly from Windows by clicking **Start**, **All Programs**, **Microsoft Press**, **Excel 2003 Step by Step**. Locate the file in the chapter subfolder and double-click to open it.

The following table lists each chapter's practice files.

| Chapter | Folder | Files |
|---------|--------|-------|
| 1 | GettingToKnowXL | FileOpen, ZeroIn, DataEntry, and Replace |
| 2 | SettingUpWorkbook | Easier, DataRead, and AddPicture |
| 3 | PerformingCalculations | NameRange, Formula, and FindErrors |
| 4 | ChangingDocAppearance | Formats, CreateNew, EasyRead, Conditional, Follow, and Margins |
| 5 | UsingFilters | Filter, Calculations, and Validate |
| 6 | MultipleSources | TemplateStart, January, February, March, Linking, 2001Q1, Consolidate, TotalByHour2001, Y2001Q1, and Y2001ByMonth |
| 7 | ReorderingAndSummarizing | Sorting and Levels |
| 8 | AnalyzingAlternativeDataSets | Defining, Multiple, GoalSeek, Solver, and Descriptive |
| 9 | PivotTable | CreatePivot, EditPivot, Export, and External |
| 10 | Charts | CreateChart, Customize, TrendLine, Dynamic, and Diagrams |
| 11 | Printing | Printing, Part, and PrintChart |

*(continued)*

| Chapter | Folder | Files |
|---------|--------|-------|
| 12 | Macros | View, Record, Toolbar, Menu, and RunOnOpen |
| 13 | OtherPrograms | Include, YearEndSummary, Worksheet, SalesByCategory, Hyperlink, ProductList, PasteChart, and ChartTarget |
| 14 | Database | Lookup, Query, Products, and Summary |
| 15 | Web | Saving, Publish, Pivot, WebData, Smart, and Structured |
| 16 | Collaborating | Sharing, Comments, Tracking, MergeTarget, Owner, Buyer, Protection, and Signature |

# Uninstalling the Practice Files

After you finish working through this book, you should uninstall the practice files to free up hard disk space.

**1** On the Windows taskbar, click the **Start** button, point to **Settings**, and then click **Control Panel**.

**2** Double-click the **Add or Remove Programs** icon.

**3** Click **Microsoft Office Excel 2003 Step by Step**, and click **Change/Remove**.

**4** Click **OK** when the confirmation dialog box appears.

> **Important** If you need additional help installing or uninstalling the practice files, please see the section "Getting Help" earlier in this book. Microsoft's product support does not provide support for this book or its CD-ROM.

# Conventions and Features

You can save time when you use this book by understanding how the Step by Step series shows special instructions, keys to press, buttons to click, and so on.

| Convention | Meaning |
|---|---|
| **1**<br>**2** | Numbered steps guide you through hands-on exercises in each topic. |
| ● | A round bullet indicates an exercise that has only one step. |
| (CD icon) | This icon at the beginning of a chapter lists the files that the lesson will use and explains any file preparation that needs to take place before starting the lesson. |
| OPEN: Practice File | Practice files that you'll need to use in a topic's procedure are shown. |
| *Microsoft Office Specialist* | This icon indicates a section that covers a Microsoft Office Specialist (MOS) exam objective. |
| *New in Office 2003* | This icon indicates a new or greatly improved feature in this version of Microsoft Excel. |
| **Tip** | This section provides a helpful hint or shortcut that makes working through a task easier. |
| **Important** | This section points out information that you need to know to complete the procedure. |
| **Troubleshooting** | This section shows you how to fix a common problem. |
| (Save button icon)<br>Save | When a button is referenced in a topic, a picture of the button appears in the margin area with a label. |
| [Alt]+[Tab] | A plus sign (+) between two key names means that you must press those keys at the same time. For example, "Press [Alt]+[Tab]" means that you hold down the Alt key while you press Tab. |

*(continued)*

| Convention | Meaning |
| --- | --- |
| **Boldface type** | Program features that you click or press are shown in black boldface type. |
| *Blue italic type* | Terms that are explained in the glossary at the end of the book are shown in blue italic type within the chapter. |
| Blue type | Text that you are supposed to type appears in blue boldface type in the procedures. |

# Microsoft Office Specialist Skills Standards

Each Microsoft Office Specialist certification has a set of corresponding skill standards that describe areas of individual, Microsoft Office program use. You should master each skill standard to fully prepare for the corresponding Microsoft Office Specialist certification exam.

This book will fully prepare you for the Microsoft Office Specialist certification at either the Specialist or the Expert level. Throughout this book, content that pertains to a Microsoft Office Specialist skills standard is identified with the following Microsoft Office Specialist logo in the margin:

**Microsoft Office Specialist**

## Microsoft Office Specialist Skill Standards

| Skill Number | Skill Set and Skills | Page |
|---|---|---|
| **XL03S-1** | **Creating Data and Content** | |
| XL03S-1-1 | Enter and edit cell content | 11, 17 |
| XL03S-1-2 | Navigate to specific cell content | 17, 291 |
| XL03S-1-3 | Locate, select, and insert supporting information | 17 |
| XL03S-1-4 | Insert, position, and size graphics | 34 |
| **XL03S-2** | **Analyzing Data** | |
| XL03S-2-1 | Filter lists using AutoFilter | 84 |
| XL03S-2-2 | Sort lists | 120 |
| XL03S-2-3 | Insert and modify formulas | 44 |
| XL03S-2-4 | Use statistical, date and time, financial, and logical functions | 44 |
| XL03S-2-5 | Create, modify, and position diagrams and charts based on worksheet data | 174, 190 |

*(continued)*

| Skill Number | Skill Set and Skills | Page |
|---|---|---|
| **XL03S-3** | **Formatting Data and Content** | |
| XL03S-3-1 | Apply and modify cell formats | 58 |
| XL03S-3-2 | Apply and modify cell styles | 62 |
| XL03S-3-3 | Modify row and column formats | 25, 58 |
| XL03S-3-4 | Format worksheets | 101 |
| **XL03S-4** | **Collaborating** | |
| XL03S-4-1 | Insert, view, and edit comments | 291 |
| **XL03S-5** | **Managing Workbooks** | |
| XL03S-5-1 | Create new workbooks from templates | 98 |
| XL03S-5-2 | Insert, delete, and move cells | 25 |
| XL03S-5-3 | Create and modify hyperlinks | 239 |
| XL03S-5-4 | Organize worksheets | 25, 101 |
| XL03S-5-5 | Preview data in other views | 101, 197 |
| XL03S-5-6 | Customize window layout | 32, 98 |
| XL03S-5-7 | Set up pages for printing | 73, 76 |
| XL03S-5-8 | Print data | 197 |
| XL03S-5-9 | Organize workbooks using file folders | 3, 266 |
| XL03S-5-10 | Save data in appropriate formats for different uses | 3 |

# Microsoft Office Specialist Expert Skill Standards

| Skill Number | Skill Set and Skills | Page |
|---|---|---|
| **XL03E-1** | **Organizing and Analyzing Data** | |
| XL03E-1-1 | Use subtotals | 89 |
| XL03E-1-2 | Define and apply advanced filters | 84 |
| XL03E-1-3 | Group and outline data | 124 |
| XL03E-1-4 | Use data validation | 91 |
| XL03E-1-5 | Create and modify list ranges | 280 |
| XL03E-1-6 | Add, show, close, edit, merge, and summarize scenarios | 132 |

*(continued)*

# Taking a Microsoft Office Specialist Certification Exam

As desktop computing technology advances, more employers rely on the objectivity and consistency of technology certification when screening, hiring, and training employees to ensure the competence of these professionals. As a job seeker or employee, you can use technology certification to prove that you have the skills businesses need, and can save them the trouble and expense of training. Microsoft Office Specialist is the only Microsoft certification program designed to assist employees in validating their Microsoft Office skills.

## About the Microsoft Office Specialist Program

A Microsoft Office Specialist is an individual who has demonstrated, worldwide standards of Microsoft Office skill via a certification exam in one or more of the Microsoft Office desktop programs including Microsoft Word, Excel, PowerPoint, Outlook, Access, and Project. Microsoft Office Specialist certifications are available at the Specialist and Expert skill levels. Visit *http://www.microsoft.com/officespecialist* to locate skill standards for each certification and an Authorized Testing Center in your area.

### What Does This Logo Mean?

This Microsoft Office Specialist logo means this courseware has been approved by the Microsoft Office Specialist Program to be among the finest available for learning Excel 2003. It also means that upon completion of this courseware, you may be prepared to become a Microsoft Office Specialist.

## Selecting a Microsoft Office Specialist Certification Level

In selecting the Microsoft Office Specialist certification(s) level that you would like to pursue, you should assess the following:

- The Office program ("program") and version(s) of that program with which you are familiar

- The length of time you have used the program

- Whether you have had formal or informal training in the use of that program

Candidates for Specialist-level certification are expected to successfully complete a wide range of standard business tasks, such as formatting a document or spreadsheet. Successful candidates generally have six or more months of experience with the program, including either formal instructor-led training or self-study using Microsoft Office Specialist–approved books, guides, or interactive computer-based materials.

Candidates for Expert-level certification are expected to complete more complex, business-oriented tasks utilizing the program's advanced functionality, such as importing data and recording macros. Successful candidates generally have one or more years of experience with the program, including formal instructor-led training or self-study using Microsoft Office Specialist–approved materials.

# Microsoft Office Specialist Skills Standards

Every Microsoft Office Specialist certification exam is developed from a set of exam skills standards that are derived from studies of how the Office program is used in the workplace. Because these skills standards dictate the scope of each exam, they provide you with critical information on how to prepare for certification.

---

**See Also**   See "Microsoft Office Specialist Skills Standards" on page xvii for a complete list of skills standards for Excel.

---

Microsoft Office Specialist–Approved Courseware, including the Microsoft Press Step by Step series, are reviewed and approved on the basis of their coverage of the Microsoft Office Specialist skills standards.

# The Exam Experience

Microsoft Office Specialist certification exams for Office 2003 programs are performanced-based exams that require you to complete 15 to 20 standard business tasks using an interactive simulation (that is, digital models) of a Microsoft Office program. Exam questions can have one, two, or three task components, which, for example, require you to create or modify a document or spreadsheet:

Modify the existing brochure by completing the following three tasks:

**1**   Left-align the heading *Premium Real Estate*.

**2**   Insert a footer with right-aligned page numbering. (Note: accept all other default settings.)

**3**   Save the document with the file name **Broker Brochure** in the My Documents folder.

Candidates should also be aware that each exam must be completed within an alloted time of 45 minutes and that, in the interest of test security and fairness, the Office Help system (including the Office Assistant) cannot be accessed during the exam.

Passing standards (that is, minimum required score) for Microsoft Office Specialist certification exams range from 60 to 85 percent correct, depending on the exam.

## The Exam Interface and Controls

The exam interface and controls, including the test question, appear across the bottom of the screen.

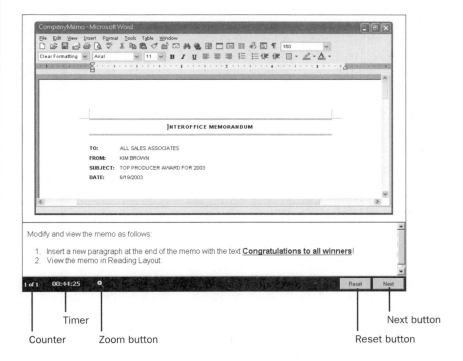

- The **Counter** is located in the left corner of the exam interface and tracks the number of questions completed and how many questions remain.

- The **Timer** is located to the right of the **Counter** and starts when the first question appears on the screen. The **Timer** displays the remaining exam time. If the **Timer** is distracting, click the **Timer** to remove the display.

  **Important**   Transition time between questions is not counted against total allotted exam time.

- The **Zoom** icon is located to the right of the **Timer** on the exam interface. It lets you increase or decrease the font size of the question text by clicking the plus or minus symbol.

■ The **Reset** button is located to the left of the **Next** button and will restart a question if you believe you have made an error. The **Reset** button will not restart the entire exam nor extend the total allotted exam time.

■ The **Next** button is located in the right corner. When you complete a question, click the **Next** button to move to the next question. It is not possible to move back to a previous question on the exam.

# Test-Taking Tips

■ Follow all instructions provided in each question completely and accurately.

■ Enter requested information as it appears in the instructions, but without duplicating the format. For example, all text and values that you will be asked to enter will appear in the instructions with bold and underlined text formats (for example, **text**); however, you should enter the information without applying these formats unless you are specifically instructed to do otherwise.

■ Close all dialog boxes before proceeding to the next exam question unless you are specifically instructed otherwise.

■ There is no need to close task panes before proceeding to the next exam question unless you are specifically instructed otherwise.

■ There is no need to save your work before moving on to the next question unless you are specifically instructed to do otherwise.

■ For questions that ask you to print a document, spreadsheet, chart, report, slide, and so on, please be aware that nothing will actually be printed.

■ Responses are scored based on the result of your work, not the method you use to achieve that result (unless a specific method is indicated in the instructions), and not the time you take to complete the question. Extra keystrokes or mouse clicks do not count against your score.

■ If your computer becomes unstable during the exam (for example, if the exam does not respond or the mouse no longer functions) or if a power outage occurs, contact a testing center administrator immediately. The administrator will restart the computer and return the exam to the point where the interruption occurred with your score intact.

## Certification

At the conclusion of the exam, you will receive a score report, which you can print with the assistance of the testing center administrator. If your score meets or exceeds the passing standard (that is, minimum required score), you will also be mailed a printed certificate within approximately 14 days.

## College Credit Recommendation

The American Council on Education (ACE) has issued a one-semester-hour college credit recommendation for each Microsoft Office Specialist certification. To learn more, visit *www.microsoft.com/traincert/mcp/officespecialist/credit.asp.*

# For More Information

To learn more about Microsoft Office Specialist certification, visit *www.microsoft.com/ officespecialist.*

# Quick Reference

**3** In the **Replace with** box, type the word or text you want to substitute for the text in the **Find what** box.

**4** Click **Find Next**.

**5** Click **Replace** to replace the value in the highlighted cell.

Page 5 **To replace cell data manually**

**1** Click the cell with the data to be replaced.

**2** Type the new data, and press Enter.

Page 6 **To modify cell data manually**

**1** Click the cell with the data to be modified.

**2** Click anywhere in the formula bar.

**3** Edit the cell contents in the formula bar, and press Enter.

Page 20 **To change an action**

**1** Click the **Undo** button to remove the last change.

**2** Click the **Redo** button to reinstate the last change you removed.

Page 20 **To check spelling**

● On the Standard toolbar, click the **Spelling** button.

Page 21 **To improve word choice using the Thesaurus**

**1** On the **Tools** menu, click **Research**.

**2** In the **Research** task pane, type the word to look up in the **Search For** box.

**3** Click the **Reference** down arrow, select **Thesaurus: English (U.S.)** from the list, and click the **Start Searching** button.

Page 21 **To use online research tools**

**1** On the **Tools** menu, click **Research**.

**2** In the **Research** task pane, type the word to look up in the **Search For** box.

**3** Click the **Reference** down arrow, select the source in which you want to research from the list, and click the **Start Searching** button.

Chapter 2 **Setting Up a Workbook**

Page 29 **To name a worksheet**

**1** In the lower left corner of the workbook window, right-click the desired sheet tab.

**2** From the shortcut menu that appears, click **Rename**.

**3** Type the new name for the worksheet, and press Enter.

**To reposition a worksheet**

● Click the sheet tab of the worksheet you want to move, and drag it to the new position on the tab bar.

**To change the default number of worksheets**

**1** On the **Tools** menu, click **Options**.

**2** In the **Options** dialog box, click the **General** tab, and, in the **Sheets In New Workbook** box, type the number of worksheets you want in your new workbooks.

**3** Click **OK**.

**To adjust column width**

● Position the mouse pointer over an edge of the column head of the column to be resized, and drag the edge to the side.

**To adjust row height**

● Position the mouse pointer over an edge of the row head in the row to be resized, and drag the edge up or down.

**To merge cells**

**1** Select the cells to be merged.

**2** On the Formatting toolbar, click the **Merge and Center** toolbar button.

**To add cells to a worksheet**

**1** On the **Insert** menu, click **Cells**.

**2** In the **Insert** dialog box, select the option button indicating whether to shift the cells surrounding the inserted cell down (if your data is arranged as a column) or to the right (if your data is arranged as a row).

**3** Click **OK**.

**To move cells within a worksheet**

**1** Select the cells and click the **Cut** toolbar button.

**2** On the **Insert** menu, click **Cut Cells**.

**3** In the **Insert Paste** dialog box, select the option button indicating whether to shift the cells surrounding the inserted cell down (if your data is arranged as a column) or to the right (if your data is arranged as a row).

**4** Click **OK**.

**To delete cells from a worksheet**

**1** Select the cells to delete and, on the **Edit** menu, click **Delete**.

**2** In the **Delete** dialog box, select the option button indicating whether to shift the cells surrounding the deleted cells up (if your data is arranged as a column) or to the left (if your data is arranged as a row).

**3** Click **OK**.

**To add a row or column**

**1** Click any cell in the row below which you want the new row to appear, or click any cell in the column to the right of which you want the new column to appear.

**2** On the **Insert** menu, click **Rows** or **Columns**.

**To hide a row or column**

**1** Select any cell in the row or column to be hidden.

**2** On the **Format** menu, point to **Row** or **Column** and then click **Hide**.

**To unhide a row or column**

● On the **Format** menu, point to **Row** or **Column** and then click **Unhide**.

**To prevent text spillover**

**1** Click the desired cell.

**2** On the **Format** menu, click **Cells**.

**3** If necessary, click the **Alignment** tab.

**4** Select the **Wrap Text** check box, and click **OK**.

**To control how text appears in a cell**

**1** Click the desired cell.

**2** On the **Format** menu, click **Cells**.

**3** Use the controls in the **Format Cells** dialog box to change the appearance of the cell text.

**To freeze column headings**

**1** Click the first cell in the row below the rows you want to freeze.

**2** On the **Window** menu, click **Freeze Panes**.

**To unfreeze column headings**

● On the **Window** menu, click **Unfreeze Panes**.

Page 35    **To add a picture to a worksheet**

    **1**    Click the cell into which you want to add the picture.

    **2**    On the **Insert** menu, point to **Picture** and then click **From File**.

    **3**    Navigate to the folder with the picture file, and then double-click the file name.

Page 36    **To change a picture's properties**

    **1**    Right-click the graphic, and from the shortcut menu that appears, click **Format Picture**.

    **2**    Use the controls in the **Format Picture** dialog box to change the picture's properties.

Page 37    **To control contrast of an image**

    **1**    Right-click the graphic, and from the shortcut menu that appears, click **Format Picture**.

    **2**    Click the **Picture** tab.

    **3**    In the **Image Control** section of the dialog box, clear the contents of the **Contrast** box, and type the new contrast value.

Page 37    **To control the brightness of an image**

    **1**    Right-click the graphic, and from the shortcut menu that appears, click **Format Picture**.

    **2**    Click the **Picture** tab.

    **3**    In the **Image Control** section of the dialog box, clear the contents of the **Brightness** box, and type the new brightness value.

Page 37    **To scale and resize graphics**

    **1**    Right-click the graphic, and from the shortcut menu that appears, click **Format Picture**.

    **2**    Click the **Size** tab.

    **3**    Select the **Lock Aspect Ratio** check box if you want to maintain the relationship between the image's height and its width.

    **4**    Type the percentage value you would like the new image to be in the **Height** box.

    **5**    Click **OK**.

Page 37    **To rotate an image**

    **1**    Right-click the graphic, and from the shortcut menu that appears, click **Format Picture**.

    **2**    Click the **Size** tab.

**3**     Type the number of degrees to rotate the image in the **Rotation** box.

Page 37   **To crop an image**

**1**     Right-click the graphic, and from the shortcut menu that appears, click **Format Picture**.

**2**     Click the **Picture** tab.

**3**     In the **Crop From** section of the tab page, type the amount of the image you want to crop in the **Top**, **Bottom**, **Left**, and **Right** boxes.

Page 37   **To add a background image to a worksheet**

**1**     On the **Format** menu, point to **Sheet**, and click **Background**.

**2**     In the **Sheet Background** dialog box, click the image that you want to serve as the background pattern for your worksheet, and click **OK**.

Chapter 3   **Performing Calculations on Data**

Page 42   **To name a range of cells**

**1**     Select the cells to be included in the range.

**2**     Click in the Name box.

**3**     Type the name of the range, and press [Enter].

Page 43   **To name a range of cells using adjacent cell labels**

**1**     Ensure that the desired name for the cell range is in the topmost or leftmost cell of the range.

**2**     Select the cells to be part of the range.

**3**     On the **Insert** menu, point to **Name** and then click **Create**.

**4**     Select the check box indicating the location of the cell with the name for the range, and then click **OK**.

Page 48   **To write a formula**

**1**     Click the cell into which the formula will be written.

**2**     Type an equal sign, and then type the remainder of the formula.

Page 48   **To enter a range into a formula**

**1**     Click the cell into which the formula will be written.

**2**     Type an equal sign, and then type the first part of the formula.

**3**     Select the cells to be used in the formula.

**4**     Finish typing the formula.

**To add cell shading**

**1**   Click the cell to be shaded.

**2**   On the Formatting toolbar, click the **Fill Color** button.

**3**   In the **Fill Color** color palette, click the desired square, and then click **OK**.

**To change row or column alignment**

**1**   Click the header of the row or column you want to change.

**2**   On the Formatting toolbar, click the button corresponding to the alignment you want to apply.

**To create a style**

**1**   On the **Format** menu, click **Style**.

**2**   In the **Style name** box, delete the existing value and then type a name for the new style.

**3**   Click **Modify**, and define the style with the controls of the **Format Cells** dialog box.

**4**   Click **OK** in the **Format Cells** dialog box and the **Styles** dialog box.

**To copy a format**

**1**   Click the cell with the format to be copied.

**2**   On the Standard toolbar, click the **Format Painter** button.

**3**   Click the cell or cells to which the styles will be copied.

**To apply an AutoFormat**

**1**   Select the cells to which you want to apply the **AutoFormat**.

**2**   On the **Format** menu, click **AutoFormat**.

**3**   Select the AutoFormat you want to apply, and then click **OK**.

**To format a number**

**1**   Click the cell with the number to be formatted.

**2**   On the **Format** menu, click **Cells**.

**3**   If necessary, click the **Number** tab.

**4**   In the **Category** list, click the general category for the formatting.

**5**   In the **Type** list, click the specific format, and then click **OK**.

**To format a number as a dollar amount**

**1**   Click the cell with the number to be formatted.

**2**   On the Formatting toolbar, click the **Currency Style** button.

Page 68 **To create a custom format**

**1**  On the **Format** menu, click **Cells**.

**2**  In the **Category** list, click **Custom**.

**3**  In the **Type** list, click the item to serve as the base for the custom style.

**4**  In the **Type** box, modify the item, and then click **OK**.

Page 71 **To create a conditional format**

**1**  Click the cell to be formatted.

**2**  On the **Format** menu, click **Conditional Formatting**.

**3**  In the second list box, click the down arrow and then click the operator to use in the test.

**4**  Type the arguments to use in the condition.

**5**  Click the **Format** button, and use the controls in the **Format Cells** dialog box to create a format for this condition.

**6**  Click **OK**.

Page 72 **To set multiple conditions for a cell**

**1**  Click the cell to be formatted.

**2**  Create a conditional format, and then click **Add**.

**3**  Create a new condition and format in the spaces provided.

Page 74 **To add a header or a footer**

**1**  On the **View** menu, click **Header and Footer**.

**2**  Click the **Custom Header** or **Custom Footer** button.

**3**  Add text or images, and click **OK**.

Page 74 **To add a graphic to a header or footer**

**1**  Create a header or footer.

**2**  Click anywhere in one of the section boxes, and then click the **Insert Picture** button.

**3**  Navigate to the folder with the image file, double-click the file name, and then click **OK**.

Page 78 **To change margins**

**1**  On the Standard toolbar, click the **Print Preview** button.

**2**  Click **Margins**.

**3**  Drag the margin lines in the window to the desired positions.

**To select a random row from a list**

**1**   In the cell next to the first cell with data in it, type **=RAND()<#%**, replacing # with the number that represents the approximate percentage of rows you want to mark as *TRUE*.

**2**   Press [Tab].

**3**   Click the cell into which you entered the **RAND()** formula, grab the fill handle, and drag to the cell next to the last cell in the data column.

**To extract a list of unique values**

**1**   Click the top cell in the column to filter.

**2**   On the **Data** menu, point to **Filter** and then click **Advanced Filter**.

**3**   Select the **Unique records only** check box, and then click **OK**.

**To find a total**

●   Select the cells with the values to be summed. The total appears on the status bar, in the lower right corner of the Excel window.

**To edit a function**

**1**   Click the cell with the function to be edited.

**2**   On the **Insert** menu, click **Function**.

**3**   Edit the function in the **Function** dialog box.

**To set acceptable values for a cell**

**1**   Click the cell to be modified.

**2**   On the **Data** menu, click **Validation**.

**3**   In the **Allow** box, click the down arrow, and from the list that appears, click the type of data to be allowed.

**4**   In the **Data** box, click the down arrow, and from the list that appears, click the comparison operator to be used.

**5**   Type values in the boxes to complete the validation statement.

**6**   Click the **Input Message** tab.

**7**   In the **Title** box, type the title for the message box that appears when the cell becomes active.

**8**   In the **Input Message** box, type the message the user will see in the message box.

**9**   Click the **Error Alert** tab.

**10** In the **Style** box, click the down arrow, and from the list that appears, choose the type of box you want to appear.

**11** In the **Title** box, type the title for the message box that appears when a user enters invalid data.

**12** Type a reminder in the **Error message** box explaining the restriction.

**13** Click **OK**.

**To allow only numeric values in a cell**

**1** Click the cell to be modified.

**2** On the **Data** menu, click **Validation**.

**3** In the **Allow** box, click the down arrow, and from the list that appears, click **Whole number**.

**4** Click **OK**.

**To circle invalid data in a worksheet**

**1** On the **Tools** menu, point to **Formula Auditing**, and click **Show Formula Auditing Toolbar**.

**2** On the **Formula Auditing** toolbar, click the **Circle Invalid Data** button.

**To hide data validation circles**

**1** On the **Tools** menu, point to **Formula Auditing**, and click **Show Formula Auditing Toolbar**.

**2** On the **Formula Auditing Toolbar**, click the **Clear Validation Circles** button.

## Combining Data from Multiple Sources

**To delete a worksheet**

● On the tab bar, in the lower left corner of the workbook window, right-click the tab of the sheet to be deleted, and from the shortcut menu that appears, click **Delete**.

**To save a document as a template**

**1** On the **File** menu, click **Save As**.

**2** Click the **Save as type** down arrow, and click **Template (.xlt)**.

**To edit a template**

**1** Click the template you want to edit, and click **Open**.

**2** Edit the template as if it were any other file.

Page 101    **To change the default location for templates**

1    On the **Tools** menu, click **Options**.

2    If necessary, click the **General** tab.

3    In the **At startup, open all files in** box, type the path of the folder where Excel should look for the files.

4    Click **OK**.

Page 103    **To open multiple workbooks**

1    On the Standard toolbar, click the **Open** button.

2    Hold down [Ctrl] while you click the files to open, and then click **Open**.

Page 104    **To change how a workbook is displayed in Excel**

1    Open the files to be displayed.

2    On the **Window** menu, click **Arrange**.

3    In the **Arrange Windows** dialog box, click the option button corresponding to the desired display pattern and click **OK**.

Page 104    **To insert a worksheet in an existing workbook**

1    On the tab bar, right-click the tab of the sheet to move, and then, from the shortcut menu that appears, click **Move or Copy**.

2    Click the **To book** down arrow, and then, from the list that appears, click the book to which you want to move the worksheet.

3    In the **Before sheet** list, click the sheet to appear behind the moved sheet.

4    At the bottom of the **Move or Copy** dialog box, select the **Create a copy** check box.

5    Click **OK**.

Page 106    **To change worksheet tab colors**

1    On the tab bar, right-click the tab to be changed, and then, from the shortcut menu that appears, click **Tab Color**.

2    Click the square of the desired color, and click **OK**.

Page 108    **To link to a cell in another worksheet**

1    Click the cell from which to link, and then type =.

2    Click the title bar of the workbook containing the cell to link to.

3    Click the cell to link to.

4    Click the title bar of the workbook from which to link, and then press [Enter].

**4** Click the **Then by** down arrow, and then, from the list that appears, click the next column to sort by.

**5** Repeat step 4 with the next **Then by** down arrow.

**6** Click **OK**.

**To set a custom sort order**

**1** Type a custom list and highlight its cells.

**2** On the **Tools** menu, click **Options**.

**3** Click the **Custom Lists** tab.

**4** Click **Import**, and click **OK**.

**To find a subtotal**

**1** Select the rows for which you want to calculate a subtotal.

**2** On the **Data** menu, click **Subtotals**.

**3** Click **OK**.

**To create an outline**

**1** Select the row heads of the rows to be included in the outline.

**2** On the **Data** menu, point to **Group and Outline** and then click **Group**.

**To create an outline with multiple levels**

**1** Select the row heads of the rows to be included in the first, smaller level of the outline.

**2** Select the row heads of the rows to be included in the second, larger level of the outline.

**To hide levels of detail**

● Click the **Hide Detail** button for the level you want to hide.

**To show levels of detail**

● Click the **Show Detail** button for the level you want to show.

**Analyzing Alternative Data Sets**

**To create a scenario**

**1** On the **Tools** menu, click **Scenarios**.

**2** In the **Scenario Manager** dialog box, click **Add**.

**3** In the **Scenario name** box, type the name of the new scenario.

**4** At the right edge of the **Changing cells** box, click the **Collapse Dialog** button.

**5**    Delete the contents of the **Add Scenario** dialog box, and then hold down Ctrl while you click the cells to include in the scenario.

**6**    At the right edge of the **Changing cells** box, click the **Expand Dialog** button.

**7**    Click **OK**.

**8**    In the **Scenario Values** dialog box, enter the alternative values for each cell in the scenario.

**9**    Click **OK**, click **Show**, and then click **Close**.

Page 134    **To edit a scenario**

**1**    On the **Tools** menu, click **Scenarios**.

**2**    In the **Scenario Manager** dialog box, click the name of the scenario to be edited.

**3**    Click **Edit**.

**4**    To change the scenario name, edit the text in the **Scenario name** box.

**5**    To add or delete cells from the scenario, at the right edge of the **Changing cells** box, click the **Collapse Dialog** button.

**6**    Click **OK**.

**7**    In the **Scenario Values** dialog box, enter the alternative values for each cell in the scenario.

**8**    Click **OK**, and click **Close**.

Page 136    **To create multiple scenarios**

**1**    On the **Tools** menu, click **Scenarios**.

**2**    In the **Scenario Manager** dialog box, click **Add**.

**3**    In the **Scenario name** box, type the name of the new scenario.

**4**    At the right edge of the **Changing cells** box, click the **Collapse Dialog** button.

**5**    Delete the contents of the **Add Scenario** dialog box, and then hold down Ctrl while you click the cells to include in the scenario.

**6**    At the right edge of the **Changing cells** box, click the **Expand Dialog** button.

**7**    Click **OK**.

**8**    In the **Scenario Values** dialog box, enter the alternative values for each cell in the scenario.

**9**    Click **OK**.

**10**    Repeat steps 2 through 9 for each additional scenario.

7   Click the down arrow in the middle box, and select the operation you want to use in the constraint.

8   Click in the **Constraint** box, and either type in the value for the constraint, or click the cell with the value to be used as the constraint.

9   Click **Add**.

10  Repeat steps 6 through 9 as necessary to add further constraints.

11  Click **Cancel** to return to the **Solver** dialog box.

12  Click **Solve**.

13  Click **Cancel** to close Solver without saving your changes, click **Save Scenario** to save the solution as a scenario, or click **OK** to keep the Solver solution.

Page 147   **To use the Analysis ToolPak**

1   On the **Tools** menu, click **Data Analysis**.

2   Click the item representing the type of analysis you want to perform.

3   Click **OK**.

4   Use the controls in the dialog box that appears to set up your analysis.

5   Click **OK**.

Chapter 9   **Creating Dynamic Lists with PivotTables**

Page 157   **To create a PivotTable**

1   Click any cell in the data list.

2   On the **Data** menu, click **PivotTable and PivotChart Report**.

3   Ensure that the **Microsoft Excel list or database** option button is selected in the top pane, identifying your worksheet as the data source, and that the **PivotTable** option button is selected in the bottom pane.

4   Click **Next** to move to the next page of the wizard.

5   Ensure that the proper cell range appears in the **Range** box.

6   Click **Next** to move to the next page of the wizard.

7   Click **Finish**.

8   From the **PivotTable Field List** dialog box, drag the fields for the horizontal axis to the **Drop Column Fields Here** box.

9   From the **PivotTable Field List** dialog box, drag the fields for the vertical axis to the **Drop Row Fields Here** box.

**10** From the **PivotTable Field List** dialog box, drag the data field to the **Drop Data Field Here** box.

**11** From the **PivotTable Field List** dialog box, drag the fields for the page area to the **Drop Page Fields Here** box.

Page 164 **To filter a PivotTable**

**1** Click the down arrow at the right edge of any field heading.

**2** From the list of values that appears, click the value to use as the filter.

**3** If the list appears as a list of values with check boxes next to the values, select the check boxes beside the values to appear in the PivotTable.

**4** Click **All** from the list to remove a filter.

Page 158 **To format PivotTable data**

**1** Select the cells in the PivotTable data area.

**2** On the **Format** menu, click **Cells**.

**3** Use the controls in the **Format Cells** dialog box to format the cells in the PivotTable, and click **OK**.

Page 158 **To apply a predefined format to a PivotTable**

**1** If the **PivotTable** toolbar is hidden, right-click any toolbar and then, from the shortcut menu that appears, click **PivotTable**.

**2** Click any cell in the PivotTable.

**3** On the **PivotTable** toolbar, click the **Format Report** button.

**4** Click the desired **AutoFormat**.

Page 164 **To add a field to a PivotTable**

**1** Click any cell in the PivotTable.

**2** If the **PivotTable** toolbar is hidden, right-click any toolbar and then, from the shortcut menu that appears, click **PivotTable**.

**3** If the **PivotTable Field List** dialog box is hidden, on the **PivotTable** toolbar, click the **Show Field List** button.

**4** From the **PivotTable Field List** dialog box, drag the new field to the desired area of the PivotTable.

Page 165 **To change a PivotTable's layout**

**1** On the **PivotTable** toolbar, click **PivotTable** and then click **Wizard**.

**2** Click **Layout**.

**3** Drag fields to new areas.

**4**    Click **OK**, and click **Finish**.

**5**    You can also drag fields directly on the PivotChart to change the layout.

Page 166  **To refresh PivotTable data**

**1**    Click any cell in the PivotTable.

**2**    If the **PivotTable** toolbar is hidden, right-click any toolbar and then, from the shortcut menu that appears, click **PivotTable**.

**3**    On the **PivotTable** toolbar, click the **Refresh External Data** button.

Page 166  **To show or hide underlying PivotTable data**

●    Double-click a column or row head in a PivotTable to collapse or expand the rows or columns defined by the column head.

Page 166  **To create a link to a PivotTable field**

**1**    Click the cell you want to link to the PivotTable field, and type =.

**2**    On the tab bar, click the sheet tab of the worksheet with the PivotTable.

**3**    Click the PivotTable cell to supply the data for the other cell.

**4**    Press ⌈Enter⌉ to accept the *GETPIVOTDATA* formula Excel creates.

Page 169  **To import a text file**

**1**    On the **Data** menu, point to **Import External Data** and then click **Import Data**.

**2**    Navigate to the folder with the file to be imported, and double-click the file name.

**3**    If necessary, select the **Delimited** or **Fixed Width** option button to identify how columns are marked in the text file. Click **Next** to accept the **Text Import Wizard's** summary of the text file's data, and move to the second page of the wizard.

**4**    If necessary, select the check box next to the proper delimiter for the text file. Click **Next** to accept the **Text Import Wizard's** analysis of the text file's data, and move to the third page of the wizard.

**5**    Click **Finish** to accept the values and data types as assigned by the wizard.

**6**    Click **OK** to paste the imported data into the active worksheet, beginning at the active cell.

Chapter 10  **Creating Charts**

Page 177  **To create an embedded chart**

**1**    Select the cells to provide data for the chart.

**2**    On the Standard toolbar, click the **Chart Wizard** button.

**3** In the **Chart type** section, click the desired chart type; and then, in the **Chart sub-type** section, click the desired subtype.

**4** Click **Next** to move to the next wizard page.

**5** Verify that the axis and data series names are correct.

**6** Click **Next** to move to the next wizard page.

**7** In the **Chart title** box, type the name of the chart and then press ⟨Tab⟩.

**8** Type names for the chart title and axes in the boxes provided, and then click **Next**.

**9** Click **Finish** to accept the default choice to create the chart as part of the active worksheet.

Page 178 **To resize a chart**

● Grab the sizing handle at the edge of the chart, and drag it to resize the chart.

Page 179 **To change a chart's background**

**1** Right-click anywhere in the Chart Area of the chart, and then, from the shortcut menu that appears, click **Format Chart Area**.

**2** In the **Area** section of the **Format Chart Area** dialog box, click the **Fill Effects** button.

**3** Click the **Texture** tab to display the **Texture** tab page.

**4** Click the desired texture.

**5** Click **OK** twice to close the **Fill Effects** dialog box and the **Format Chart Area** dialog box.

Page 182 **To customize chart labels**

**1** Double-click the chart label to be customized.

**2** Use the controls in the dialog box that appears to customize the chart label.

**3** To change the text of a chart label, click the label and edit it in the text box that appears.

Page 182 **To customize chart number formats**

**1** Double-click the axis of the chart with the numbers to be customized.

**2** In the **Format Axis** dialog box that appears, click the **Number** tab.

**3** Use the controls on the **Number** tab page to format the chart numbers.

**4** Click **OK**.

**Page 185**  **To perform trendline analysis**

**1** In a chart, right-click a data point in the body of the chart and then, from the short-cut menu that appears, click **Add Trendline**.

**2** If necessary, in the **Trend/Regression type** section, click **Linear**.

**3** Click the **Options** tab.

**4** In the **Forecast** section, type the number of horizontal axis units to look ahead in the **Forward** box. Then click **OK**.

**Page 188**  **To create a PivotChart**

**1** Click any cell in the data list.

**2** On the **Data** menu, click **PivotTable and PivotChart Report**.

**3** Ensure that the **Microsoft Excel list or database** option button is selected in the top pane, identifying your worksheet as the data source, and that the **PivotChart report (with PivotTable report)** option button is selected in the bottom pane.

**4** Click **Next** to move to the next page of the wizard.

**5** Ensure that the proper cell range appears in the **Range** box.

**6** Click **Next** to move to the next page of the wizard.

**7** Click **Finish**.

**8** From the **PivotTable Field List** dialog box, drag the fields for the horizontal axis to the **Drop Column Fields Here** box.

**9** From the **PivotTable Field List** dialog box, drag the fields for the vertical axis to the **Drop Row Fields Here** box.

**10** From the **PivotTable Field List** dialog box, drag the data field to the **Drop Data Field Here** box.

**11** From the **PivotTable Field List** dialog box, drag the fields for the page area to the **Drop Page Fields Here** box.

**Page 189**  **To save a PivotChart as a custom chart type**

**1** On the **Chart** menu, click **Chart Type**.

**2** If necessary, click the **Custom Types** tab to display the **Custom Types** tab page.

**3** In the **Select from** section, select the **User-defined** option button and then click **Add**.

**4** In the **Name** box, type a name for the chart type.

**5** In the **Description** box, type a description for the chart type. Then click **OK**.

**To print a multipage worksheet**

> **1** On the **File** menu, click **Print**.
>
> **2** In the **Print range** section, select the **All** option button.
>
> **3** Click **Print**.

**To print nonadjacent worksheets in a workbook**

> **1** On the tab bar, hold down Ctrl while you click the sheet tabs of the worksheets to print.
>
> **2** On the Standard toolbar, click the **Print** button.

**To suppress error messages when printing**

> **1** On the **File** menu, click **Page Setup**.
>
> **2** Click the **Sheet** tab to display the **Sheet** tab page.
>
> **3** In the **Print** section, click the **Cell errors as** box and then, from the list that appears, click the desired representation.

**To print selected pages of a multipage worksheet**

> **1** On the **File** menu, click **Print**.
>
> **2** In the **Print range** section, select the **Page(s)** option button.
>
> **3** In the **From** box, type the first page to print.
>
> **4** In the **To** box, type the last page to print.
>
> **5** Click **OK**.

**To print a worksheet on a specific number of pages**

> **1** On the **File** menu, click **Page Setup**.
>
> **2** Click the **Page** tab.
>
> **3** In the **Scaling** section, select the **Fit to** option button and then type the desired number of pages in the **page(s) wide by** and **tall** boxes.
>
> **4** Click **OK**.

**To define a print area and center it on a page**

> **1** Select the cells to be printed.
>
> **2** On the **File** menu, point to **Print Area** and then click **Set Print Area**.
>
> **3** On the Standard toolbar, click the **Print Preview** button.
>
> **4** Click the **Setup** button.
>
> **5** Click the **Margins** tab to display the **Margins** tab page.

**6** In the **Center on page** section, select the **Horizontally** check box and the **Vertically** check box.

**7** Click **OK**.

Page 208 **To hide columns or rows during printing**

**1** Select the column or row heads of the columns or rows to be hidden.

**2** On the **Format** menu, point to **Columns** or **Rows** and then click **Hide**.

Page 208 **To unhide columns or rows during printing**

● On the **Format** menu, point to **Columns** or **Rows** and then click **Unhide**.

Page 206 **To repeat rows or columns at the top or left of printed pages**

**1** On the **File** menu, click **Page Setup**.

**2** Click the **Sheet** tab to display the **Sheet** tab page.

**3** Click the **Collapse Dialog** button next to the **Rows to repeat at top** or **Columns to repeat at left** box.

**4** Select the rows or columns to repeat.

**5** Click the **Expand Dialog** button.

**6** Click **OK**.

Page 210 **To print a chart without printing the worksheet**

**1** Click the chart.

**2** On the **File** menu, click **Print**.

**3** In the **Print what** section, ensure that the **Selected Chart** option button is selected.

**4** Click **OK** to print the chart.

Page 210 **To print a worksheet without printing a chart**

**1** Right-click the **Chart Area** of the chart, and then, from the shortcut menu that appears, click **Format Chart Area**.

**2** Click the **Properties** tab.

**3** Clear the **Print object** check box, and then click **OK**.

**4** Click on the worksheet so the chart is no longer selected, and then print the worksheet.

Page 212 **To print a chart at its actual size**

**1** Click the chart to select it.

**2** On the Standard toolbar, click the **Print Preview** button.

**3**  Click the **Setup** button.

**4**  Click the **Chart** tab.

**5**  Select the **Custom** option button, and then click **OK**.

**To open and view a macro**

**1**  Open a workbook with a macro attached.

**2**  Click **Enable Macros** to allow macros to run.

**3**  On the **Tools** menu, point to **Macro** and then click **Macros**.

**4**  In the **Macro Name** pane, click the name of the macro to view.

**5**  Click **Edit**.

**6**  Click **Close** to close the macro.

**To step through a macro**

**1**  On the **Tools** menu, point to **Macro** and then click **Macros**.

**2**  In the **Macro Name** list, click the name of the macro to step through.

**3**  Click **Step Into**.

**4**  Right-click the taskbar, and then, from the shortcut menu that appears, click **Tile Windows Vertically**.

**5**  Press [F8] to execute each macro step.

**6**  After the last macro step, in the Microsoft Visual Basic Editor, click the **Close** button.

**To run a macro**

**1**  On the **Tools** menu, point to **Macro** and then click **Macros**.

**2**  In the **Macro Name** list, click the name of the macro to run.

**3**  Click **Run**.

**To create a macro**

**1**  On the **Tools** menu, point to **Macro** and then click **Record New Macro**.

**2**  In the **Macro name** box, delete the existing name and then type a name for the new macro.

**3**  Click **OK**.

**4**  Execute the steps that make up the macro.

**5**  On the **Stop Recording** toolbar, click the **Stop Recording** button.

Page 221  **To modify an existing macro**

**1**  On the **Tools** menu, point to **Macro** and then click **Macros**.

**2**  In the **Macro name** list, click the macro name and then click **Edit**.

**3**  Change the VBA code that makes up the macro.

**4**  On the Visual Basic Editor's Standard toolbar, click the **Save** button to save your change.

**5**  Click the **Close** button.

Page 225  **To create a toolbar**

**1**  On the **Tools** menu, click **Customize**.

**2**  If necessary, click the **Toolbars** tab to display the **Toolbars** tab page.

**3**  Click **New**.

**4**  In the **Toolbar name** box, type the name of the new toolbar.

**5**  Click **OK**.

Page 225  **To add a macro button to a toolbar**

**1**  On the **Tools** menu, click **Customize**.

**2**  In the **Customize** dialog box, click the **Commands** tab.

**3**  In the **Categories** list, click **Macros**.

**4**  Drag the **Custom Button** command to the target toolbar.

**5**  On the **Custom Macros** toolbar, right-click the **Custom** button and then, from the shortcut menu that appears, click **Name**.

**6**  Type a name for the button, and then press `Enter`.

**7**  On the target toolbar, right-click the new button and then, from the shortcut menu that appears, click **Assign Macro**.

**8**  Click the name of the macro to be assigned to the button.

**9**  Click **OK**.

**10**  In the **Customize** dialog box, click **Close**.

Page 226  **To delete a custom toolbar**

**1**  On the **Tools** menu, click **Customize**.

**2**  If necessary, click the **Toolbars** tab.

**3**  In the **Toolbars** list, click the name of the toolbar to be deleted.

**4**  Click **Delete**.

**5**     Click **OK** in the warning dialog box that appears.

**6**     Click **Close** to close the **Customize** dialog box.

Page 228 **To create a new menu**

**1**     On the **Tools** menu, click **Customize**.

**2**     If necessary, click the **Commands** tab to display the **Commands** tab page.

**3**     In the **Categories** list, click **New Menu**.

**4**     Drag **New Menu** from the **Commands** list to the spot on the main menu bar where you want the new menu to appear.

**5**     Right-click the **New Menu** heading, and then, from the shortcut menu that appears, click **Name**.

**6**     Type a new name for the menu, and then press `Enter`.

**7**     In the **Customize** dialog box, click **Close**.

Page 229 **To add a macro to a menu**

**1**     On the **Tools** menu, click **Customize**.

**2**     If necessary, click the **Commands** tab to display the **Commands** tab page.

**3**     In the **Categories** list of the **Customize** dialog box, click **Macros**.

**4**     In the **Commands** list, drag the **Custom Menu Item** command to the new menu head. When a box appears under the menu head, drag **Custom Menu Item** onto it.

**5**     On the new menu, right-click **Custom Menu Item** and then, from the shortcut menu that appears, click **Name**.

**6**     Type a name for the item, and then press `Enter`.

**7**     On the new menu, right-click the new menu item and then, from the shortcut menu that appears, click **Assign Macro**.

**8**     In the **Macro name** box, click the name of the macro to assign to the menu item.

**9**     Click **OK**.

**10**     Click **Close** to close the **Customize** dialog box.

Page 229 **To delete a custom menu**

**1**     On the **Tools** menu, click **Customize**.

**2**     Right-click the menu head of the menu to be deleted, and then, from the shortcut menu that appears, click **Delete**.

**3**     In the **Customize** dialog box, click **Close**.

**To run a macro when a workbook is opened**

**1** On the **Tools** menu, point to **Macro** and then click **Record New Macro**.

**2** In the **Macro name** box, type a name that begins with *Auto_*, such as Auto_Open.

**3** Click **OK**.

**4** Carry out the steps to be saved in the macro.

**5** On the **Stop Recording** toolbar, click the **Stop Recording** button.

**Chapter 13 Working with Other Microsoft Office Programs**

**To link to an external document**

**1** On the **Insert** menu, click **Object**.

**2** Click the **Create from File** tab to display the **Create from File** tab page.

**3** Click **Browse**.

**4** Navigate to the target folder, and double-click the file to include in the workbook.

**5** Select the **Link to file** check box.

**6** Click **OK**.

**To edit a linked file**

● Right-click the linked file, and then, from the shortcut menu that appears, point to **Presentation Object** (in the case of a Microsoft PowerPoint presentation) and then click **Edit**.

**To store a workbook as part of another file**

**1** Open the other Office file.

**2** On the **Insert** menu, click **Object**.

**3** Select the **Create from File** option button.

**4** Click the **Browse** button.

**5** Navigate to the target folder, and double-click the workbook to include in the file.

**6** Click **OK**.

**To edit an embedded workbook**

● Right-click the linked file, and then, from the shortcut menu that appears, point to **Worksheet Object** (in the case of a PowerPoint presentation) and then click **Edit**.

**To create a hyperlink to another location within the same document**

**1**    Right-click the cell into which you want to insert the hyperlink, and then, from the shortcut menu that appears, click **Hyperlink**.

**2**    Click the **Place in This Document** button.

**3**    In the **Or select a place in this document** box, click the target for the hyperlink.

**4**    If desired, type a cell reference in the **Type the Cell Reference** box.

**5**    In the **Text to display** box, type the text to be shown as the link.

**6**    Click **OK**.

**To create a hyperlink between documents**

**1**    Right-click the cell into which you want to insert the hyperlink, and then, from the shortcut menu that appears, click **Hyperlink**.

**2**    If necessary, click the **Existing File or Web Page** button.

**3**    Navigate to the folder with the target file.

**4**    Click the name of the target file.

**5**    In the **Text to display** box, type the text to be shown as the link.

**6**    Click **OK**.

**To paste a chart into another document**

**1**    Right-click a blank spot on the chart, and then, from the shortcut menu that appears, click **Copy** to copy the chart image to the Clipboard.

**2**    Open the file into which the chart will be pasted.

**3**    Right-click a blank spot in the active document, and from the shortcut menu that appears, click **Paste**.

**Chapter 14**  **Working with Database Data**

**To find a value**

**1**    Create a data range in which the leftmost column contains a unique value for each row.

**2**    In a cell, type =VLOOKUP(*cell2*, *range*, *column*, FALSE) (where *cell2* is the cell for someone to enter a value for Excel to find in the leftmost column, *range* is the range or name of the range, and *column* is the number of the column—counting from the left—for the value to be returned), and press Enter. *FALSE* finds only exact matches, while *TRUE* would find the nearest match equal to or less than the specified value.

**3**    In *cell2*, type the value to be found in the named range, and press Enter.

Page 253   **To define a new Microsoft Access data source**

1   On the **Data** menu, point to **Import External Data** and then click **New Database Query**.

2   If necessary, click the **Databases** tab in the **Choose Data Source** dialog box.

3   Click **<New Data Source>**, and then click **OK**.

4   In the first box, type the name of the source.

5   In the second box, click the down arrow and then, from the list that appears, click **Microsoft Access Driver (*.mdb)**.

6   Click **Connect**.

7   Click **Select**.

8   Navigate to the target folder, click the target database, and then click **OK**.

9   Click **OK** again.

10   In the fourth box, click the down arrow and then, from the list that appears, click the default table for the data source.

11   Click **OK**.

Page 254   **To create a database query**

1   On the **Data** menu, point to **Import External Data** and then click **New Database Query**.

2   If necessary, click the **Databases** tab in the **Choose Data Source** dialog box.

3   Click the name of the data source, and then click **OK**.

4   Add the table columns you want to use in your query by clicking the column name and then clicking **Add**.

5   Click **Next**.

6   In the **Column To Filter** pane, click the name of the column by which you want to filter the results.

7   In the first comparison operator box, click the down arrow and then, from the list that appears, click the comparison operator to be used.

8   In the first value box, type the first value to use in the comparison.

9   If necessary, type a second value in the second value box.

10   Click **Next**.

11   In the **Sort by** box, click the down arrow and then, from the list that appears, click the name of the column by which to sort the query results, and click **Ascending** or **Descending**.

**12** Click **Next**.

**13** Click **Save Query**.

**14** In the **File name** box, type a name for the query and then click **Save**.

**15** Click **Finish**.

**16** In the **Import Data** dialog box, click **OK**.

Page 258 **To summarize data with a database function**

**1** Create a data list.

**2** Above or to the side of the data list, copy the headings from the columns in the data list.

**3** In the cells directly below the copied headings, type the rules to use as criteria to limit the list rows considered by the database formulas.

**4** In any blank cell above or to the side of the data list, type the database formula following the pattern *DFUNCTION(data*, <;$QD>*field*<;$QD>, *criteria*), where:

   ■ *DFUNCTION* is the database function (e.g., DSUM or DAVERAGE)

   ■ *data* is the range of cells containing the data list (including column headings)

   ■ <;$QD>*field*<;$QD> is the name of the field (enclosed in quotes) to be used in calculating the formula's result

   ■ *criteria* is the range of cells containing the rules (including column headings) to be used in limiting the cells considered by the formula.

Chapter 15 **Publishing Information on the Web**

Page 265 **To save a workbook as an HTML document**

**1** On the **File** menu, click **Save as Web Page**.

**2** If necessary, in the **Save** pane, select the **Entire Workbook** option button.

**3** Enter a file name in the **File name** box, and then click **Save**.

Page 265 **To view a workbook saved as an HTML file**

**1** Start Microsoft Internet Explorer.

**2** In Internet Explorer, open the **File** menu and then click **Open**.

**3** Click **Browse**.

**4** Navigate to the target folder, and then double-click the file to be viewed.

**5** Click **OK**.

Page 267 **To publish a worksheet on the Web**

**1** On the **File** menu, click **Save as Web Page**.

**2** Navigate to the directory to which you want to publish the worksheet.

**3** In the **Save** section of the dialog box, select the **Selection: Sheet** option button to publish the active worksheet on the Web.

**4** In the **Publish as** section of the dialog box, click the **Change** button.

**5** In the **Title** box, type a new title for the page and then click **OK**.

Page 268 **To update Microsoft Excel Web pages automatically**

**1** On the **File** menu, click **Save as Web Page**.

**2** In the **Save** section of the dialog box, select the **Selection: Sheet** option button to publish the active worksheet on the Web.

**3** In the **Publish as** section of the dialog box, click the **Change** button.

**4** In the **Title** box, type a new title for the page and then click **OK**.

**5** Select the **AutoRepublish every time this workbook is saved** check box.

Page 268 **To edit a workbook over the Web**

**1** On the **File** menu, click **Save as Web Page**.

**2** Navigate to the Web directory to which you want to publish the workbook.

**3** In the **Save** section of the dialog box, select the **Selection: Sheet** option button to publish the active worksheet on the Web.

**4** In the **Save** section of the dialog box, select the **Add interactivity** check box and then click **OK**.

**5** Open the file in Internet Explorer.

**6** Use the tools on the **Interactivity** toolbar to edit the worksheet.

Page 271 **To save a PivotTable to the Web**

**1** Click any cell in the PivotTable.

**2** On the **File** menu, click **Save as Web Page**.

**3** In the **Save** section of the dialog box, select the **Selection: Sheet** option button.

**4** In the **Save** section of the dialog box, select the **Add interactivity** check box and then click **Publish**.

**5** If necessary, click the **Choose** down arrow, and then, from the list that appears, click **Items on Pivot**.

**6** In the list below the **Choose** box, click the item beginning with *PivotTable*.

**7** Click **Publish**.

Page 272 **To work with a PivotTable via the Web**

**1** Open the Web page with the PivotTable in Internet Explorer.

**2** Use the down arrows and column heads to modify the PivotList's organization.

Page 274 **To link to Web data**

**1** In Internet Explorer, open the Web page with the table data to which you want to link.

**2** Select the table data, and then press [Ctrl]+[C] to copy the data to the Clipboard.

**3** In Excel, click the desired cell, and then, on the Standard toolbar, click the **Paste** button.

**4** Click the **Paste Options** button, and then, from the list that appears, click **Create Refreshable Web Query**.

**5** Click the table icon next to the data you want to import, and then click **Import**.

Page 276 **To acquire real-time data**

**1** On the **Tools** menu, click **AutoCorrect Options**.

**2** Click the **Smart Tags** tab to display the **Smart Tags** tab page.

**3** Select the **Label data with smart tags** check box.

**4** Verify that the five check boxes in the **Recognizers** list are selected.

**5** Select the **Embed smart tags in this workbook** check box.

**6** Click **Check Workbook**.

**7** Move the mouse pointer over a cell with the Smart Tag indicator.

**8** Click the **Smart Tag Actions** button, and then, from the list that appears, click the desired action.

**9** Select the **Starting at cell** option button, verify that the proper cell appears in the **Starting at cell** box, and then click **OK**.

Page 278 **To export an Excel document as XML**

**1** On the **File** menu, click **Save As**.

**2** Click the **Save as type** down arrow, and then, from the list that appears, click **XML Spreadsheet (*.xml)**.

**3** Click **Save**.

**4** Click **Yes** to clear the message box and save the workbook as an XML spreadsheet.

Page 279    **To import an XML file into Excel**

**1**    On the Standard toolbar, click the **Open** button.

**2**    Navigate to the target folder, and double-click the target file with the .xml extension.

Page 283    **To apply an XML data map to a worksheet**

**1**    On the **Data** menu, point to **XML**, and then click **XML Source**.

**2**    Click **Workbook Maps**.

**3**    Click **Add**.

**4**    Navigate to the folder, click the .xsd file that contains the schema, and click **Open**.

**5**    If necessary, click the entry representing the schema, and click **OK**.

**6**    Drag the elements you want to add from the **XML Source** task pane to the body of the worksheet.

Page 284    **To import XML data into a worksheet with a data map**

**1**    On the **Data** menu, point to **XML**, and then click **Import**.

**2**    Click the name of the file that contains the XML data, and click **Import**.

Page 284    **To change the viewing options of an XML data map**

**1**    Click a cell in the list you want to modify.

**2**    On the **Data** menu, point to **XML**, and then click **XML Source**.

**3**    Click **Options** in the **XML Source** task pane, and click the viewing option you want to apply to the list.

Page 284    **To remove an element from an XML data map**

**1**    On the **Data** menu, point to **XML**, and then click **XML Source**.

**2**    In the **XML Source** task pane, right-click the element to remove and click **Remove Element**.

**3**    Click **OK** to acknowledge that the deletion will cause data to be lost.

Page 284    **To remove an XML data map assignment**

**1**    On the **Data** menu, point to **XML**, and then click **XML Source**.

**2**    In the **XML Source** task pane, click **Workbook Maps**.

**3**    Click the data map to remove, click **Delete**, and click **OK** to clear the message box that appears.

## Chapter 16  Collaborating with Colleagues

**Page 289**  **To turn workbook sharing on**

1    On the **Tools** menu, click **Share Workbook**.

2    Select the **Allow changes by more than one user at the same time** check box, and then click the **Advanced** tab.

3    Click **OK** to accept the default settings.

4    Click **OK** if a message box appears, and then save the workbook.

**Page 289**  **To send a workbook to colleagues by e-mail**

1    From the Microsoft Windows **Start** menu, open Microsoft **Outlook Express**.

2    Click the **New Mail** button.

3    Click the **Attach** button.

4    Navigate to the target folder, and double-click the file to attach.

5    Click **Send**.

**Page 292**  **To add a comment**

1    Click the cell to which to add the comment.

2    On the **Insert** menu, click **Comment**.

3    In the comment field, type the comment.

4    Click a different cell to close the comment.

**Page 292**  **To view a comment**

●    Move the mouse pointer over a cell with a comment.

**Page 292**  **To delete a comment**

●    Right-click the cell with the comment, and then, from the shortcut menu that appears, click **Delete Comment**.

**Page 294**  **To turn on change tracking**

1    On the **Tools** menu, point to **Track Changes** and then click **Highlight Changes**.

2    Select the **Track changes while editing** check box.

3    If necessary, clear the **When** check box.

4    If necessary, clear the **Who** check box.

5    If necessary, select the **Highlight changes on screen** check box.

6    Click **OK**.

Page 296   **To accept or reject changes in a single workbook**

**1**   On the **Tools** menu, point to **Track Changes** and then click **Accept or Reject Changes**.

**2**   Click **OK** to save the workbook and clear the message box that appears.

**3**   Verify that the **When** check box is selected and that *Not yet reviewed* appears in the **When** box.

**4**   Click **OK**.

**5**   Click **Accept** to accept the change, or click **Reject** to reject the change.

Page 295   **To add a history worksheet to a workbook**

**1**   On the **Tools** menu, point to **Track Changes** and then click **Highlight Changes**.

**2**   Select the **List changes on a new sheet** check box.

**3**   Click **OK**.

Page 297   **To merge changes from multiple workbooks**

**1**   On the **Tools** menu, click **Compare and Merge Workbooks**.

**2**   Hold down [Ctrl] as you click the files with the changes to be merged, and then click **OK**.

**3**   On the Standard toolbar, click the **Save** button to save your work.

**4**   On the **Tools** menu, point to **Track Changes** and then click **Accept or Reject Changes**.

**5**   Verify that the **When** check box is selected and that *Not yet reviewed* appears in the **When** box, that the **Who** check box is cleared, and that the **Where** check box is cleared.

**6**   Click **OK**.

Page 300   **To password-protect a workbook**

**1**   On the **File** menu, click **Save As**.

**2**   Click the **Tools** menu head, and then click **General Options**.

**3**   In the **Password to open** box, type a password and then click **OK**.

**4**   In the **Reenter password to proceed** box, type the same password and then click **OK**.

**5**   Click **Save**.

**6**   Click **Yes** if a message box appears.

Page 299 **To remove a password from a workbook**

**1**     On the **File** menu, click **Save As**.

**2**     Click the **Tools** menu head, and then click **General Options**.

**3**     In the **Password to open** box, erase the existing password and then click **OK**.

Page 301 **To password-protect a worksheet**

**1**     Activate the worksheet to be protected.

**2**     On the **Tools** menu, point to **Protection** and then click **Protect Sheet**.

**3**     In the **Password to unprotect sheet** box, type the password and then click **OK**.

**4**     In the **Confirm Password** dialog box, type the same password in the space provided, and then click **OK**.

Page 301 **To remove protection from a worksheet**

**1**     On the **Tools** menu, point to **Protection** and then click **Unprotect Sheet**.

**2**     In the **Password** box, type the password and then click **OK**.

Page 301 **To password-protect a range**

**1**     Select the cells to be protected.

**2**     On the **Tools** menu, point to **Protection** and then click **Allow Users to Edit Ranges**.

**3**     Click **New**.

**4**     In the **Title** box, type the name for the new range.

**5**     In the **Range password** box, type a password and then click **OK**.

**6**     In the **Confirm password** box, type the same password and then click **OK**.

Page 301 **To remove a password from a cell range**

**1**     On the **Tools** menu, point to **Protection** and then click **Allow Users to Edit Ranges**.

**2**     In the **Ranges** box, click the range to be unprotected and then click **Delete**.

**3**     Click **OK**.

Page 304 **To create a self-signed digital certificate**

**1**     On the **Start** menu, click **Run**.

**2**     In the **Open** box, type C:\Program Files\Microsoft Office\OFFICE11\Selfcert.exe and press Enter. If Office was not installed in the default directory, modify the path to reflect the directory in which it was installed.

**3**     In the **Create Digital Certificate** dialog box, type a name for your certificate.

**4**     Click **OK**.

Page 305 **To digitally sign a workbook**

   **1**   On the **Tools** menu, click **Options**.

   **2**   In the **Options** dialog box, click the **Security** tab, and click **Digital Signatures**.

   **3**   In the **Select Certificate** dialog box, click the certificate with which you want to sign the workbook and click **OK**.

   **4**   Click **OK** to close the **Digital Signatures** dialog box, and again to close the **Options** dialog box.

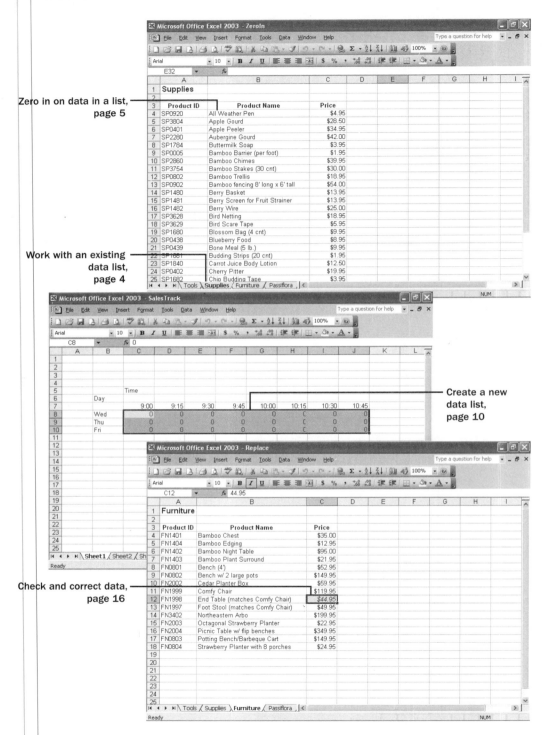

Zero in on data in a list, page 5

Work with an existing data list, page 4

Create a new data list, page 10

Check and correct data, page 16

# Chapter 1 at a Glance

# 1 Getting to Know Excel

**In this chapter you will learn to:**

✔ Work with an existing data list.

✔ Zero in on data in a list.

✔ Create a data list.

✔ Check and correct data.

One thing all businesses have in common is the need to keep accurate records. As the range of products, services, and customers expands, businesses require a computer-based system to keep up with an avalanche of financial and other data.

Microsoft Excel is a spreadsheet program that lets you organize your data into lists and then summarize, compare, and present your data graphically. For example, you can have Excel find the sum, average, or maximum value for sales on a given day; create a graph showing what percentage of sales were in a particular range; and show how the total sales compared with the total sales of other days in the same week. In short, Excel saves you from having to create these summaries by hand.

The exercises in this book are based on data for The Garden Company, the fictional business used in the *Step by Step* series. In addition to taking care of the plants and gardening supplies offered by the company, the owner, Catherine Turner, and her employees need to maintain the data lists that let Catherine and The Garden Company's head buyer make informed decisions about the products the company carries.

In this chapter, you'll learn how to work with an existing data list and specific data within a data list, create a data list, and check and correct data.

**See Also**   Do you need a quick refresher on the topics in this chapter? See the quick reference entries on pages xxvii–xxix.

 **Important**   Before you can use the practice files in this chapter, be sure you install them from the book's companion CD to their default location. See "Using the Book's CD-ROM" on page xi for more information.

## Introducing Excel

When you start Excel, a blank document appears. From this point, you can add data, change how the data looks, have Excel summarize data, or find information in Excel's help files. The following graphic points out the most important parts of Excel: the workbook window, the main menu bar, the formula bar, the Standard and Formatting toolbars, the status bar, the Ask A Question box, and the task pane.

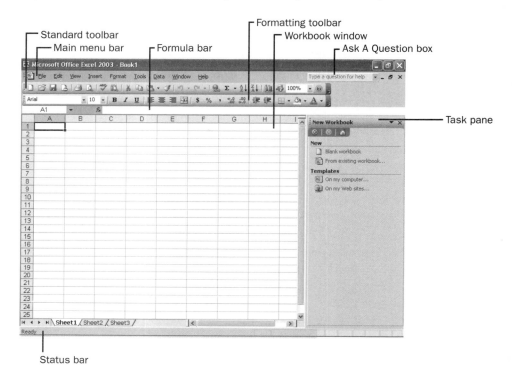

Standard toolbar
Main menu bar
Formula bar
Formatting toolbar
Workbook window
Ask A Question box
Task pane
Status bar

**Important**    Depending on the screen resolution you have set on your computer and which toolbar buttons you use most often, it's possible that not every button on every toolbar will appear on your Excel toolbars. If a button mentioned in this book doesn't appear on a toolbar, click the **Toolbar Options** down arrow at the right end of that toolbar to display the rest of the buttons available on that toolbar.

The most basic part of an Excel document is the box that holds an element of data— in Excel, that box is called a *cell*. Each cell is at the intersection of a *row* (a sequence of cells along a horizontal line) and a *column* (a sequence of cells along a vertical line); rows are identified by a number and columns by a letter. The row number and column letter that designate a specific cell are called a *cell reference*. For example, the cell in the upper left corner of the workbook window has the cell reference A1. A single set of columns and rows makes up a *worksheet*, which appears as a page in an Excel document. A *workbook*, in turn, is a collection of one or more worksheets.

**Tip**    When you create an Excel document, you create a workbook with three worksheets.

The workbook that owner Catherine Turner has developed for The Garden Company has three worksheets, with each worksheet holding data about products available at the company's retail location. She has named the workbook *Products*, and she records data about furniture items on one worksheet, gardening supplies on another worksheet, and tools on a third worksheet. On each worksheet, she uses three columns to record each product's identification code, description, and price. This collection of related information is called a *data list*.

You can include more than three categories in a workbook for a given subject by simply creating additional worksheets; if you want to store data about an entirely different subject, however, you should create a new workbook. For example, if Catherine wanted to record more data about different categories of products sold by The Garden Company, such as varieties of plants, she could create a new worksheet in the Products workbook and add the data to the worksheet. However, if she wanted to store data on a different subject, perhaps her customers and their contact information, she would create a new workbook.

**Tip**  Each workbook should contain information about a unique subject, such as Products, Customers, or Sales, while each worksheet should hold information about a subset of items in that category, meaning different types of products, preferred customers vs. non-preferred customers, or sales information for a given month.

The Excel help system is a great source of information about the program. Rather than get help through the **Help** menu, you can type a question in the **Ask A Question** box and have Excel display the help topics that match your request. The benefit of placing the Ask A Question box in the main Excel window is that you can quickly and easily get help while your question is fresh in your mind, without adding any steps that might distract you from your question.

The task pane lets you open files, paste data from the Clipboard, create blank workbooks, and create Excel workbooks based on existing files. A great advantage of the task pane is that it groups many common actions, such as opening or creating new files, in one place and lets you perform them with a single mouse click. The only drawback of the task pane is that it takes up valuable screen space. Fortunately, you can show or hide the task pane easily. On the **View** menu, click **Task Pane**; Excel hides the task pane if it is currently displayed or shows it if it is currently hidden.

# Working with an Existing Data List

***Microsoft Office Specialist***

When you start Excel, the program displays a blank worksheet and has the task pane open on the right side of the screen. You can begin to enter data in the worksheet's cells or open an existing workbook. In the exercises that follow, you'll be working with some of the workbooks that have already been created for The Garden Company. After you've made any desired changes to a workbook, you should save the workbook.

When you save a file, you overwrite the previous copy of the file. If you have made changes that you want to save but you want to keep a copy of the file as it was previously, you can use the **Save As** command to specify a name for the new file.

**Tip** Readers frequently ask, "How often should I save my files?" It's good practice to save your changes every half hour, or even every five minutes, but the best time to save a file is whenever you have made a change you would hate to have to make again.

You can also use the controls in the **Save As** dialog box to specify a different format for the new file and a different location in which to save the new version of the file. For example, Catherine Turner, the owner of The Garden Company, might want to save an Excel file in a different format if she needs to share the file with the company's accountant, who happens to use another spreadsheet program.

After you save a file, you can change a *property* (or properties) of the file to make it easier for your colleagues to find when they search your company's network. In the Microsoft Windows operating systems, you can search for files based on the file's author or title, or by keywords associated with the file. A file tracking sales of furniture products might have the keywords *furniture* and *sales* associated with it. Those properties are available on the **Summary** tab page of the **Properties** dialog box. Other properties, such as Checked By, Date Completed, and Language are available on the **Custom** tab page of the dialog box.

In this exercise, you start Excel from the **Start** menu and then use the **Open** dialog box to open an existing workbook. Once you have opened the workbook, you update the price of an item and save the workbook twice: once as an Excel workbook, where you will also change the file's properties, before saving the file as a Lotus file in a new directory.

**1** On the taskbar, click the **Start** button, point to **Programs, Microsoft Office,** and then click **Microsoft Office Excel 2003.**

The main Excel program window appears.

**2** On the Standard toolbar, click the **Open** button.

The **Open** dialog box appears.

**Tip** When the task pane is displayed, you can also open a file by looking under the **Getting Started** heading and either clicking the name of the workbook you want to open or clicking **More** to display the **Open** dialog box.

**3** Click the **Look In** down arrow, and select the hard disk where you installed the Step by Step practice files.

The files and folders on your hard disk appear.

Open

**4** Locate the SBS folder, and then double-click the **Excel** folder.

The files and folders in the Excel folder appear.

**5** Double-click the **GettingToKnowXL** folder.

The files and folders in the GettingToKnowXL folder appear.

**6** Double-click the **FileOpen.xls** file.

The FileOpen.xls file opens.

**7** Click cell C16, type **15.95**, and press `Enter`.

The data in cell C16 changes to $15.95.

Save

**8** On the Standard toolbar, click the **Save** button.

Excel saves your changes.

**9** On the **File** menu, click **Properties**.

The **Properties** dialog box appears.

**10** If necessary, click the **Summary** tab, and type **Practice** in the **Keywords** box.

**11** Click the **Custom** tab and select **Date completed**.

**12** Click the **Type** down arrow and select **Date**.

**13** Type the current date in the **Value** box in the form *mm/dd/yyyy*, and click **OK**.

**14** On the **File** menu, click **Save As**.

The **Save As** dialog box appears.

**15** Click in the **File name** box, delete the existing file name, and type **SaveAs**.

Up One Level

**16** Click the **Up One Level** button to move from the GettingToKnowXL folder to the Excel folder.

**17** Click the **Save as type** down arrow to expand the list, and click **WK4 (1-2-3) (*.wk4)**.

**18** Click the **Save** button.

A dialog box appears, indicating that some features might be lost. Click **Yes** to have Excel save a new copy of your data in a Lotus file named SaveAs.wk4.

CLOSE: SaveAs.wk4.

# Zeroing In on Data in a List

Once you have opened a workbook, you can examine and modify its contents. To change specific data, such as the price of a pair of shears, you can move to that cell directly and then make your changes. Once in that cell, you can move to another cell in the same worksheet or move to another worksheet in the workbook. Moving to another worksheet is accomplished by clicking its *sheet tab*, located at the lower left edge of the workbook window.

You can move to a specific cell in lots of ways, but the most direct method is to click the cell to which you want to move. The cell you click will be outlined in black, and its contents, if any, will appear in the formula bar. When a cell is outlined, it is the *active cell*, meaning that you can modify its contents. You use a similar method to select multiple cells (referred to as a *cell range*)—just click the first cell in the range, and drag the mouse pointer over the remaining cells you want to select. Once you have selected the cell or cells you want to work with, you can cut, copy, delete, or change the format of the contents of the cell or cells. For instance, Catherine Turner, the owner of The Garden Company, might want to copy the prices of her five most popular garden furniture pieces to a new page that summarizes the best-selling items in each product category that the company offers.

**Important** If you select a group of cells, the first cell you click is designated the active cell.

You're not limited to selecting cells individually or as part of a range. You can select any number of noncontiguous cells by pressing Ctrl and clicking each cell you want to select. Or, you might need to move a column of price data one column to the right to make room for a column of headings that indicate to which product category (Furniture, Tools, Supplies, and so forth) items belong. To move an entire column (or entire columns) of data at a time, you click the column's header, located at the top of the worksheet. Clicking a column header highlights every cell in that column and lets you copy or cut the column and paste it elsewhere in the workbook.

The *Paste Options* button appears next to data you copy from a cell and paste into another cell.

Paste Options button

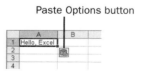

Clicking the **Paste Options** button displays a list of actions Excel can take regarding the pasted cells. The options in the list are summarized in the following table.

| Option | Action |
|---|---|
| Keep Source Formatting | Paste the contents of the Clipboard (which holds the last information selected via Cut or Copy) into the target cells, and format the data as it was formatted in the original cells. |
| Match Destination Formatting | Paste the contents of the Clipboard into the target cells, and format the data using the existing format in the target cells. |
| Values and Number Formatting | Paste the contents of the Clipboard into the target cells, keeping any numeric formats. |
| Keep Source Column Widths | Paste the contents of the Clipboard into the target cells, and resize the columns of the target cells to match the widths of the columns of the source cells. |
| Formatting Only | Apply the format of the source cells to the target cells, but do not copy the contents of the source cells. |
| Link Cells | Display the contents of the source cells in the target cells, updating the target cells whenever the content of the source cells changes. |
| Values Only | Paste the values from a column into the target column; use the existing format of the target column. |
| Values and Source Formatting | Paste a column of cells into the target column; apply the format of the copied column to the new column. |

**Troubleshooting**   If the **Paste Options** button doesn't appear, you can turn the feature on by clicking **Options** on the **Tools** menu. In the dialog box that appears, click the **Edit** tab and then select the **Show Paste Options buttons** check box.

In this exercise, you move from one worksheet to another to examine data about products The Garden Company sells and then select a range of cells whose contents you want to copy to the Summary sheet in your workbook. After you have copied and pasted that information, you select the first three columns of your Summary worksheet, copy them to the Clipboard, and move the columns (and their contents) over one column to make the first column available to add text indicating which worksheet specific sets of data came from.

**OPEN:** ZeroIn from the *SBS\Excel\GettingToKnowXL* folder.

**1**  In the lower left corner of the Excel window, click the **Furniture** sheet tab.

The Furniture worksheet appears.

**2**  On the tab bar, right-click the arrow buttons, and then, from the shortcut menu that appears, click **Passiflora**.

The Passiflora worksheet appears.

**3**  Click the **Tools** sheet tab to make the Tools worksheet the active worksheet in the workbook.

**4**  Click cell A3.

Cell A3 becomes the active cell in the worksheet. The value in cell A3, *Product ID*, appears in the formula bar, and the cell identifier appears in the Name box.

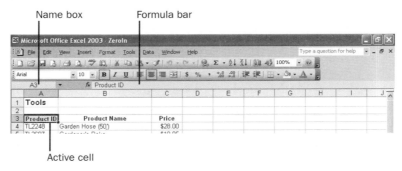

**5**  Drag from cell A3 to cell C6.

The selected cells are highlighted.

Copy

**6**  On the Standard toolbar, click the **Copy** button.

The contents of the selected cells are copied to the Clipboard. The selected cells retain their contents and are surrounded by a marquee outline (an outline that seems to move around the edge of the cells).

**7**  Click the **Summary** sheet tab.

Paste

**8**  The Summary sheet appears. Click cell A3, and then, on the Standard toolbar, click the **Paste** button.

The values in the cells you copied appear in cells A3 to C6 of the Summary worksheet.

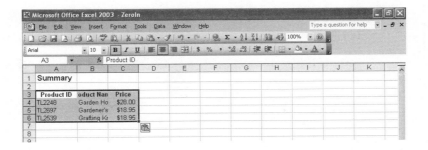

**Tip** Prior to Excel 2002, you had to select the cells that were the destination for the values you copied. If the destination area wasn't the same size as the copied area, Excel wouldn't let the paste proceed. In this version of Excel, all you need to do is click the cell in the upper left corner of the group of cells that you want to hold the data and then paste the data into the sheet. The exception, which you will encounter later in this chapter, occurs when you cut and paste entire columns or rows.

**9** Click the **Tools** sheet tab.

The Tools worksheet appears.

**10** Click the Name box.

The value in the Name box is highlighted.

**11** In the Name box, type **B9**, and press [Enter].

Cell B9 is highlighted with the value *Long-handled Loppers*.

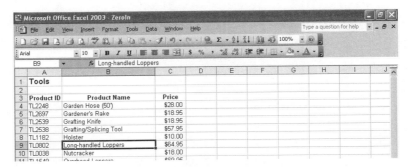

**12** Click the Name box, type **B14**, and press [Enter].

Cell B14 is highlighted with the value *Pruning Saw*.

**13** Click the **Summary** sheet tab.

The Summary worksheet appears.

**14** Click the column heading for column A.

Every cell in column A, including the column heading, is highlighted.

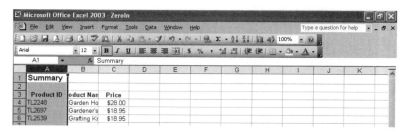

**15** Drag to the column heading for column C.

Every cell in columns A through C, including the column headings, is highlighted.

**16** On the Standard toolbar, click the **Cut** button.

**17** Click the column heading for column B, and drag to the column heading for column D.

Every cell in columns B through D, including the column headings, is highlighted.

**18** On the **Edit** menu, click **Paste**.

The contents of the Clipboard appear in columns B through D.

**19** On the Standard toolbar, click the **Save** button to save your changes.

CLOSE: ZeroIn.xls.

**Tip** To select cell A1 in the active worksheet (that is, to return to the top of a worksheet immediately), press [Ctrl]+[Home].

# Creating a Workbook

Every time you want to gather and store data that isn't closely related to any of your existing data, you should create a new workbook. The default new workbook in the current version of Excel has three worksheets, although you can add more worksheets or delete existing worksheets if you want. Creating a new workbook is a straightforward process—you just click the appropriate button on the toolbar.

Once you have created a workbook, you can begin entering data. The simplest way to enter data is to click a cell and type a value, a method that works very well when you're entering a few pieces of data but that is less than ideal when you're entering long sequences or series of values. For example, Catherine Turner, the owner of The Garden Company, might want to create a worksheet listing hourly company sales figures for weekdays from 1:00 p.m. to 7:00 p.m. To record those numbers, she would need to create a worksheet with the following layout.

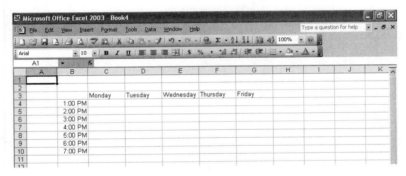

Typing the sequence *Monday, Tuesday, Wednesday, Thursday, Friday* repeatedly can be handled by copying and pasting the first occurrence of the sequence, but there's an easier way to do it using *AutoFill*. With AutoFill, you enter the first element in a recognized series, grab the *fill handle* at the lower right corner of the cell, and drag the fill handle until the series extends far enough to accommodate your data. A similar tool, *FillSeries*, lets you enter two values in a series and use the fill handle to extend the series in your worksheet. For example, if you want to create a series starting at 2 and increasing by two, you would put *2* in the first cell and *4* in the second cell, select both cells, and then use the fill handle to extend the series to your desired end value.

Other data entry techniques you'll use in this section are *AutoComplete*, which detects when a value you're entering is similar to previously entered values; *Pick from List*, which lets you choose a value from existing values in a column; and Ctrl + Enter, which lets you enter a value in multiple cells simultaneously.

The following table summarizes these data entry techniques.

| Method | Action |
| --- | --- |
| AutoFill | Enter the first value in a recognized series, and use the fill handle to extend the series. |
| FillSeries | Enter the first two values in a series, and use the fill handle to extend the series. |
| AutoComplete | Type the first few letters in a cell, and if a similar value exists in the same column, Excel will suggest the existing value. |
| Pick from List | Right-click a cell, and from the shortcut menu that appears, choose **Pick from List**. A list of existing values in the cell's column will appear. |
| Ctrl + Enter | Select a range of cells to contain the same data, type the data in the active cell, and press Ctrl + Enter. |

**Troubleshooting** If an AutoComplete suggestion doesn't appear as you begin typing a cell value, the option may be turned off. To turn on AutoComplete, choose **Options** from the **Tools** menu, click the **Edit** tab, and select the **Enable AutoComplete for Cell Values** check box.

Another handy feature in the current version of Excel is the **Auto Fill Options** button that appears next to data you add to a worksheet using either AutoFill or FillSeries.

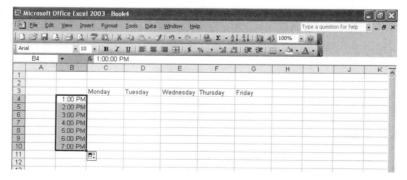

Clicking the **Auto Fill Options** button displays a list of actions Excel can take regarding the cells affected by your Fill operation. The options in the list are summarized in the following table.

| Option | Action |
|---|---|
| **Copy Cells** | Copy the contents of the selected cells to the cells indicated by the Fill operation. |
| **Fill Series** | Fill the cells indicated by the Fill operation with the next items in the series. |
| **Fill Formatting Only** | Copy the format of the selected cell to the cells indicated by the Fill operation, but do not place any values in the target cells. |
| **Fill Without Formatting** | Fill the cells indicated by the Fill operation with the next items in the series, but ignore any formatting applied to the source cells. |
| **Fill** *Days*, *Weekdays*, **etc.** | This option changes according to the series you extend. For example, if you extend the cells *Wed*, *Thu*, and *Fri*, Excel presents two options, Fill Days and Fill Weekdays, and lets you select which you intended. If you do not use a recognized sequence, the option does not appear. |

**Troubleshooting**   If the **Auto Fill Options** button doesn't appear, you can turn the feature on by clicking **Options** on the **Tools** menu. In the dialog box that appears, click the **Edit** tab and then select the **Show Paste Options buttons** check box.

In this exercise, you create a workbook to track the number of customers of The Garden Company making purchases during a two-hour period for three days. The workbook will eventually have sheets recording the total number of customers making purchases (by quarter hour), items sold, and number of items in a given transaction. You use the data entry methods described earlier in this section, such as AutoFill, FillSeries, and [Ctrl]+[Enter], to fill in the worksheets.

**1**   On the Standard toolbar, click the **New** button.

A blank workbook appears.

**2**   On the Standard toolbar, click the **Save** button.

The **Save** dialog box appears.

**3**   If necessary, navigate to the SBS\Excel\GettingToKnowXL folder on your hard disk.

**4**   In the **File name** box, type SalesTrack.

**5**   Click **Save**.

Excel saves your file as SalesTrack.xls.

New

Save

**6**   Click cell B6, and type Day.

**7**   Click cell C5, and type Time.

**8**   Click cell B8, and type Wed.

A black box appears around cell B8.

**9**   Move the mouse pointer over the lower right corner of cell B8.

The mouse pointer changes to a black plus sign.

**10**   Click the black plus sign at the lower right corner of cell B8, and drag it to cell B10.

Excel fills cell B9 with the value *Thu* and cell B10 with *Fri*. As you drag over cells B9 and B10, Excel displays a ScreenTip indicating which value will appear in each cell.

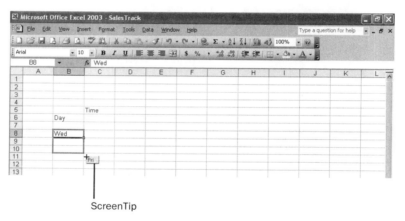

ScreenTip

**11**   Click cell C6, and type 9:00; then click cell D6, and type 9:15.

**Tip**   You give Excel two values when you use FillSeries: the first value sets the starting point for the series, and the second sets the increment. In this example, 9:15 is 15 minutes greater than the starting value of 9:00, so Excel adds 15 minutes to the current cell to generate the value for the next cell in the series.

**12**   Click cell C6, and drag to cell D6.

A black box appears around cells C6 and D6.

**13**   Move the mouse pointer over the lower right corner of cell D6.

When the mouse pointer is over the lower right corner of the cell, it changes to a black plus sign.

**14**   Click the black plus sign at the lower right corner of cell D6, and drag it to cell J6.

Excel fills the six cells from E6 through J6 with the next values in the series, namely 9:30 to 10:45, in 15-minute increments.

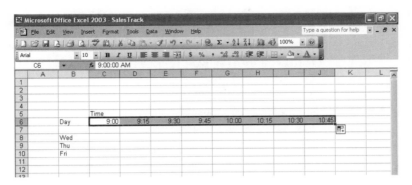

**15**  On the Standard toolbar, click the **Save** button to save your changes.

**CLOSE: SalesTrack.xls.**

Open

**16**  On the Standard toolbar, click the **Open** button.

The **Open** dialog box appears.

**17**  Click **DataEntry**, and then click **Open**.

DataEntry.xls appears.

**18**  Click the **Sheet2** sheet tab.

Sheet2 appears.

**19**  Click cell C8 and type **Bamboo S**, but do not press [Enter].

Just after you type the S, Excel searches the existing items in the column and, finding a match, adds the highlighted text *takes (30 cnt)* to the contents of the cell.

**20**  To accept the suggested value, *Bamboo Stakes (30 cnt)*, for the cell, press the [Enter] key.

Excel completes the cell entry.

> **Important** Pressing ⌫[Del] before pressing [Enter] (or [Tab]) will delete the highlighted text and keep *Bamboo S* as the value of the cell you were editing.

**21** Click cell C9 and type **Bamboo T**, but do not press [Enter].

Just after you type the *T*, Excel adds the highlighted text *rellis*.

**22** Press [Tab] to accept the suggested value, *Bamboo Trellis*.

*Bamboo Trellis* appears in cell C9.

**23** Right-click cell C10, and on the shortcut menu that appears, click **Pick from List**.

A list of existing values in the column appears.

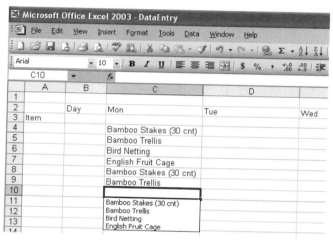

**24** Click **Bird Netting**.

*Bird Netting* appears in cell C10.

**25** Click the **Sheet1** sheet tab.

Sheet1 appears.

**26** Drag from cell C8 to cell J10.

Excel highlights the cells in the rectangle defined at the upper left by cell C8 and at the lower right by cell J10. Note that cell C8 is still the active cell.

**27** Type **0**, and press [Ctrl]+[Enter].

The value *0* appears in every selected cell.

**28** On the Standard toolbar, click the **Save** button to save your changes.

CLOSE: DataEntry.

# Checking and Correcting Data

*Microsoft
Office
Specialist*

Once you've entered your data, you should take the time to check and correct it. You do need to verify visually that each piece of numeric data is correct, but you can make sure that the text is spelled correctly by using Excel's spelling checker. When the spelling checker encounters a word it doesn't recognize, it will highlight the word and offer suggestions representing its best guess of the correct word. You can then edit the word directly, pick the proper word from the list of suggestions, or have the spelling checker ignore the misspelling. You can also use the spelling checker to add any words that aren't in the standard dictionary so that Excel will recognize them later, saving you time by not requiring you to identify the words as correct every time they occur in your worksheets. Once you've made a change, you can remove the change as long as you haven't closed the workbook where you made the change. To undo a change, you click the appropriate toolbar button or open the **Edit** menu and choose the **Undo** command. If you decide you want to keep a change, you can use the **Redo** command to restore it.

*New in
Office 2003*

If you're not sure of your word choice, or if you use a word that is almost but not quite right for your meaning, you can check for alternative words using the Thesaurus. A number of other Research tools are also available, such as the Encarta Encyclopedia, which you can refer to as you create your workbook.

You can use a distinct text format to identify data you might need to change later. As an example, a sales representative for one of The Garden Company's suppliers might give The Garden Company's owner, Catherine Turner, a list of prices for upcoming products, with a note that those prices could change at any time. Catherine could format the changeable prices differently from the rest of the prices in the worksheet and call the representative to update her worksheet just before the products became available. After receiving the new prices, she could use **Find Format** in the **Find and Replace** dialog box to locate the old prices and then change them by hand.

In this exercise, you have just found out that the manufacturer of the *Comfy Chair* has changed the name of the product to the *Cushy Chair*. You use **Find** to determine whether there are any occurrences of the word *Comfy*, and if there are, you use **Replace** to change them to *Cushy*. After you have made that change, you use **Find Format** to locate specially formatted data and change it. Finally you use the spelling checker to ensure that your text data has been entered correctly.

OPEN: Replace from the *SBS\Excel\GettingToKnowXL* folder.

**1** If necessary, click the **Furniture** sheet tab to display the Furniture worksheet.

**2** On the **Edit** menu, click **Find**.

The **Find and Replace** dialog box appears and opens to the **Find** tab.

**Tip** You can also open the **Find and Replace** dialog box by pressing Ctrl + F .

**3** In the **Find what** box, type Comfy, and then click **Find Next**.

The first cell containing *Comfy* is highlighted.

**4** In the **Find and Replace** dialog box, click **Find Next** again.

The second cell containing *Comfy* is highlighted.

**Tip** Clicking **Find All** would generate a list of matching cells and their contents below the dialog box. Clicking one of the matches moves you to that instance of the matching word or phrase.

**5** Click the **Replace** tab.

The **Find what** box still shows the word *Comfy*.

**6** In the **Replace with** box, type Cushy.

**7** Click **Replace All**.

A dialog box appears, indicating that Excel has completed the operation and that three replacements were made.

**8** Click **OK**.

The three occurrences of the word *Comfy* have been switched to *Cushy*.

**Important** You can change the occurrences of the word *Comfy* one at a time by clicking the **Replace** button instead of the **Replace All** button. You might do so to ensure that there are no instances in which you don't want to replace the original word.

**9** In the **Find and Replace** dialog box, click the **Find** tab.

The **Find** tab page appears.

**10** Clear the **Find what** box.

**11** Click the **Options** button to expand the options on the **Find** tab page.

The **Find** tab page options appear.

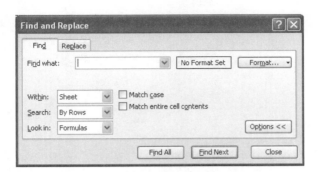

**12** Click the **Format** button.

The **Find Format** dialog box appears.

**13** If necessary, click the **Font** tab.

The **Font** tab page appears.

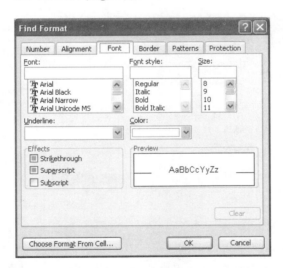

**14** In the **Font style** list, click **Italic**, and then click **OK**.

The **Find Format** dialog box disappears.

**15** In the **Find and Replace** dialog box, click **Find Next**.

Excel highlights the first cell containing italicized text.

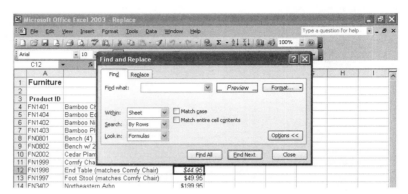

**16** In the **Find and Replace** dialog box, click **Close**.

The **Find and Replace** dialog box disappears.

*I*
Italic

**17** On the Formatting toolbar, click the **Italic** button.

Excel removes italics from the text in the selected cell.

**18** Type **47.95** and press Enter.

Excel replaces the previous value in the cell with the value you just entered. You will now undo the change you just made.

Undo

**19** On the Standard toolbar, click the **Undo** button.

The contents of cell C12 revert to 44.95.

**20** Click the **Undo** button.

The contents of cell C12 are once again italicized.

Redo

**21** Click the **Redo** button.

The contents of cell C12 are no longer italicized.

**22** On the **Tools** menu, click **Spelling**.

The **Spelling** dialog box appears. The first misspelled word Excel detects appears in the **Not in Dictionary** box, while the list of suggested replacements appears in the **Suggestions** list.

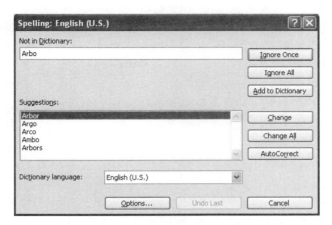

**23** If necessary, in the **Suggestions** list, click **Arbor** and then click **Change**.

Excel changes *Arbo* to *Arbor* and displays a dialog box asking if you want to continue checking spelling from the beginning of the worksheet.

**Tip** If you click **Change**, Excel inserts the suggested word. If you wanted Excel to ignore this occurrence of *Arbo*, you could have clicked **Ignore Once**; clicking **Ignore All** would cause Excel to skip over any occurrence of *Arbo* in the worksheet. Clicking **Add to Dictionary** means Excel would forever recognize *Arbo* as a word that did not need to be corrected.

**24** Click **Yes**.

A dialog box appears, indicating that the spelling checker found no more misspellings.

**25** Click **OK**.

The dialog box disappears.

**26** Click cell A1 and then, on the **Tools** menu, click **Research**.

The **Research** task pane appears.

**27** In the **Research** task pane, click the **Reference** down arrow (the down arrow next to the box with the default *All Reference Books* value), select **Thesaurus: English (U.S.)** from the list, and click the **Start Searching** button.

The results of your search appear in the **Research** task pane.

**28** In the **Research** task pane, click the **Reference** down arrow, and select **Encarta Encyclopedia: English (North America)** from the list.

The results of your search appear in the **Research** task pane.

CLOSE: Replace.xls.

# Key Points

- You can save a workbook in any folder you have permission to use, and in any of several file formats.

- To make it easier to search for relevant files using the Windows search tool, be sure to add some keywords to your workbook's properties.

- The Paste Options button gives you control over how your pasted data appears in your workbook—be sure to use it!

- If you need to enter a series of data, use AutoFill to save time.

- Use the spelling checker to ensure everything in your workbook is spelled correctly.

- If you're not sure of your word choice, or would like to explore a topic, the Thesaurus and the other online research tools can help you find more information.

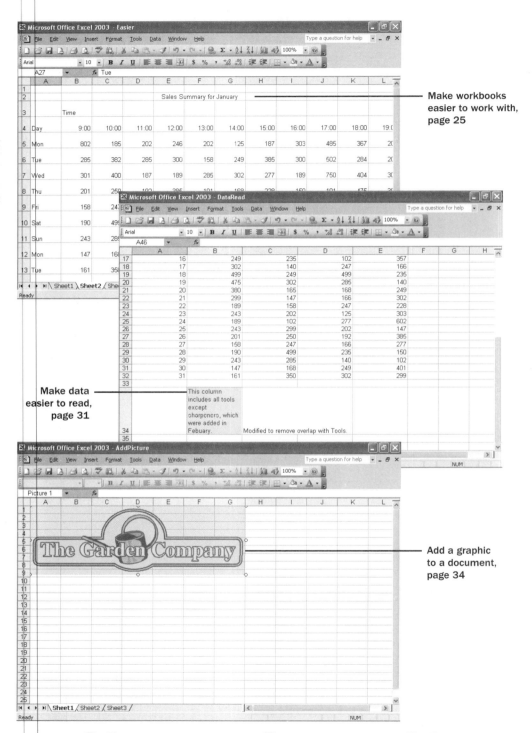

Make workbooks
easier to work with,
page 25

Make data
easier to read,
page 31

Add a graphic
to a document,
page 34

# Chapter 2 at a Glance

# 2 Setting Up a Workbook

**In this chapter you will learn to:**

✔ Make workbooks easier to work with.

✔ Make data easier to read.

✔ Add a graphic to a document.

One of the real strengths of Microsoft Excel is that the program helps you manage large quantities of data with ease. Part of the reason managing large data collections is so easy with Excel is that you can change how Excel displays your data within a worksheet. If you want more space between the rows or columns of a worksheet, want to temporarily limit which data is shown on the screen, or even just want to add descriptions that make it easier for you and your colleagues to understand the data that's stored in a worksheet, you can do so quickly. You can also change how those descriptions appear in a cell, setting them apart from the data in the worksheet.

Another way you can customize your worksheets is to add graphics, such as your company's logo or the image of a product, to a worksheet. Adding graphics to worksheets promotes awareness of your company, identifies the data as belonging to your company, and, in the case of a product image, gives viewers valuable information they need to make a purchase decision.

In this chapter, you'll learn how to make workbooks easier to work with, make data easier to read, and add a graphic to a document.

**See Also**   Do you need a quick refresher on the topics in this chapter? See the quick reference entries on pages xxix–xxxiii.

**Important**   Before you can use the practice files in this chapter, be sure you install them from the book's companion CD to their default location. See "Using the Book's CD" on page xi for more information.

## Making Workbooks Easier to Work With

*Microsoft Office Specialist*

An important component of making workbooks easy to work with is to give users an idea of where to find the data they're looking for. Excel provides several ways to set up signposts directing users toward the data they want. The first method, discussed in Chapter 1, "Getting to Know Excel," is to give each workbook a descriptive name. Once users have opened the proper workbook, you can guide them to a specific worksheet by giving each worksheet a name; the names are displayed on the sheet tabs in the lower left corner of the workbook window. To change a worksheet's name, you right-click the sheet tab of the worksheet you want and, from the shortcut menu that appears, choose **Rename**. Choosing **Rename** opens the worksheet name for editing. You can also change the order of worksheets in a workbook by dragging the sheet tab of a worksheet to the desired position on the navigation bar, bringing the most popular worksheets to the front of the list.

If you need more than three worksheets in most of the workbooks you create, you can change the default number of worksheets in your new workbooks. To change the default number of worksheets, on the **Tools** menu, click **Options**. In the **Options** dialog box, click the **General** tab, and, in the **Sheets In New Workbook** box, type the number of worksheets you want in your new workbooks, and click **OK**.

After you have put up the signposts that make your data easy to find, you can take other steps to make the data in your workbooks easier to work with. For instance, you can change the width of a column or the height of a row in a worksheet by dragging the column or row's border to the desired position. Increasing a column's width or a row's height increases the space between cell contents, making it easier to select a cell's data without inadvertently selecting data from other cells as well.

**Tip**   You can apply the same change to more than one row or column by selecting the rows or columns you want to change and then dragging the border of one of the selected rows or columns to the desired location. When you release the mouse button, all of the selected rows or columns will change to the new height or width.

Modifying column width and row height can make a workbook's contents easier to work with, but you can also insert a row or column between the edge of a worksheet and the cells that contain the data to accomplish this as well. Adding space between the edge of a worksheet and cells, or perhaps between a label and the data to which it refers, makes the workbook's contents less crowded and easier to work with. You insert rows by clicking a cell and then, on the **Insert** menu, clicking **Rows**. Excel inserts a row above the active cell. You insert a column in much the same way by clicking **Columns** on the **Insert** menu. When you do this, Excel inserts a column to the left of the active cell.

Likewise, you can insert individual cells into a worksheet. To insert a cell, click the cell that is currently in the position where you want the new cell to appear, and on the **Insert** menu, click **Cells** to display the **Insert** dialog box. In the **Insert** dialog box, you can choose whether to shift the cells surrounding the inserted cell down (if your data is arranged as a column) or to the right (if your data is arranged as a row). When you click **OK**, the new cell appears, and the contents of affected cells shift down or to the right, as appropriate. In a similar vein, if you want to delete a block of cells, select the cells, and on the **Edit** menu, click **Delete** to display the **Delete** dialog box, complete with option buttons that let you choose how to shift the position of the cells around the deleted cells.

**Tip** The **Insert** dialog box also includes option buttons you can select to insert a new row or column; the **Delete** dialog box has similar buttons that let you delete an entire row or column.

In some cases, the values you want to put in the new cells might already exist in your worksheet. For example, Catherine Turner might have typed some sales data into a blank worksheet in anticipation of modifying the sheet once the rest of the data was entered. You can move cells from another part of your worksheet, rather than just copy or cut the values from the cells and paste them into other cells, by using a variation of the standard cut-and-paste operation. After you select the cells and click the **Cut** toolbar button on the **Standard** toolbar, on the **Insert** menu, click **Cut Cells**. The **Insert Paste** dialog box will appear, allowing you to choose how to shift the cells surrounding the cells you're inserting.

**Tip** If you click the **Copy** toolbar button instead of the **Cut** toolbar button, the menu item on the **Insert** menu will be **Copy Cells** instead of **Cut Cells**.

Merge and
Center

Sometimes adding cells or even changing a row's height or a column's width isn't the best way to improve your workbook's usability. For instance, even though a column label might not fit within a single cell, increasing that cell's width (or every cell's width) might throw off the worksheet's design. While you can type individual words in cells so that the label fits in the worksheet, another alternative is to merge two or more cells. Merging cells tells Excel to treat a group of cells as a single cell as far as content and formatting go. To merge cells into a single cell, you click the **Merge and Center** toolbar button. As the name of the button implies, Excel centers the contents of the merged cell.

**Tip** Clicking a merged cell and then clicking the *Merge and Center* toolbar button removes the merge.

If you want to delete a row or column, you right-click the row or column head and then, from the shortcut menu that appears, click **Delete**. You can temporarily hide a number of rows or columns by selecting those rows or columns and then, on the **Format** menu, pointing to **Row** or **Column** and then clicking **Hide**. The rows or columns you selected disappear, but they aren't gone for good, as they would be if you'd used **Delete**. Instead, they have just been removed from the display until you call them back; to return the hidden rows to the display, on the **Format** menu, point to **Row** or **Column** and then click **Unhide**.

When you insert a row, column, or cell in a worksheet with existing formatting, the **Insert Options** button appears. As with the **Paste Options** button and the **Auto Fill Options** button, clicking the **Insert Options** button displays a list of choices you can make about how the inserted row or column should be formatted. The options are summarized in the following table.

| Option | Action |
|---|---|
| **Format Same as Above** | Apply the format of the row above the inserted row to the new row. |
| **Format Same as Below** | Apply the format of the row below the inserted row to the new row. |
| **Format Same as Left** | Apply the format of the column to the left of the inserted column to the new column. |
| **Format Same as Right** | Apply the format of the column to the right of the inserted column to the new column. |
| **Clear Formatting** | Apply the default format to the new row or column. |

In this exercise, you make the worksheet containing last January's sales data easier to read. First you name the worksheet and bring it to the front of the list of worksheets in its workbook. Next you increase the column width and row height of the cells holding the sales data. In addition, you merge and center the worksheet's title and then add a row between the title and the row that holds the times for which The Garden Company recorded sales. Then you add a column to the left of the first column of data and then hide rows containing data for all but the first week of the month.

OPEN: Easier.xls from the *SBS\Excel\SettingUpWorkbook* folder.

1    Select cells C1 to D3 and, on the **Standard** toolbar, click the **Cut** button.

2    Select cells B5 to C7.

3    On the **Insert** menu, click **Cut Cells**.

    The **Insert Paste** dialog box appears.

4    If necessary, select the **Shift Cells Right** option button, and click **OK**.

    The cut cells appear in cells B5 to C7, pushing the existing cells to the right. The values in cells C5 to C7 are repeated incorrectly in cells D5 to D7.

5    Select cells D5 to D7 and, on the **Edit** menu, click **Delete**.

    The **Delete** dialog box appears.

6    If necessary, select the **Shift Cells Left** option button, and click **OK**.

    Cells D5 to D7 are deleted.

**7** In the lower left corner of the workbook window, right-click the **Sheet2** sheet tab.

**8** From the shortcut menu that appears, click **Rename**.

Sheet2 is highlighted.

**9** Type January, and press `Enter`.

The name of the worksheet changes from *Sheet2* to *January*.

| | | | | | | |
|---|---|---|---|---|---|---|
| 20 | Tue | 202 | 102 | 277 | 187 | 187 |
| 21 | Wed | 300 | 401 | 150 | 125 | 385 |
| 22 | Thu | 189 | 299 | 102 | 283 | 277 |
| 23 | Fri | 101 | 166 | 401 | 166 | 201 |
| 24 | Sat | 135 | 235 | 299 | 202 | 125 |
| 25 | Sun | 206 | 140 | 382 | 243 | 444 |

Ⅰ◀ ◀ ▶ ▶Ⅰ \ Sheet1 \ **January** / Sheet3 /

Ready

**10** Click the **January** sheet tab, and drag it to the left of the **Sheet1** sheet tab.

The **January** sheet tab moves to the left of the **Sheet1** sheet tab. As the sheet tab moves, an inverted black triangle marks the sheet's location in the workbook.

**11** Click the column head for column A, and drag to column M.

Columns A through M are highlighted.

**12** Position the mouse pointer over the right edge of column A, and drag the edge to the right until the ScreenTip reads *Width: 10.00 (75 pixels)*.

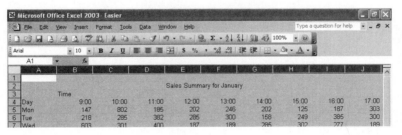

**13** The width of the selected columns changes.

**14** Select rows 3 through 35.

Rows 3 through 35 are highlighted.

**15** Position the mouse pointer over the bottom edge of row 3, and drag the edge down until the ScreenTip says *Height: 25.50 (34 pixels)*.

The height of the selected rows changes.

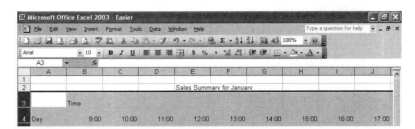

**16** Click cell E2, and drag to cell G2.

**17** On the Formatting toolbar, click the **Merge and Center** toolbar button.

Cells E2, F2, and G2 are merged into a single cell, and the new cell's contents are centered.

**Important** Depending on the screen resolution you have set on your computer and which toolbar buttons you use most often, it's possible that not every button on every toolbar will appear on your Excel toolbars. If a button mentioned in this book doesn't appear on a toolbar, click the **Toolbar Options** down arrow on that toolbar to display the rest of the buttons available on that toolbar.

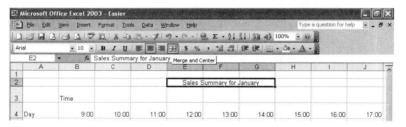

**18** Click cell A3.

**19** On the **Insert** menu, click **Rows**.

A new row, labeled row 3, appears above the row previously labeled row 3.

**20** On the **Insert** menu, click **Columns**.

A new column, labeled column A, appears to the left of the column previously labeled column A.

**21** Select rows 13 through 36.

Rows 13 through 36 are highlighted.

**22** On the **Format** menu, point to **Row**, and then click **Hide**.

Rows 13 through 36 disappear from the worksheet.

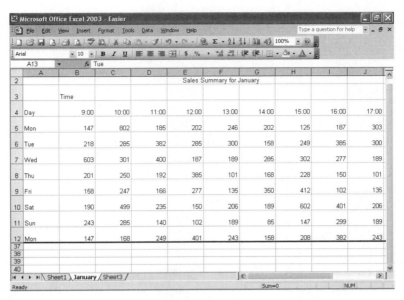

**23** On the **Format** menu, point to **Row**, and then click **Unhide**.

The hidden rows reappear in the worksheet.

**24** On the **Tools** menu, click **Options**.

The **Options** dialog box appears.

**25** Click the **General** tab.

The **General** tab page appears.

**26** In the **Sheets In New Workbook** box, type 12.

**27** Click **OK**.

**28** On the **Standard** toolbar, click the **Save** button.

Save

Excel saves the document.

CLOSE: Easier.xls.

# Making Data Easier to Read

*Microsoft Office Specialist*

After you have modified your worksheet so that it is easier to work with, you can make the data easier to read by changing how data is presented within the worksheet's cells. One case in which you might want to change how data is presented occurs if the data doesn't fit in a cell's boundaries and you don't want to merge the cells the data overlaps with. For instance, you could choose not to merge the cells because you might want to add data or comments to the neighboring cells later.

The following graphic shows what happens if there is a spillover in two adjacent cells.

| | | |
|---|---|---|
| 161 | 350 | 302 |
| This column include | Modified to remove overlap with Tools. | |

If the cell to the right were empty, the text in the left cell would simply spill over into the cell to its right. When there is data in the cell to the right, however, Excel brings it to the front, hiding any data that spills over from the adjoining cell. To avoid hiding the text in the first cell behind the text in the second cell, you can have the text wrap within the first cell, as seen in the following graphic.

| | | |
|---|---|---|
| | This column includes all tools except sharpeners, which were added in | |
| 34 | February. | Modified to remove overlap with Tools. |

**Tip**     It may be tempting to just change a column's width to accommodate your data, but remember that widening a single column will make that column stand out in the worksheet, possibly causing data in other columns to become harder to read.

Another method for making your data easier to read is to distinguish any data labels by changing how the data appears in a cell. One way to separate data labels from the data that follows them is to change the *alignment* of the labels in their cells. For example, you can center the data labels in their cells, setting the labels apart from the right-aligned data farther down in the column.

You can also make your worksheet data easier to read by ensuring that the data labels at the top of a column *freeze*, or remain on the screen regardless of how far down in the document you scroll. For instance, Catherine Turner, the owner of The Garden Company, might not remember which data is kept in which column in a worksheet. Freezing the data labels at the top of the column would let her scroll to the last row of the worksheet and still have the labels visible as a reference. Excel marks the division between frozen and unfrozen cells with a *split bar*.

Split bar

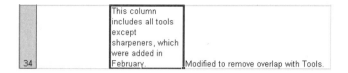

**Troubleshooting**   When you tell Excel to freeze rows in your worksheet, Excel freezes the rows above the active cell and the columns to the left of the active cell. So, if you want to freeze the top three rows of your worksheet, click the first cell in the fourth row (cell A4) and then turn on the freeze. If you wanted to freeze the top three rows and the first column, you would click the second cell in the fourth row (cell B4).

In this exercise, you prevent the text in a cell from spilling over into adjoining cells, allowing you to enter comments in those adjoining cells without obscuring the contents of the first cell. You then change the alignment of the cells containing the data labels for the columns in your worksheet and then freeze those data labels so that they remain at the top of the page as you scroll down through the worksheet.

OPEN: DataRead.xls from the *SBS\Excel\SettingUpWorkbook* folder.

**1**   If necessary, click the **SalesbyCategory** sheet tab.

**2**   Click cell B34.

**3**   On the **Format** menu, click **Cells**.

The **Format Cells** dialog box appears.

**4**   If necessary, click the **Alignment** tab.

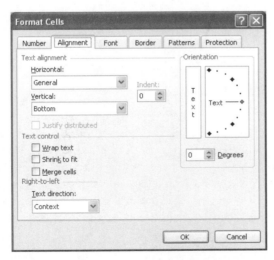

**5**   If necessary, select the **Wrap text** check box, and click **OK**.

The text in cell B34 wraps to fit within the original borders of the cell.

**6**   Click cell B1, and drag to cell E1.

**7**   On the Formatting toolbar, click the **Center** button.

Center

The contents of the selected cells are centered within those cells.

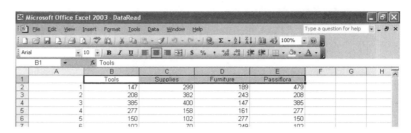

**8** Click cell A2.

**9** On the **Window** menu, click **Freeze Panes**.

A split bar appears between row 1 and row 2.

**10** On the vertical scroll bar, click the down arrow.

Row 1 stays in place while the remaining rows scroll normally.

**11** On the **Window** menu, click **Unfreeze Panes**.

The split bar disappears, and all rows scroll normally.

**12** On the Standard toolbar, click the **Save** button.

Excel saves your changes.

Save

CLOSE: DataRead.xls.

# Adding a Graphic to a Document

*Microsoft Office Specialist*

An important part of establishing a strong business is creating a memorable corporate identity. Setting aside the obvious need for sound management, two important physical attributes of a strong retail business are a well-conceived shop space and an eye-catching, easy-to-remember logo. Once you or your graphic artist has created a logo, you should add the logo to all of your documents, especially any that might be seen by your customers. Not only does the logo mark the documents as coming from your company, it also serves as an advertisement, encouraging anyone who sees your worksheets to call or visit your company.

One way to add a picture to a worksheet is to go through the **Insert** menu and click the **Picture** item. Clicking **Picture** shows a submenu that lists several sources from which you can choose a picture to add; in this case, where you're adding a logo you've saved as a graphics file, you can click the **From File** item to open a dialog box that lets you locate the picture you want to add from your hard disk.

**Tip** When you insert a picture, the **Picture** toolbar might appear. The **Picture** toolbar contains buttons that let you change the picture's contrast, brightness, and so on. You can use those buttons to change your picture's appearance, but you don't get as much control as when you use the **Format Picture** dialog box, presented later in this section.

Once you've added the picture to your worksheet, you can change the picture's location on the worksheet by dragging it to the desired spot. You can also change the appearance of the picture by opening the **Format** menu and choosing **Picture**. Then, in the **Format Picture** dialog box, you can modify the image's size or brightness, rotate the image on the page, or crop away any portion of the image that you don't want to show.

You can also resize a picture by clicking it and then dragging one of the handles that appears on the graphic. Using the **Format Picture** dialog box helps ensure that the *aspect ratio*, or relationship between the picture's height and width, doesn't change. If you do accidentally resize a graphic by dragging a handle, just click the **Undo** button to remove your change.

If you'd like to generate a repeating image in the background of a worksheet, forming a tiled pattern behind your worksheet's data, you can open the **Format** menu, point to **Sheet**, and click **Background**. In the **Sheet Background** dialog box, click the image that you want to serve as the background pattern for your worksheet, and click **OK**.

**Tip** To remove a background image from a worksheet, open the **Format** menu, point to **Sheet**, and click **Delete Background**.

In this exercise, you add the new logo for The Garden Company to an existing worksheet, change the graphic's location on the worksheet, reduce the size of the graphic, change the image's brightness and contrast, rotate and crop the image, delete the image, and then set the image as a repeating background for the worksheet.

OPEN: AddPicture.xls from the *SBS\Excel\SettingUpWorkbook* folder.

1   Click cell A1.

2   On the **Insert** menu, point to **Picture**, and then click **From File**.

The **Insert Picture** dialog box appears.

3   If necessary, navigate to the SettingUpWorkbook folder and then double-click **tgc_logo.gif**.

The chosen graphic appears in the AddPicture.xls file.

**4** Right-click the graphic, and from the shortcut menu that appears, click **Format Picture**.

The **Format Picture** dialog box appears.

**5** Click the **Size** tab.

The **Size** tab page appears. Notice that the **Lock aspect ratio** check box is selected.

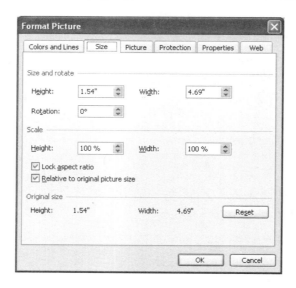

**6** In the **Scale** section of the tab page, clear the contents of the **Height** box, and type 50%.

**7** In the **Size and Rotate** section of the tab page, clear the contents of the **Rotation** box, type 180, and click **OK**.

The picture is resized, maintaining the original aspect ratio, and rotated.

**8** Click the center of the graphic, and drag it so that it is centered horizontally on the screen and the top of the graphic is just below row 1.

The graphic moves with your mouse pointer.

**Troubleshooting** Remember that dragging one of the handles at the edge of the graphic will resize the graphic. If you accidentally resize the logo instead of moving it, click the **Undo** button.

**9** On the **Format** menu, click **Picture**.

The **Format Picture** dialog box appears.

**10** Click the **Picture** tab.

The **Picture** tab page appears.

**11** In the **Image Control** section of the dialog box, clear the contents of the **Brightness** box, and type 40.

**12** In the **Image Control** section of the dialog box, clear the contents of the **Contrast** box, and type 40.

**13** In the **Crop From** section of the dialog box, clear the contents of the **Top** box, type .5, and click **OK**.

The image changes to reflect the properties you set.

**14** If necessary, select the image, and, on the **Standard** toolbar, click the **Cut** button.

The image disappears.

**15** On the **Format** menu, point to **Sheet**, and click **Background**.

The **Sheet Background** dialog box appears.

**16** If necessary, navigate to the SettingUpWorkbook folder and then double-click **tgc_logo.gif**.

The image repeats in the background of the active worksheet.

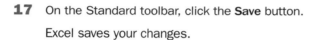

**17** On the Standard toolbar, click the **Save** button.

Save

Excel saves your changes.

CLOSE: AddPicture.xls.

# Key Points

- You can control how many worksheets appear in new workbooks you create. If you always use workbooks where each worksheet represents a month of the year, change the default number of worksheets to 12!

- Making sure your data is easily readable is one of the best things you can do for your colleagues. Be sure your worksheet columns and rows are roomy enough to accommodate your data.

- Remember that you can add or delete individual cells from a worksheet. Rather than go through a lengthy cut-and-paste routine when you forgot to type a cell value, just add a cell where you need it.

- If you add a graphic to your worksheet, you can change the graphic's size and appearance using the Format Picture dialog box.

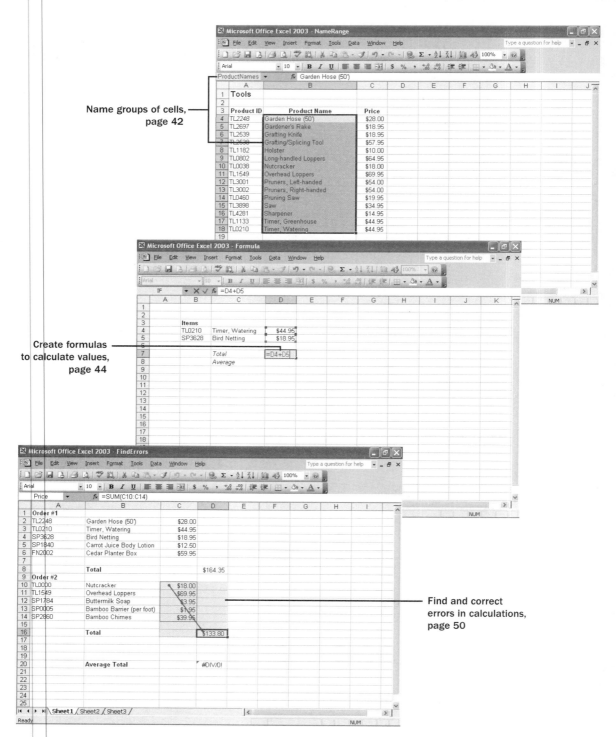

Name groups of cells, page 42

Create formulas to calculate values, page 44

Find and correct errors in calculations, page 50

# Chapter 3 at a Glance

# 3 Performing Calculations on Data

**In this chapter you will learn to:**

✔ Name groups of cells.

✔ Create formulas to calculate values.

✔ Find and correct errors in calculations.

Microsoft Excel workbooks give you a handy place to store and organize your data, but you can also do a lot more with your data in Excel. One important task you can perform in Excel is to calculate totals for the values in a series of related cells. You can also use Excel to find out other information about the data you select, such as the maximum or minimum value in a group of cells. Finding the maximum or minimum value in a group can let you identify your best salesperson, product categories you might need to pay more attention to, or suppliers that consistently give you the best deal. Regardless of your bookkeeping needs, Excel gives you the ability to find the information you want. And if you should make an error, you can find the cause and correct it quickly.

Many times you can't access the information you want without referencing more than one cell, and it's also often true that you'll use the data in the same group of cells for more than one calculation. Excel makes it easy to reference a number of cells at once, letting you define your calculations quickly.

In this chapter, you'll learn how to streamline references to groups of data in your worksheets and how to create and correct formulas that summarize the sales and product data from The Garden Company.

**See Also** Do you need a quick refresher on the topics in this chapter? See the quick reference entries on pages xxxiii–xxxv.

 **Important** Before you can use the practice files in this chapter, be sure you install them from the book's companion CD-ROM to their default location. See "Using the Book's CD-ROM" on page xi for more information.

# Naming Groups of Data

**Microsoft
Office
Specialist**

When you work with large amounts of data, it's easier to identify groups of cells that contain related data. In the following graphic, for example, cells C2 through C6 hold the prices of items from a customer's order.

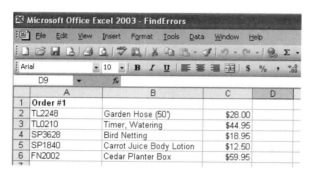

Rather than specify the cells individually every time you want to use the data they contain, you can define those cells as a *range* (also called a *named range*). For instance, you could group the items from the previous graphic into a range named *OrderItems1*. Whenever you want to use the contents of that range in a calculation, you can simply use the name of the range instead of specifying each cell individually.

You can create a named range in a number of ways, two of which you can access through the **Insert** menu. The first method works well if you have a column of data with a label at the head of the column, as in the following graphic.

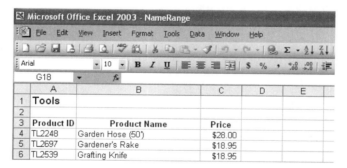

In this case, you access the **Create Names** dialog box by pointing to **Name** on the **Insert** menu and clicking **Create**. In the **Create Names** dialog box, you can define a named range by having Excel use the label in the top cell as the range's name. You can also create and delete named ranges through the **Define Name** dialog box, which you access by pointing to **Define** on the **Insert** menu and clicking **Name**.

A final way to create a named range is to select the cells you want in the range, click in the **Name** box next to the formula bar, and then type the name for the range. You can display the ranges available in a workbook by clicking the **Name** box's down arrow.

**Important**   Every range in a workbook must have a unique name. Assigning the name of an existing range to a new range removes the original reference, likely affecting how your worksheet behaves.

In this exercise, you will create named ranges to streamline references to groups of cells.

OPEN: NameRange from the *SBS\Excel\PerformingCalculations* folder.

**1**   If necessary, click the **Tools** sheet tab.

**2**   Click cell C3 and drag to cell C18.

The selected cells are highlighted.

**3**   On the **Insert** menu, point to **Name**, and then click **Create**.

The **Create Names** dialog box appears.

**4**   If necessary, select the **Top row** check box.

**5**   Click **OK**.

Excel assigns the name *Price* to the cell range.

**6**   In the lower left corner of the workbook window, click the **Supplies** sheet tab.

The Supplies worksheet appears.

**7**   Click cell C4 and drag to cell C29.

**8**   On the **Insert** menu, point to **Name**, and then click **Define**.

The **Define Name** dialog box appears.

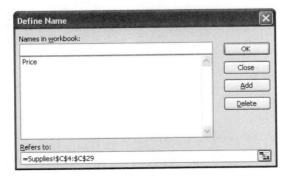

**9** In the **Names in Workbook** box, type SuppliesPrice and then click **OK**.

Excel assigns the name *SuppliesPrice* to the cell range, and the **Define Name** dialog box disappears.

**10** In the lower left corner of the workbook window, click the **Furniture** sheet tab.

The Furniture worksheet appears.

**11** Click cell C4 and drag to cell C18.

**12** Click in the Name box.

The contents of the Name box are highlighted.

**13** Type FurniturePrice, and press [Enter].

Excel assigns the name *FurniturePrice* to the cell range.

**14** On the **Insert** menu, point to **Name**, and then click **Define**.

The **Define Name** dialog box appears.

**15** In the **Names in workbook** list of the **Define Name** dialog box, click **Price**.

*Price* appears in the **Names in workbook** box.

**16** In the **Names in workbook** box, delete *Price*, type ToolsPrice, and then click **OK**.

The **Define Name** dialog box disappears.

**17** On the Standard toolbar, click the **Save** button.

Save

CLOSE: NameRange.

# Creating Formulas to Calculate Values

*Microsoft Office Specialist*

Once you've added your data to a worksheet and defined ranges to simplify data references, you can create a *formula*, or an expression that performs calculations on your data. For example, you can calculate the total cost of a customer's order, figure the average sales for all Wednesdays in the month of January, or find the highest and lowest daily sales for a week, month, or year.

To write an Excel formula, you begin the cell's contents with an equal sign—when Excel sees it, it knows that the expression following it should be interpreted as a calculation and not text. After the equal sign, you type the formula. For instance, you can find the sum of the numbers in cells C2 and C3 using the formula =C2+C3. After you have entered a formula into a cell, you can revise it by clicking the cell and then editing the formula in the formula bar. For example, you can change the preceding formula to =C3-C2, which calculates the difference between the contents of cells C2 and C3.

**Troubleshooting**   If Excel treats your formula as text, make sure you haven't accidentally put a space before the equal sign. Remember, the equal sign must be the first
character!

Typing the cell references for 15 or 20 cells in a calculation would be tedious, but
Excel makes it easy to handle complex calculations. To create a new calculation, you
click **Function** on the **Insert** menu. The **Insert Function** dialog box appears, with a list
of *functions*, or predefined formulas, from which you can choose.

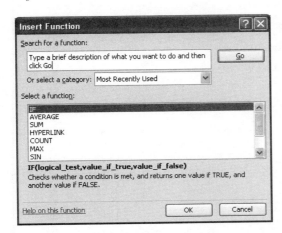

The most useful functions in the list are described in the following table.

| Item | Description |
| --- | --- |
| SUM | Returns the sum of the numbers in the specified cells |
| AVERAGE | Finds the average of the numbers in the specified cells |
| COUNT | Finds the number of entries in the specified cells |
| MAX | Finds the largest value in the specified cells |
| MIN | Finds the smallest value in the specified cells |

Two other functions you might use are the NOW() and PMT() functions. The NOW()
function returns the time the workbook was last opened, so the value will change
every time the workbook is opened. The proper form for this function is *=NOW()*; to
update the value to the current date and time, just save your work, close the workbook, and then reopen it. The PMT() function is a bit more complex. It calculates
payments due on a loan, assuming a constant interest rate and constant payments. To
perform its calculations, the PMT() function requires an interest rate, the number of

months of payments, and the starting balance. The elements to be entered into the function are called *arguments* and must be entered in a certain order. That order is written *PMT(rate, nper, pv, fv, type)*. The following table summarizes the arguments in the PMT() function.

| Argument | Description |
| --- | --- |
| rate | The interest rate, to be divided by 12 for a loan with monthly payments |
| nper | The total number of payments for the loan |
| pv | The amount loaned (pv is short for present value, or principal) |
| fv | The amount to be left over at the end of the payment cycle (usually left blank, which indicates 0) |
| type | 0 or 1, indicating whether payments are made at the beginning or at the end of the month (usually left blank, which indicates 0, or the end of the month) |

If you wanted to borrow $20,000 at an 8 percent interest rate and pay the loan back over 24 months, you could use the PMT() function to figure out the monthly payments. In this case, the function would be written *=PMT(8%/12, 24, 20000)*, which calculates a monthly payment of $904.55.

You can also add the names of any ranges you've defined to a formula. For example, if the named range *Order1* refers to cells C2 through C6, you can calculate the average of cells C2 through C6 with the formula *=AVERAGE(Order1)*. If you want to include a series of contiguous cells in a formula but you haven't defined the cells as a named range, you can click the first cell in the range and drag to the last cell. If the cells aren't contiguous, hold down the ⌃Ctrl key and click the cells to be included. In both cases, when you release the mouse button, the references of the cells you selected appear in the formula.

Another use for formulas is to display messages when certain conditions are met. For instance, Catherine Turner, the owner of The Garden Company, might provide a free copy of a gardening magazine to customers making purchases worth more than $150. This kind of formula is called a *conditional formula,* and it uses the IF function. To create a conditional formula, you click the cell to hold the formula and open the **Insert Function** dialog box. From within the dialog box, you select **IF** from the list of available functions and then click **OK**. The **Function Arguments** dialog box appears.

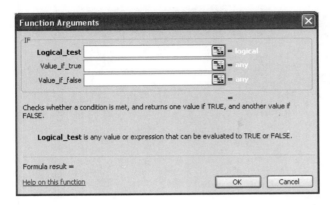

When you work with an IF function, the **Function Arguments** dialog box will have three boxes: **Logical_test**, **Value_if_true**, and **Value_if_false**. The **Logical_test** box holds the condition you want to check. To check whether the total for an order is greater than $150, the expression would be *SUM(Order1)>150*.

Now you need to have Excel display messages indicating whether the customer should receive a free magazine. To have Excel print a message from an IF function, you enclose the message in quotes in the **Value_if_true** or **Value_if_false** box. In this case, you would type *"Qualifies for a free magazine!"* in the **Value_if_true** box and *"Thanks for your order!"* in the **Value_if_false** box.

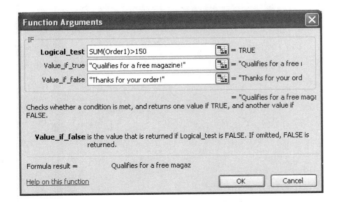

Once you've created a formula, you can copy it and paste it into another cell. When you do, Excel will try to change the formula so that it works in the new cells. For instance, in the following graphic, cell D8 contains the formula *=SUM(C2:C6)*.

Clicking cell D8, copying the cell's contents, and then pasting the result into cell D16 writes *=SUM(C10:C14)* into cell D16. Excel has reinterpreted the formula so that it fits the surrounding cells! Excel knows it can reinterpret the cells used in the formula because the formula uses a *relative reference*, or a reference that can change if the formula is copied to another cell. Relative references are written with just the cell row and column (for example, *C14*). If you want a cell reference to remain constant when the formula using it is copied to another cell, you can use an absolute reference. To write a cell reference as an absolute reference, you type *$* before the row name and the column number. If you wanted the formula in cell D16 to show the sum of values in cells C10 through C14 regardless of the cell into which it is pasted, you would write the formula as *=SUM($C$10:$C$14)*.

**Tip** If you copy a formula from the formula bar, use absolute references, or use only named ranges in your formula. Excel won't change the cell references when you copy your formula to another cell.

In this exercise, you create a formula to find the total cost of an order, copy that formula to another cell, and then create a formula to find the average cost of items in the order. The cells with the cost of products in this order are stored in the named range *OrderItems*.

OPEN: Formula from the *SBS\Excel\PerformingCalculations* folder.

1  Click cell D7.

   D7 becomes the active cell.

2  In the formula bar, type =SUM, drag from cell D4 to D5, and press [Enter].

   The value $63.90 appears in cell D7.

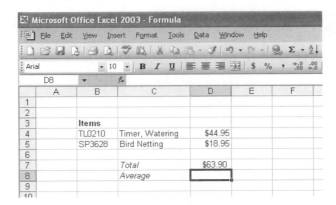

Copy

Paste

**3** Click cell D7, and then, on the Standard toolbar, click the **Copy** button.

Excel copies the formula in cell D7 to the Clipboard.

**4** Click cell D8, and then, on the Standard toolbar, click the **Paste** button.

The value *$18.95* appears in cell D8, and *=SUM(D5:D6)* appears in the formula bar.

**5** Press ⌑.

The formula in cell D8 disappears.

**6** On the **Insert** menu, click **Function**.

The **Insert Function** dialog box appears.

**7** Click **AVERAGE**, and then click **OK**.

The **Function Arguments** dialog box appears, with the contents of the **Number 1** box highlighted.

**8** Type OrderItems, and then click **OK**.

The **Function Arguments** dialog box disappears, and *$31.95* appears in cell D8.

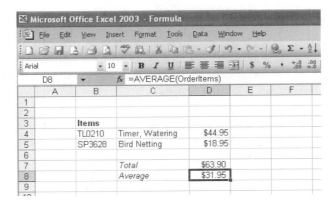

**9** Click cell C10.

**10** On the **Insert** menu, click **Function**.

The **Insert Function** dialog box appears.

**11** In the **Select a function** list, click **IF** and then click **OK**.

The **Function Arguments** dialog box appears.

**12** In the **Logical_test** box, type **D7>50**.

**13** In the **Value_if_true** box, type **"5% discount"**.

**14** In the **Value_if_false** box, type **"No discount"** and then click **OK**.

The **Function Arguments** dialog box disappears, and *5% discount* appears in cell C10.

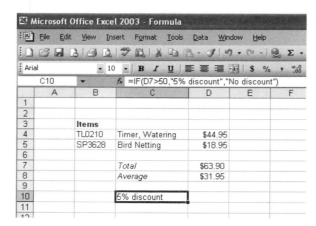

**15** On the Standard toolbar, click the **Save** button.

Save

Excel saves your changes.

CLOSE: Formula.

# Finding and Correcting Errors in Calculations

*Microsoft Office Specialist*

Including calculations in a worksheet gives you valuable answers to questions about your data. As is always true, however, it is possible for errors to creep into your formulas. Excel makes it easy to find the source of errors in your formulas by identifying the cells used in a given calculation and describing any errors that have occurred. The process of examining a worksheet for errors in formulas is referred to as *auditing*.

Excel identifies errors in several ways. The first way is to fill the cell holding the formula generating the error with an *error code*. In the following graphic, cell D8 has the error code *#NAME?*.

Error

When a cell with an erroneous formula is the active cell, an **Error** button appears next to it. You can click the button's down arrow to display a menu with options that provide information about the error and offer to help you fix it. The following table lists the most common error codes and what they mean.

| Error Code | Description |
| --- | --- |
| ##### | The column isn't wide enough to display the value. |
| #VALUE! | The formula has the wrong type of argument (such as text where a TRUE or FALSE value is required). |
| #NAME? | The formula contains text that Excel doesn't recognize (such as an unknown named range). |
| #REF! | The formula refers to a cell that doesn't exist (which can happen whenever cells are deleted). |
| #DIV/0! | The formula attempts to divide by zero. |

Another technique you can use to find the source of formula errors is to ensure that the appropriate cells are providing values for the formula. For example, you might want to calculate the total sales for a product category, but say you accidentally create a formula referring to the products' names, not their prices. You can identify that kind of error by having Excel trace a cell's *precedents*, which are the cells with values used in the active cell's formula. Excel identifies a cell's precedents by drawing a blue tracer arrow from the precedent to the active cell.

You can also audit your worksheet by identifying cells with formulas that use a value from a given cell. For example, you might have the total cost of a single order used in a formula that calculates the average cost of all orders placed on a given day. Cells that use another cell's value in their calculations are known as *dependents*, meaning that they depend on the value in the other cell to derive their own value. As with tracing precedents, you can point to **Formula Auditing** on the **Tools** menu and then click **Trace Dependents** to have Excel draw blue arrows from the active cell to those cells that have calculations based on that value.

If the cells identified by the tracer arrows aren't the correct cells, you can hide the arrows and correct the formula. To hide the tracer arrows on a worksheet, you point to **Formula Auditing** on the **Tools** menu and click **Remove All Arrows**.

If you prefer to have the elements of a formula error presented as text in a dialog box, you can use the **Error Checking** dialog box (which you display by clicking **Error Checking** on the **Tools** menu) to view the error and the formula in the cell where the error occurs. You can also use the controls in the **Error Checking** dialog box to move through the formula one step at a time, to choose to ignore the error, or to move to the next or the previous error. If you click the **Options** button, you can also use the controls in the **Options** dialog box to change how Excel determines what is an error and what isn't.

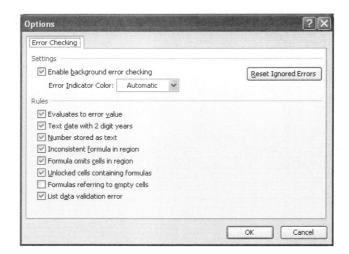

**Tip** One change worth noting is that you can have the **Error Checking** tool ignore formulas that don't use every cell in a region (such as a row or column). If you clear the **Formula Omits Cells In Region** check box, you can create formulas that don't add up every value in a row or column (or rectangle) without Excel marking them as an error.

For times when you just want to display the results of each step of a formula and don't need the full power of the Error Checking tool, you can use the **Evaluate Formula** dialog box to move through each element of the formula. To display the **Evaluate Formula** dialog box, you point to **Formula Auditing** on the **Tools** menu and click

**Evaluate Formula**. The Evaluate Formula dialog box is much more useful for examining formulas that don't produce an error but aren't generating the result you expect.

Finally, you can monitor the value in a cell regardless of where in your workbook you are by opening a watch window that displays the value in the cell. For example, if one of your formulas uses values from cells in other worksheets, or even other workbooks, you can set a watch on the cell that contains the formula and then change the values in the other cells. To set a watch, click the cell you want to monitor, point to **Formula Auditing** on the **Tools** menu, and then click **Show Watch Window**. Click **Add Watch** to have Excel monitor the selected cell.

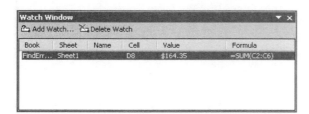

As soon as you type in the new value, the watch window displays the new result of the formula. When you're done watching the formula, select the watch, click **Delete Watch**, and close the watch window.

In this exercise, you use the formula auditing capabilities in Excel to identify and correct errors in a formula.

OPEN: FindErrors from the *SBS\Excel\PerformingCalculations* folder.

**1**   Click cell D20.

**2**   On the **Tools** menu, point to **Formula Auditing**, and then click **Show Watch Window**.

**3**   Click **Add Watch,** and then click **Add** in the **Add Watch** dialog box.

Cell D20 appears in the watch window.

**4**   Click cell D8.

*=SUM(C2:C6)* appears in the formula bar.

**5**   On the **Tools** menu, point to **Formula Auditing**, and then click **Trace Precedents**.

A blue arrow appears between cell D8 and the group of cells from C2 to C6, indicating that cells in the C2:C6 range are precedents of the value in cell D8.

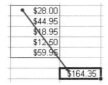

**6** On the **Tools** menu, point to **Formula Auditing**, and then click **Remove All Arrows**.

The arrow disappears.

**7** Click cell A1.

**8** On the **Tools** menu, click **Error Checking**.

The **Error Checking** dialog box appears.

**9** Click **Next**.

The error in cell D8 appears in the **Error Checking** dialog box.

**10** Click the **Close** button to close the **Error Checking** dialog box.

**11** On the **Tools** menu, point to **Formula Auditing**, and then click **Trace Error**.

Blue arrows appear, pointing to cell D20 from cells D7 and D15. These arrows indicate that using the values (or lack of values, in this case) in the indicated cells is generating the error in cell D20.

**12** On the **Tools** menu, point to **Formula Auditing**, and then click **Remove All Arrows**.

The arrows disappear.

**13** In the formula bar, delete the existing formula, type **=AVERAGE(D8,D16)**, and press [Enter].

The value *$149.08* appears in cell D20.

**14** Click cell D20.

**15** On the **Tools** menu, point to **Formula Auditing**, and then click **Evaluate Formula**.

The **Evaluate Formula** dialog box appears, with the formula from cell D20 displayed.

**16** Click **Evaluate**.

The result of the formula in cell D20 appears.

**17** Click **Close**.

**18** In the watch window, click the watch in the list.

**19** Click **Delete Watch**.

The watch disappears.

**20** On the **Tools** menu, point to **Formula Auditing**, and then click **Hide Watch Window**.

The watch window disappears.

**21** On the Standard toolbar, click the **Save** button.

Save

Excel saves your changes.

**CLOSE: FindErrors.**

# Key Points

■ You can add a group of cells to a formula by typing the formula and then, at the spot in the formula where you want to name the cells, selecting the cells using the mouse.

■ Creating named ranges lets you refer to entire blocks of cells with a single term, saving you lots of time and effort.

■ When you write a formula, be sure you use absolute referencing ($A$1) if you want the formula to remain the same when it's copied from one cell to another, or relative referencing (A1) if you want the formula to change to reflect its new position in the worksheet.

■ Rather than type in a formula from scratch, you can use the **Insert Function** dialog box to help you on your way.

■ You can monitor how the value in a cell changes by adding a watch to the watch window.

■ To see which formulas refer to the values in the selected cell, use **Trace Dependents**; if you want to see which cells provide values for the formula in the active cell, use **Trace Precedents**.

■ You can step through the calculations of a formula in the **Evaluate Formula** dialog box, or go through a more rigorous error-checking procedure using the **Error Checking** tool.

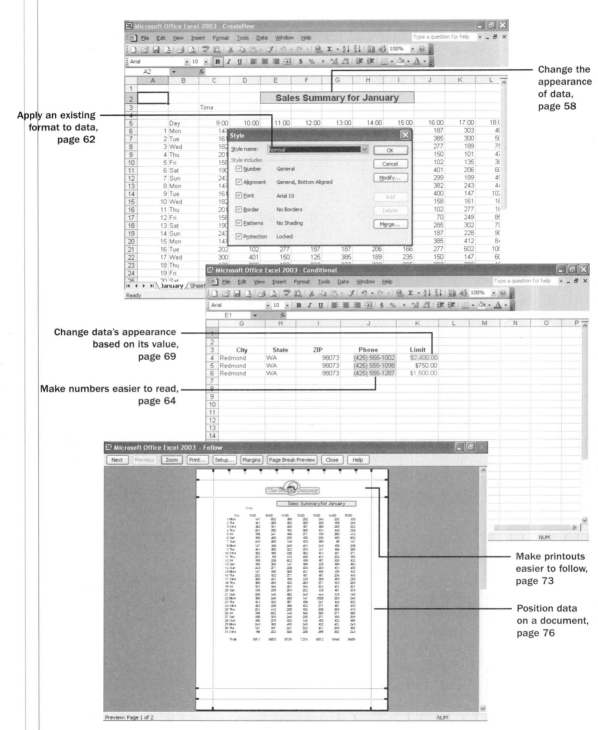

Change the appearance of data, page 58

Apply an existing format to data, page 62

Change data's appearance based on its value, page 69

Make numbers easier to read, page 64

Make printouts easier to follow, page 73

Position data on a document, page 76

# Chapter 4 at a Glance

# 4 Changing Document Appearance

**In this chapter you will learn to:**

✔ Change the appearance of data.

✔ Apply an existing format to data.

✔ Make numbers easier to read.

✔ Change data's appearance based on its value.

✔ Make printouts easier to follow.

✔ Position data in a document.

An important aspect of working with data entered into a workbook is ensuring that the data is easy to read. Microsoft Excel gives you a wide variety of ways to make your data easier to understand; for example, you can change the font, letter size, or color used to present a cell's contents. You can also change how your data appears on the printed page, such as by changing your printer's margins or adding information at the top or bottom of every page.

Changing how data appears on a worksheet helps set the contents of a cell apart from the contents of surrounding cells. The simplest example is that of a data label. If a column on your worksheet has a list of days, you can set a label—for example, *Day*—apart easily by presenting it in bold type that's noticeably larger than the type used to present the data to which it refers. To save time, you can define a number of custom formats and then apply them quickly to the desired cells.

You might also want to specially format a cell's contents to reflect the value in that cell. For instance, Catherine Turner, the owner of The Garden Company, might grant some credit to The Garden Company's better customers, use Excel to track each customer's purchases, and use that information to determine which customers are nearing their credit limit. A quick way to distinguish when a customer is close to his or her credit limit is to change how their outstanding balance is presented in its cell. Catherine might, for example, change the color of the font from the standard black to blue when a customer is within 10 percent of his or her limit.

In addition to changing how data appears in the cells of your worksheet, you can also use headers and footers to add page numbers, current data, or graphics to the top and bottom of every printed page.

In this chapter, you'll learn how to change the appearance of data, apply existing formats to data, make numbers easier to read, change data's appearance based on its value, make printouts easier to follow, and position your data on the printed page.

---

**See Also** Do you need a quick refresher on the topics in this chapter? See the quick reference entries on pages xxxv–xxxviii.

---

**Important** Before you can use the practice files in this chapter, be sure you install them from the book's companion CD-ROM to their default location. See "Using the Book's CD-ROM" on page xi for more information.

# Changing the Appearance of Data

*Microsoft Office Specialist*

Excel spreadsheets can hold and process lots of data, but when you manage numerous spreadsheets it can be hard to remember from a worksheet's title exactly what data is kept in that worksheet. Data labels give you and your colleagues information about data in a worksheet, but it's important to format the labels so that they stand out visually. To make your data labels or any other data stand out, you can change the format of the cells in which the data is stored.

| Time | | | |
|---|---|---|---|
| Day | 9:00 | 10:00 | 11:00 |
| 1 Mon | 147 | 802 | 185 |
| 2 Tue | 161 | 285 | 382 |
| 3 Wed | 182 | 301 | 400 |
| 4 Thu | 201 | 250 | 192 |

Most of the tools you need to change a cell's format can be found on the Formatting toolbar.

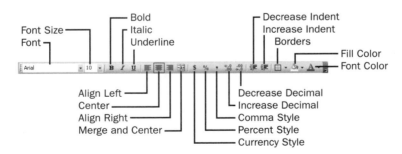

**Important** Depending on the screen resolution you have set on your computer and which toolbar buttons you use most often, it's possible that not every button on every toolbar will appear on your Excel toolbars. If a button mentioned in this book doesn't appear on a toolbar, click the **Toolbar Options** button on that toolbar to display the rest of its buttons.

Bold

You can apply the formatting represented by a toolbar button by selecting the cells you want to apply the style to and then clicking the appropriate button. If you want to set your data labels apart by making them appear bold, click the **Bold** button. If you have already made a cell's contents bold, selecting the cell and clicking the **Bold** button will remove the formatting.

**Tip**   Deleting a cell's contents doesn't delete the cell's formatting. To delete a cell's formatting, select the cell and then, on the **Edit** menu, point to **Clear** and click **Formats**.

Items on the Formatting toolbar that give you choices, such as the **Font Color** control, have a down arrow at the right edge of the control. Clicking the down arrow displays a list of options accessible for that control, such as the fonts available on your system or the colors you can assign to a cell.

Borders

Another way you can make a cell stand apart from its neighbors is to add a border around the cell. In versions of Excel prior to Excel 2002, you could select the cell or cells to which you wanted to add the border and use the options available under the Formatting toolbar's **Borders** button to assign a border to the cells. For example, you could select a group of cells and then choose the border type you wanted. That method of adding borders is still available in Excel, but it has some limitations. The most important limitation is that, while creating a simple border around a group of cells is easy, creating complex borders makes you select different groups of cells and apply different types of borders to them. The current version of Excel makes creating complex borders easy by letting you draw borders directly on the worksheet.

To use the new border-drawing capabilities, display the **Borders** toolbar.

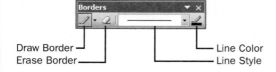

Draw Border ——
Erase Border ———
————— Line Color
————— Line Style

To draw a border around a group of cells, click the mouse pointer at one corner of the group and drag it to the diagonal corner. You will see your border expand as you move the mouse pointer. If you want to add a border in a vertical or horizontal line, drag the mouse pointer along the target grid line—Excel will add the line without expanding it to include the surrounding cells. You can also change the characteristics of the border you draw by using the options on the **Borders** toolbar.

Another way you can make a group of cells stand apart from its neighbors is to change their shading, or the color that fills the cells. On a worksheet with monthly sales data for The Garden Company, for example, owner Catherine Turner could change the fill color of the cells holding her data labels to make the labels stand out even more than by changing the formatting of the text used to display the labels.

If you want to change the attributes of every cell in a row or column, you can click the header of the row or column you want to format and select your desired format.

One task you can't perform using the tools on the Formatting toolbar is to change the standard font for a workbook, which is used in the Name box and in the formula bar. The standard font when you install Excel is Arial, a simple font that is easy to read on a computer screen and on the printed page. If you want to choose another font, click **Options** on the **Tools** menu, which displays the **General** tab page, and use the **Standard Font** and **Size** controls to set the new default for your workbook.

**Important**   The new standard font won't take effect until you quit Excel and restart the program.

In this exercise, you emphasize a worksheet's title by changing the format of cell data, adding a border to a cell, and then changing a cell's fill color. After those tasks are complete, you change the default font for the workbook.

OPEN: Formats from the *SBS\Excel\ChangingDocAppearance* folder.

**1**   If necessary, click the **January** sheet tab.

**2**   Click cell E2.

Cell E2 is highlighted.

**3**   On the Formatting toolbar, click the **Font Size** down arrow and, from the list that appears, click **14**.

The text in cell E2 changes to 14-point type, and row 2 expands vertically to accommodate the text.

**4**   On the Formatting toolbar, click the **Bold** button.

The text in cell E2 appears bold.

**5**   Click the row head for row 5.

Row 5 is highlighted.

Center

**6** On the Formatting toolbar, click the **Center** button.

The contents of the cells in row 5 are centered.

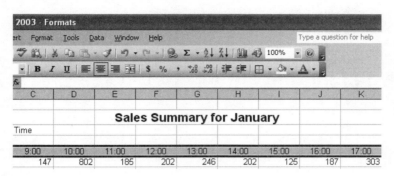

**7** Click cell E2.

Cell E2 is highlighted.

Borders

**8** On the Formatting toolbar, click the down arrow at the right of the **Borders** button and then, from the list that appears, click **Draw Borders**.

The **Borders** toolbar appears, and the mouse pointer changes to a pencil.

**9** Click the left edge of cell E2 and drag to the right edge.

A border appears around cell E2.

**10** On the **Borders** toolbar, click the **Close** button.

The **Borders** toolbar disappears.

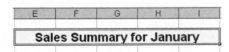
Fill Color

**11** On the Formatting toolbar, click the **Fill Color** down arrow.

The **Fill Color** color palette appears.

**12** In the **Fill Color** color palette, click the yellow square.

Cell G2 fills with a yellow background.

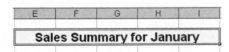

**13** On the **Tools** menu, click **Options**.

The **Options** dialog box appears.

**14** If necessary, click the **General** tab. Click the **Standard Font** down arrow and select **Courier New**.

**15** Click the **Size** down arrow, select **9**, and click **OK**.

**16** Click **OK** to clear the dialog box that appears.

**17** On the Standard toolbar, click the **Save** button.

Excel saves your changes.

Save

CLOSE: Formats.

# Applying an Existing Format to Data

As you work with Excel, you will probably develop preferred formats for data labels, titles, and other worksheet elements. Rather than add the format's characteristics one element at a time to the target cells, you can have Excel store the format and recall it as needed. You can find the predefined formats available to you in the **Style** dialog box.

You can apply an existing style to a cell from within the **Style** dialog box. If none of the existing styles are what you want, you can create your own by typing the name of your new style in the **Style name** box and then clicking **Modify**. The **Format Cells** dialog box appears.

Once you've set the characteristics of your new style, click **OK** to make your style available permanently.

Format Painter

The **Style** dialog box is quite versatile, but it's overkill if all you want to do is apply formatting changes you made to a cell to the contents of another cell. To do so, you can use the Standard toolbar's **Format Painter** button; just click the cell with the format you want to copy, click the **Format Painter** button, and select the target cells.

Of course, if you want to change the formatting of an entire worksheet, the **Format Painter** and the **Style** dialog box are not the most efficient tools available to you. Instead, Excel lets you apply *AutoFormats*, which are pre-defined format patterns for a group of cells (as opposed to styles, which are pre-defined formats for individual cells). To apply an AutoFormat, you select the cells you want to format and click **AutoFormat** on the **Format** menu. In the **AutoFormat** dialog box, select the AutoFormat you want to apply and click **OK**.

In this exercise, you create a style, apply the new style to a data label, and then use the Format Painter to apply the style to the contents of another cell. Finally you assign an AutoFormat.

**OPEN: CreateNew from the *SBS\Excel\ChangingDocAppearance* folder.**

**1**    If necessary, click the **January** sheet tab.

**2**    Click cell C3.

**3**    On the **Format** menu, click **Style**.

The **Style** dialog box appears, with *Normal* in the **Style name** box.

**4**    In the **Style name** box, delete the existing value and then type Emphasis.

The **Add** button is activated.

**5**    Click **Modify**.

The **Format Cells** dialog box appears.

**6**    If necessary, click the **Font** tab.

The **Font** tab page appears.

**7**    In the **Font style** box, click **Bold Italic**.

The text in the Preview pane, in the lower right corner of the dialog box, changes to reflect your choice.

**8**    Click the **Alignment** tab.

The **Alignment** tab page appears.

**9**    In the **Horizontal** box, click the down arrow and, from the list that appears, click **Center**.

**10** Click **OK**.

The **Format Cells** dialog box disappears.

**11** Click **OK**.

The **Style** dialog box disappears, and the text in cell C3 takes on the chosen style.

**12** On the Standard toolbar, click the **Format Painter** button.

The mouse pointer changes to a white cross with a paintbrush icon next to it.

**13** Click cell B5.

Cell B5 takes on the format of cell C3.

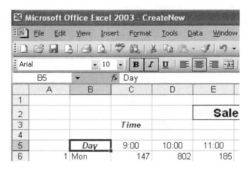

**14** Select cells A3 to P38.

**15** On the **Format** menu, click **AutoFormat**.

The **AutoFormat** dialog box appears.

**16** Scroll the list, click the **List 3** AutoFormat, and click **OK**.

The **AutoFormat** dialog box disappears, and the cells take on the selected AutoFormat.

**17** On the Standard toolbar, click the **Save** button.

Excel saves your changes.

Save

CLOSE: CreateNew.

# Making Numbers Easier to Read

Microsoft
Office
Specialist

Changing the format of the cells in your worksheet can make your data much easier to read, both by setting data labels apart from the actual data and by adding borders to define the boundaries between labels and data even more clearly. Of course, using formatting options to change the font and appearance of a cell's contents doesn't help with idiosyncratic data types such as dates, phone numbers, or currency.

For example, consider U.S. phone numbers. These numbers are 10 digits long and have a three-digit area code, a three-digit exchange, and a four-digit line number written in the form *(###) ###-####*. While it's certainly possible to type a phone number with the expected formatting in a cell, it's much simpler to type a sequence of 10 digits and have Excel change the data's appearance.

You can tell Excel to expect a phone number in a cell by opening the **Format Cells** dialog box to the **Number** tab and displaying the formats available under the **Special** category.

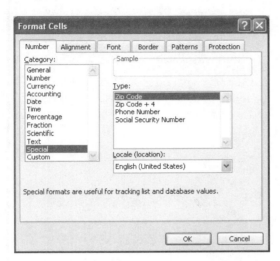

Clicking **Phone Number** from the **Type** list tells Excel to format 10-digit numbers in the standard phone number format. As you can see by comparing the contents of the active cell and the contents of the formula bar in the next graphic, the underlying data isn't changed, just its appearance in the cell.

| *fx* | 4255550122 | | | |
| --- | --- | --- | --- | --- |
| | G | H | I | J |
| | | | | |
| | | | | |
| | City | State | ZIP | Phone |
| | | | | (425) 555-0122 |
| | | | | |

**Troubleshooting**   If you type a nine-digit number in a field that expects a phone number, you won't see an error message; instead, you'll see a two-digit area code. For example, the number *4255555012* would be displayed as *(425) 555-5012*. An 11-digit number would be displayed with a four-digit area code.

Just as you can instruct Excel to expect a phone number in a cell, you can also have it expect a date or a currency amount. You can make those changes from the **Format**

**Cells** dialog box by choosing either the **Date** category or the **Currency** category. The **Date** category lets you pick the format for the date (and determine whether the date's appearance changes due to the **Locale** setting of the operating system on the computer viewing the workbook). In a similar vein, selecting the **Currency** category displays controls to set the number of places after the decimal point, the currency symbol to use, and the way in which Excel should display negative numbers.

You can also create a custom numeric format to add a word or phrase to a number in a cell. For example, you can add the phrase *per month* to a cell with a formula that calculates average monthly sales for a year to ensure that you and your colleagues will recognize the figure as a monthly average. To create a custom number format, click **Cells** on the **Format** menu to open the **Format Cells** dialog box. Then, if necessary, click the **Number** tab to display the **Number** tab page.

In the **Category** list, click **Custom** to display the available custom number formats in the **Type** list. You can then click the base format you want and modify it in the **Type** box. For example, clicking the *0.00* format causes Excel to format any number in a cell with two digits to the right of the decimal point.

**Tip**  The zeros in the format indicate that that position in the format can accept any number as a valid value.

To customize the format, click in the **Type** box and add to the format any symbols or text you want. For example, typing a dollar sign to the left of the existing format and then typing *"per month"* to the right of the existing format causes the number 1500 to be displayed as *$1500.00 per month*.

**Important**  You need to enclose any text in quotes so that Excel recognizes the text as a string to be displayed in the cell.

In this exercise, you assign date, phone number, and currency formats to ranges of cells in your worksheet. After you assign the formats, you test them by entering customer data.

OPEN: EasyRead from the *SBS\Excel\ChangingDocAppearance* folder.

**1**  Click cell B4.

**2**  On the **Format** menu, click **Cells**.

The **Format Cells** dialog box appears.

**3**  If necessary, click the **Number** tab.

**4**  In the **Category** list, click **Date**.

The **Type** list appears with a list of date formats.

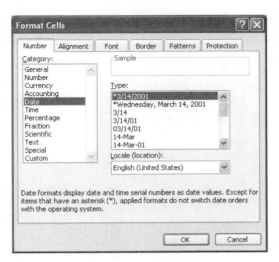

**5** In the **Type** list, click *3/14/01.

**6** Click **OK**.

Excel assigns the chosen format to the cell.

Format Painter

**7** On the Standard toolbar, click the **Format Painter** button.

Cell B4 is highlighted with a marquee outline.

**8** Click cell B5 and drag to cell B23.

Excel assigns the format from cell B4 to cells B5:B23.

**9** Click cell J4.

**10** On the **Format** menu, click **Cells**.

The **Format Cells** dialog box appears.

**11** In the **Category** list, click **Special**.

The **Type** list appears with a list of special formats.

**12** In the **Type** list, click **Phone Number** and then click **OK**.

The **Format Cells** dialog box disappears.

**13** On the Standard toolbar, click the **Format Painter** button.

Cell J4 is highlighted with a marquee outline.

**14** Click cell J5 and drag to cell J23.

Excel assigns the format from cell J4 to cells J5:J23.

**15** Click cell K4.

**16** On the **Format** menu, click **Cells**.

The **Format Cells** dialog box appears.

**17** In the **Category** list, click **Custom**.

The contents of the **Type** list are updated to reflect your choice.

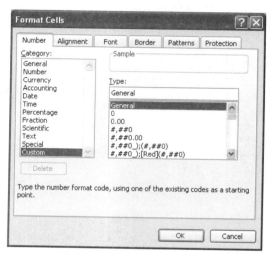

**18** In the **Type** list, click the **#,##0.00** item.

*#,##0.00* appears in the **Type** box.

**19** In the **Type** box, click to the left of the existing format and type $, and then click to the right of the format and type "total".

**20** Click **OK**.

The **Format Cells** dialog box disappears.

**21** On the Standard toolbar, click the **Format Painter** button.

Cell K4 is highlighted with a marquee outline.

**22** Click cell K5 and drag to cell K23.

Excel assigns the format from cell K4 to cells K5:K23.

**23** In cell B4, type January 25, 2004 and press ⌅ Enter.

The contents of cell B4 change to *1/25/04*, matching the format you set earlier.

**24** In cell C4, type C100001.

**25** In cell D4, type Steven.

**26** In cell E4, type Levy.

**27** In cell F4, type **6789 Elm Street**.

**28** In cell G4, type **Redmond**.

**29** In cell H4, type **WA**.

**30** In cell I4, type **87063**.

**31** In cell J4, type **4255550102**.

The contents of the cell change to *(425) 555-0102*, matching the format you chose earlier.

**32** In cell K4, type **2400**.

The contents of the cell change to *$2,400.00 total*, matching the format you created earlier.

**33** On the Standard toolbar, click **Save** to save your changes.

CLOSE: EasyRead.

# Changing Data's Appearance Based on Its Value

*Microsoft Office Specialist*

Recording sales, credit limits, and other business data in a worksheet lets you make important decisions about your operations. And as you saw earlier in this chapter, you can change the appearance of data labels and the worksheet itself to make interpreting your data easier.

Another way you can make your data easier to interpret is to have Excel change the appearance of your data based on its value. These formats are called *conditional formats* because the data must meet certain conditions to have a format applied to it. For instance, if owner Catherine Turner wanted to highlight any Saturdays on which daily sales at The Garden Company were over $4,000, she could define a conditional format that tests the value in the cell recording total sales, and that will change the format of the cell's contents when the condition is met.

To create a conditional format, you click the cells to which you want to apply the format, open the **Format** menu, and click **Conditional Formatting** to open the **Conditional**

**Formatting** dialog box. The default configuration of the **Conditional Formatting** dialog box appears in the following graphic.

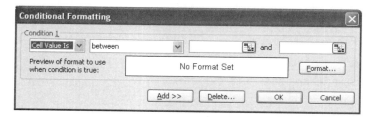

The first list box lets you choose whether you want the condition that follows to look at the cell's contents or the formula in the cell. In almost every circumstance, you will use the contents of the cell as the test value for the condition.

**Tip**   The only time you would want to set a formula as the basis for the condition would be to format a certain result, such as a grand total, the same way every time it appeared in a worksheet.

The second list box in the **Conditional Formatting** dialog box lets you select the comparison to be made. Depending on the comparison you choose, the dialog box will have either one or two boxes in which you enter values to be used in the comparison. The default comparison *between* requires two values, whereas comparisons such as *less than* require one.

After you have created a condition, you need to define the format to be applied to data that meets that condition. You do that in the **Format Cells** dialog box. From within this dialog box, you can set the characteristics of the text used to print the value in the cell. When you're done, a preview of the format you defined appears in the **Conditional Formatting** dialog box.

You're not limited to creating one condition per cell. If you like, you can create additional conditions by clicking the **Add** button in the **Conditional Formatting** dialog box. When you click the **Add** button, a second condition section appears.

**Important**   Excel doesn't check to make sure your conditions are logically consistent, so you need to be sure you enter your conditions correctly.

Excel evaluates the conditions in the order you entered them in the **Conditional Formatting** dialog box and, upon finding a condition the data meets, stops its comparisons. For example, suppose Catherine wanted to visually separate the credit limits of The Garden Company's customers into two different categories: those with limits under $1,500 and those with limits from $1,500 to $2,500. She could display her customers' credit limits with a conditional format using the conditions in the following graphic.

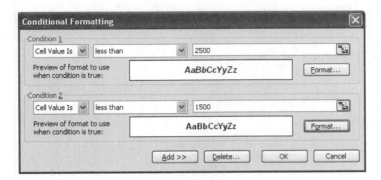

In this case, Excel would compare the value *1250* with the first condition, *<2500*, and assign that formatting to the cell containing the value. That the second condition, *<1500*, is "closer" is irrelevant—once Excel finds a condition the data meets, it stops comparing.

**Tip**   You should always enter the most restrictive condition first. In the preceding exam-ple, setting the first condition to *<1500* and the second to *<2500* would result in the proper format.

In this exercise, you create a series of conditional formats to change the appearance of data in worksheet cells displaying the credit limit of The Garden Company's customers.

OPEN: Conditional from the *SBS\Excel\ChangingDocAppearance* folder.

**1**   If necessary, click cell K4.

**2**   On the **Format** menu, click **Conditional Formatting**.

   The **Conditional Formatting** dialog box appears.

**3**   In the second list box, click the down arrow and then, from the list that appears, click **between**.

   The word *between* appears in the second list box.

**4**   In the first argument box, type 1000.

**5**   In the second argument box, type 2000.

**6**   Click the **Format** button.

   The **Format Cells** dialog box appears.

**7**   If necessary, click the **Font** tab.

   The **Font** tab page appears.

**8** In the **Color** box, click the down arrow and then, from the color palette that appears, click the blue square.

The color palette disappears, and the text in the Preview pane changes to blue.

**9** Click **OK**.

The **Format Cells** dialog box disappears.

**10** Click the **Add** button.

The **Condition 2** section of the dialog box appears.

**11** In the second list box, click the down arrow and then, from the list that appears, click **between**.

The word *between* appears in the second list box.

**12** In the first argument box, type 2000.

**13** In the second argument box, type 2500.

**14** Click the **Format** button.

The **Format Cells** dialog box appears.

**15** In the **Color** box, click the down arrow and then, from the color palette that appears, click the green square.

The color palette disappears, and the text in the Preview pane changes to green.

**16** Click **OK**.

The **Format Cells** dialog box disappears.

**17** Click **OK**.

The **Conditional Formatting** dialog box disappears.

**18** In cell K4, click the fill handle, and drag it to cell K6.

**19** The contents of cells K5 and K6 change to *$2,400.00*, and the **Auto Fill Options** button appears.

Auto Fill
Options

**20** Click the **Auto Fill Options** button, and from the list that appears, click **Fill Formatting Only**.

The contents of cells K5 and K6 revert to their previous values, and Excel applies the conditional formats to the selected cells.

| I | J | K |
|---|---|---|
| | | |
| | | |
| ZIP | Phone | Limit |
| 98073 | (425) 555-1002 | $2,400.00 |
| 98073 | (425) 555-1098 | $750.00 |
| 98073 | (425) 555-1287 | $1,500.00 |

**21**   On the Standard toolbar, click the **Save** toolbar button to save your changes.

CLOSE: Conditional.

# Making Printouts Easier to Follow

Changing how your data appears in the body of your worksheets can make your data much easier to understand, but it doesn't communicate when the worksheet was last opened or whom it belongs to. You could always add that information to the top of every printed page, but you would need to change the current date every time you opened the document; and if you wanted the same information to appear at the top of every printed page, any changes to the body of your worksheets could mean you would need to edit your workbook so that the information appeared in the proper place.

If you want to ensure that the same information appears at the top or bottom of every printed page, you can do so using headers or footers. A header is a section that appears at the top of every printed page, while a footer is a section that appears at the bottom of every printed page. To create a header or footer in Excel, you open the **Page Setup** dialog box to the **Header/Footer** tab.

**Important**   Everything you will learn about creating headers in this section applies to creating footers as well. Also, you can have both headers and footers in the same document.

The list boxes on the **Header/Footer** tab page will hold a number of standard headers and footers, such as page numbers by themselves or followed by the name of the workbook. You can create your own headers by opening the **Header** dialog box.

In the **Header** dialog box, you can add your own text or use the box's buttons to change the appearance of the text in the header or to insert a date, time, or page number. Beginning with Excel 2002, you have had the option of adding a graphic to a header or footer. Adding a graphic such as a company logo to a worksheet lets you identify the worksheet as referring to your company and helps reinforce your company's identity if you include the worksheet in a printed report distributed outside your company. After you insert a graphic into a header or footer, the **Format Picture** button will become available. Clicking that button will open a dialog box with tools to edit your graphic.

In this exercise, you create a custom header and a custom footer for a workbook. You add a graphic to the footer and then edit the graphic using the **Format Picture** dialog box.

**OPEN:** Follow from the *SBS\Excel\ChangingDocAppearance* folder.

**1** On the **View** menu, click **Header and Footer**.

The **Page Setup** dialog box appears, opened to the **Header/Footer** tab page.

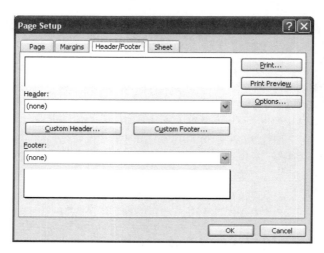

**2** Click the **Custom Footer** button.

The **Footer** dialog box appears.

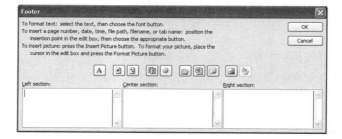

**3** Click anywhere in the **Center section** box, and then click the **Insert Picture** button.

The **Insert Picture** dialog box appears.

**4** Navigate to the ChangingDocAppearance folder, and then double-click the **tgc_logo.gif** file.

The **Insert Picture** dialog box disappears, and *&[Picture]* appears in the **Center section** box.

Insert Picture

Format Picture

**5**   Click the **Format Picture** button.

The **Format Picture** dialog box appears.

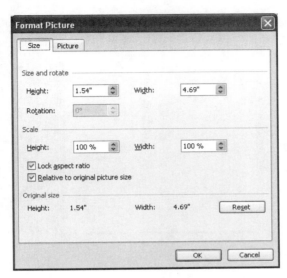

**6**   If necessary, select the **Lock aspect ratio** check box.

**7**   In the **Height** box, type 50% and then click **OK**.

The **Format Picture** dialog box disappears.

**8**   In the **Footer** dialog box, click **OK**.

The **Footer** dialog box disappears, and part of the graphic you added appears in the footer section of the **Page Setup** dialog box.

**9**   Click the **Custom Header** button.

The **Header** dialog box appears.

Date

**10**   Click anywhere in the **Left section** box, and then click the **Date** button.

*&[Date]* appears in the **Left section** box.

Page Number

**11**   Click anywhere in the **Right section** box, and then click the **Page Number** button.

*&[Page]* appears in the **Right section** box.

**12**   Click **OK**.

The **Header** dialog box disappears.

**13**   Click the **Print Preview** button.

The Print Preview window appears.

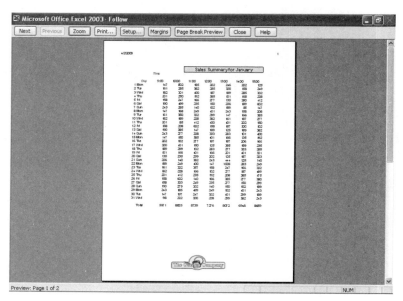

**14** Click **Close**.

The Print Preview window and the **Page Setup** dialog box disappear.

**15** Click cell E2.

**16** On the **Edit** menu, point to **Clear**, and then click **All**.

**17** The contents of the merged cell disappear, and the cells are unmerged.

Save

**18** On the Standard toolbar, click the **Save** button to save your changes.

CLOSE: Follow.

# Positioning Data on a Printout

*Microsoft*
*Office*
*Specialist*

Once you have your data and any headers or footers in your workbook, you can change your workbook's properties to ensure that your worksheets display all of your information and that printing is centered on the page.

One of the workbook properties you can change is its margins, or the boundaries between different sections of the printed page. You can view a document's margins and where the contents of the header, footer, and body appear in relation to those margins in the Print Preview window.

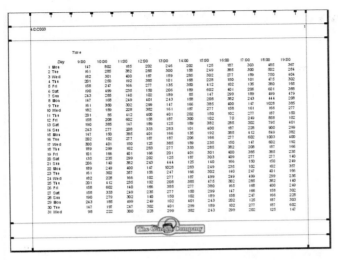

In the above graphic, the logo in the footer spills over the top margin of the footer. To remove the overlap, you can move the footer's top margin up, increasing the amount of space devoted to the footer. Increasing the size of the footer reduces the size of the worksheet body, meaning fewer rows can be printed on a page.

Another issue with printing worksheets is that the data in worksheets tends to be wider horizontally than a standard sheet of paper. For example, the data in the worksheet in the previous graphic is several columns wider than a standard piece of paper. You can use the controls in the **Page Setup** dialog box to change the alignment of the rows and columns on the page. When the columns follow the long edge of a piece of paper, the page is laid out in *portrait mode*; when the columns follow the short edge of a piece of paper, it is in *landscape mode*. The following graphic displays the contents of the previous worksheet laid out in landscape mode.

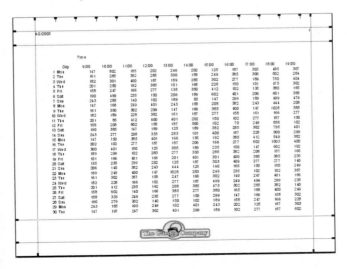

This is a better fit, but not all the data fits on the printed page. Once again, the **Page Setup** dialog box comes to the rescue. From within that dialog box, you can have Excel reduce the size of the worksheet's contents until the entire worksheet can be printed on a single page and also have Excel center the printed matter on the page so that there is an even margin around the printing.

In this exercise, you change the margins in a workbook to stop the graphic in the footer from overlapping with the data in the body of the worksheet. You then change the alignment of the workbook so that its contents are laid out in landscape mode and centered on the printed page.

**OPEN:** Margins from the *SBS\Excel\ChangingDocAppearance* folder.

Print Preview

**1**　On the Standard toolbar, click the **Print Preview** button.

　　The Print Preview window opens.

**2**　Click **Margins**.

　　Margin lines appear.

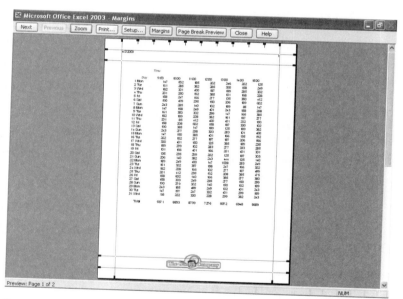

**3**　Drag the second margin line from the bottom of the page up until it clears the graphic.

　　The top edge of the footer moves above the graphic.

**4** Click **Setup**.

The **Page Setup** dialog box appears.

**5** If necessary, click the **Page** tab.

**6** Select the **Landscape** option button.

**7** Select the **Fit to** option button and set to 1 page wide by 1 page tall.

**8** Click the **Margins** tab.

The **Margins** tab page appears.

**9** In the **Center on page** section of the tab page, select both the **Horizontally** check box and the **Vertically** check box.

**10** Click **OK**.

The **Page Setup** dialog box disappears. The document view in the Print Preview window changes to reflect the new settings.

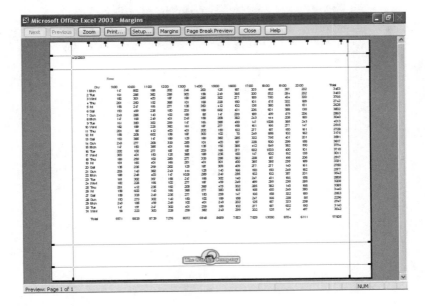

**11** Click **Close**.

The Print Preview window disappears.

**12** On the Standard toolbar, click the **Save** button to save your changes.

Save

**CLOSE:** Margins.

# Key Points

- If you don't like the default font in which Excel displays your data, you can change it.

- You can use cell formatting, including borders, alignment, and fill colors, to emphasize certain cells in your worksheets. This emphasis is particularly useful for making column and row labels stand out from the data.

- Excel comes with a number of existing styles that let you change the appearance of individual cells.

- If you want to apply the formatting from one cell to another cell, use the **Format Painter** to copy the format quickly.

- There are quite a few AutoFormats you can apply to groups of cells. If you see one you like, use it and save yourself lots of formatting time.

- Conditional formats let you set rules so that Excel will change the appearance of a cell's contents based on its value.

- Pay careful attention to how your worksheets appear when printed. Use header, footer, graphic, alignment, and margin settings to make your data look great on the page.

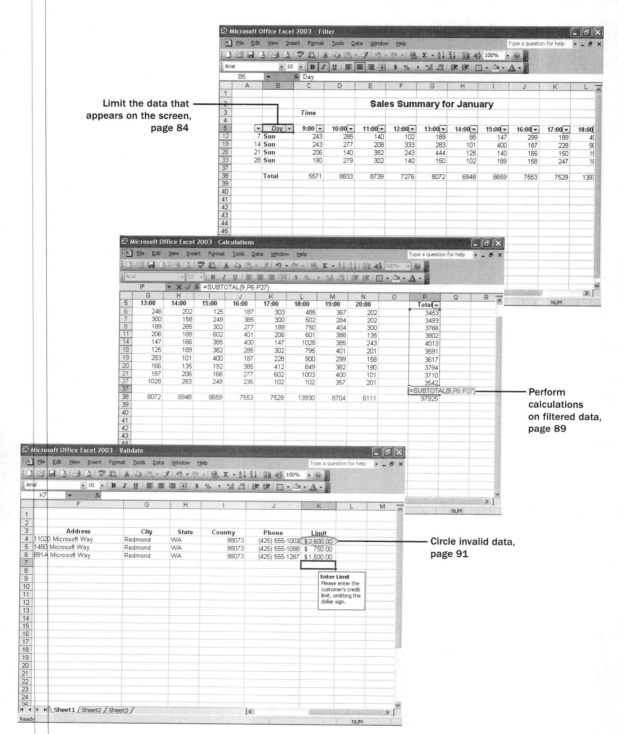

Limit the data that appears on the screen, page 84

Perform calculations on filtered data, page 89

Circle invalid data, page 91

# Chapter 5 at a Glance

# 5 Focusing on Specific Data Using Filters

**In this chapter you will learn to:**

✔ Limit the data that appears on the screen.

✔ Perform calculations on filtered data.

✔ Define a valid set of values for a range of cells.

An important aspect of working with large amounts of data is the ability to zero in on the most important data in a worksheet, whether that data represents the best 10 days of sales in a month or slow-selling product lines that you might need to reevaluate. In Microsoft Excel, you have a number of powerful, flexible tools with which you can limit the data displayed in your worksheet. Once your worksheet displays the subset of the data you need to make a decision, you can perform calculations on that data. You can discover what percentage of monthly sales were made up by the 10 best days in the month, find your total sales for particular days of the week, or locate the slowest business day of the month.

Just as you can limit the data displayed by your worksheets, you can limit the data entered into them as well. Setting rules for data entered into cells lets you catch many of the most common data entry errors, such as entering values that are too small or too large, or attempting to enter a word in a cell that requires a number. Should you add a validation rule to worksheet cells after data has been entered into them, you can circle any invalid data so that you know what to correct.

In this chapter, you'll learn how to limit the data that appears in your worksheets, perform calculations on the remaining data, and limit the data that can be entered into specific cells.

**See Also** Do you need a quick refresher on the topics in this chapter? See the quick reference entries on pages xxxviii–xl.

**Important** Before you can use the practice files in this chapter, be sure you install them from the book's companion CD-ROM to their default location. See "Using the Book's CD-ROM" on page xi for more information.

# Limiting the Data That Appears on the Screen

*Microsoft
Office
Specialist*

Excel spreadsheets can hold as much data as you need them to, but you might not want to work with all of the data in a worksheet at the same time. For example, you might want to see the sales figures for your company during the first third, second third, and final third of a month. You can limit the data shown in a worksheet by creating a *filter*, which is a rule that selects rows to be shown in a worksheet.

To create a filter, you click the cell in the group you want to filter and use the **Data** menu to turn on *AutoFilter*. When you turn on AutoFilter, which is a built-in set of filtering capabilities, a down arrow button appears in the cell that Excel recognizes as the column's label.

**Important**   When you turn on filtering, Excel treats the cells in the active cell's column as a range. To ensure that the filtering works properly, you should always add a label to the column you want to filter.

Clicking the down arrow displays a list of values and options. The first few items in the list are filtering options, such as whether you want to display the top 10 values in the column, create a custom filter, or display all values in the column (that is, remove the filter). The rest of the items in the list are the unique values in the column— clicking one of those values displays the row or rows containing that value.

Choosing the **Top 10** option from the list doesn't just limit the display to the top 10 values. Instead, it opens the **Top 10 AutoFilter** dialog box. From within this dialog box, you can choose whether to show values from the top or bottom of the list, define the number of items you want to see, and choose whether the number in the middle box indicates the number of items or the percentage of items to be shown when the filter is applied. Using the **Top 10 AutoFilter** dialog box, you can find your top 10 sales-people or identify the top five percent of your customers.

When you choose **Custom** from the **AutoFilter** list, you can define a rule that Excel uses to decide which rows to show after the filter is applied. For instance, you can create a rule that only days with total sales of less than $2,500 should be shown in your worksheet. With those results in front of you, you might be able to determine whether the weather or another factor resulted in slower business on those days.

Two related things you can do in Excel are to choose rows at random from a list and to display the unique values in a column in the worksheet (not in the down arrow's list, which you can't normally work with). Generating a list of unique values in a column can give you important information, such as from which states you have customers or which categories of products sold in an hour.

Selecting rows randomly is useful for selecting customers to receive a special offer, deciding which days of the month to audit, or picking prize winners at an employee party. To choose rows, you can use the RAND function, which generates a random value between 0 and 1 and compares it with a test value included in the statement. A statement that returns a TRUE value 30 percent of the time would be *RAND()<=30%*; that is, whenever the random value was between 0 and .3, the result would be TRUE. You could use this statement to select each row in a list with a probability of 30 percent.

In this exercise, you create a filter to show the top five sales days in January, show sales figures for Mondays during the same month, display the days with sales of at least $3,000, pick random days from the month to audit, and then generate a list of unique values in one of the worksheet's columns.

**OPEN: Filter** from the *SBS\Access\UsingFilters* folder.

**1**    If necessary, click the **January** sheet tab.

**2**    Click cell P5.

**3**    On the **Data** menu, point to **Filter**, and then click **AutoFilter**.

    A down arrow appears in cell P5.

**4**    In cell P5, click the down arrow and, from the list that appears, click **(Top 10...)**.

    The **Top 10 AutoFilter** dialog box appears.

**5**    Click in the middle box, delete *10*, type *5*, and click **OK**.

    Only the rows containing the five largest values in column P are shown.

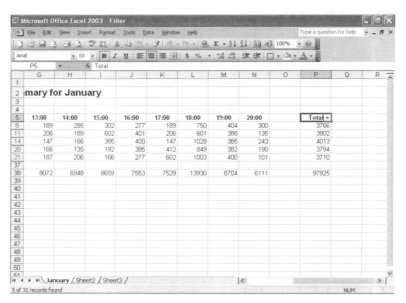

**6** On the **Data** menu, point to **Filter**, and then click **AutoFilter**.

The filtered rows reappear.

**7** Click cell B5.

**8** On the **Data** menu, point to **Filter**, and then click **AutoFilter**.

A down arrow appears in cell B5.

**9** In cell B5, click the down arrow and, from the list of unique column values that appears, click **Mon**.

Only rows with *Mon* in column B are shown in the worksheet.

**10** On the **Data** menu, point to **Filter**, and then click **AutoFilter**.

The filtered rows reappear.

**11** Click cell P5, and then, on the **Data** menu, point to **Filter**, and then click **AutoFilter**.

A down arrow appears in cell P5.

**12** In cell P5, click the down arrow and then, from the list that appears, click (**Custom…**).

The **Custom AutoFilter** dialog box appears.

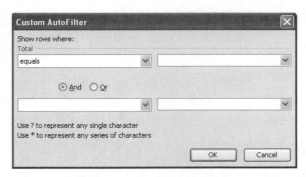

**13** In the upper left box, click the down arrow and, from the list that appears, click **is greater than or equal to**.

**14** In the upper right box, type 3000 and then click **OK**.

Only rows with totals of at least 3000 are shown in the worksheet.

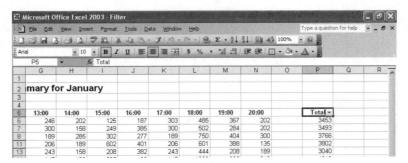

**15** On the **Data** menu, point to **Filter**, and then click **AutoFilter**.

The filtered rows reappear.

**16** On the **Data** menu, point to **Filter**, and then click **AutoFilter**.

A down arrow appears in cell P5.

**17** In cell P5, click the down arrow and then, from the list of unique column values that appears, click **2236**.

All rows except the row containing 2236 in column P disappear.

**18** On the **Data** menu, point to **Filter**, and then click **AutoFilter**.

The filtered rows reappear.

**19** In cell Q5, type Audit.

**20** In cell Q6, type **=RAND()<17%**.

If the result of the RAND function is less than *17%*, cell Q6 will display *TRUE*; otherwise, cell Q6 will display *FALSE*.

**21** Drag the **AutoFill** handle from cell Q6 to cell Q36.

*TRUE* and *FALSE* values appear in the cells from Q6 to Q36 with a frequency of approximately 16 percent and 84 percent, respectively.

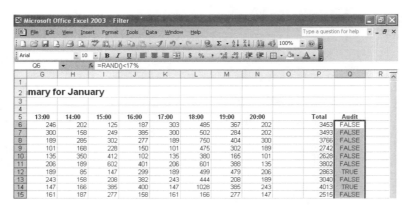

**22** On the **Data** menu, point to **Filter**, and then click **Advanced Filter**.

The **Advanced Filter** dialog box appears.

**23** Clear the **List Range** box, and then click cell B5 and drag to cell B36.

*$B$5:$B$36* appears in the **List Range** box.

**24** Select the **Unique records only** check box, and then click **OK**.

Rows with the first occurrence of a value are displayed in the worksheet.

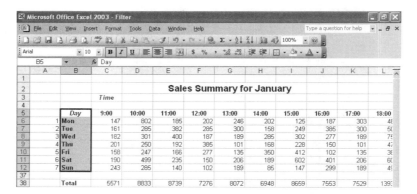

**25** On the **Data** menu, point to **Filter**, and then click **Show All**.

The filtered rows reappear.

**Save**

**26** On the **Standard** toolbar, click the **Save** button.

Excel saves your changes.

CLOSE: Filter.

# Performing Calculations on Filtered Data

*Microsoft*
*Office*
*Specialist*

When you filter your worksheet, you limit the data that appears. The ability to focus on the data that's most vital to your current needs is important, but there are a few limitations. One limitation is that any formulas you have created don't change their calculations, even if some of the rows used in the formula are hidden by the filter.

There are two ways you can find the total of a group of filtered cells. The first method is to use AutoCalculate. To use AutoCalculate, you select the cells you want to find the total for. When you do, the total for the cells appears on the status bar, at the lower edge of the Excel window.

When you use AutoCalculate, you aren't limited to finding the sum of the selected cells. To display the other functions you can use, you right-click the AutoCalculate pane and select the function you want from the shortcut menu that appears.

AutoCalculate is great for finding a quick total or average for filtered cells, but it doesn't make the result available in the worksheet. To make the value available in your worksheet, you can create a SUBTOTAL function. As with AutoCalculate, you can choose the type of calculation the function performs.

In this exercise, you use AutoCalculate to find the total of a group of cells in a filtered worksheet, create a SUBTOTAL function to make the same value available in the worksheet, and then edit the SUBTOTAL function so that it calculates an average instead of a sum.

OPEN: Calculations from the *SBS\Access\UsingFilters* folder.

**1** If necessary, click the **January** sheet tab.

**2** Click cell P5.

**3** On the **Data** menu, point to **Filter**, and then click **AutoFilter**.

A down arrow button appears in cell P5.

**4** In cell P5, click the down arrow button and then, from the list that appears, click (**Top 10...**).

The **Top 10 AutoFilter** dialog box appears.

**5** Click **OK**.

**Tip** Clicking **OK** here accepts the default setting of the **Top 10 AutoFilter** dialog box, which is to show the top 10 values in the selected cells.

**6** The **Top 10 AutoFilter** dialog box disappears, and the rows with the 10 highest values in column P are displayed.

**7** Click cell P6 and drag to cell P27.

The cells are selected, and on the status bar, in the lower right corner of the Excel window, *SUM=36781* appears in the **AutoCalculate** pane.

**8** Click cell P37, and then, on the **Standard** toolbar, click the **AutoSum** button.

The formula *=SUBTOTAL(9,P6:P36)* appears in the formula bar.

**9** Press Enter.

The value *36781* appears in cell P37. The value in cell P38 also changes to *134706*, but that calculation includes the subtotal of the filtered cells in the column.

**10** Click cell P37, and then, in the formula bar, edit the formula so that it reads *=SUBTOTAL(1,P6:P36)* and then press ⎡Enter⎤.

By changing the 9 to a 1 in the **SUBTOTAL** function, the function now calculates an average instead of a sum. The average of the top 10 values in cells P6 through P36, *3678.1* appears in cell P37. The value in cell P38 also changes to *101603.1*, but that calculation includes the average of the filtered cells in the column.

**11** If necessary, click cell P37 and then press ⎡Del⎤.

Excel deletes the **SUBTOTAL** formula from cell P37, and the total in cell P38 changes to *97925*.

**12** On the Standard toolbar, click the **Save** button.

Save

Excel saves your changes.

CLOSE: Calculations.

# Defining a Valid Set of Values for a Range of Cells

*Microsoft Office Specialist*

Part of creating efficient and easy-to-use worksheets is to do what you can to ensure that the data entered into your worksheets is as accurate as possible. While it isn't possible to catch every typographical or transcription error, you can set up a validation rule to make sure the data entered into a cell meets certain standards.

To create a validation rule, you open the **Data Validation** dialog box.

You can use the **Data Validation** dialog box to define the type of data that Excel should allow in the cell and then, depending on the data type you choose, to set the conditions data must meet to be accepted in the cell. In the following graphic, Excel knows to look for a whole number value between 1000 and 2000.

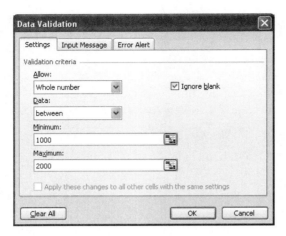

Setting accurate validation rules can help you and your colleagues avoid entering a customer's name in the cell designated to hold their phone number or setting a credit limit above a certain level. To require a user to enter a numeric value in a cell, display the **Settings** page of the **Data Validation** dialog box, click the **Allow** down arrow, and depending on your needs, choose either **Whole number** or **Decimal** from the list that appears.

Circle Invalid Data

If you want to set the same validation rule for a group of cells, you can do so by selecting the cells to which you want to apply the rule (such as a column where you enter the credit limit of customers of The Garden Company) and setting the rule using the **Data Validation** dialog box. One important fact you should keep in mind is that Excel lets you create validation rules for cells where you have already entered data. Excel doesn't tell you if any cells have data that violate your rule, but you can find out by having Excel circle any worksheet cells containing data that violates the cell's validation rule. To do so, you display the **Tools** menu, point to **Formula Auditing**, and click **Show Formula Auditing Toolbar**. On the **Formula Auditing** toolbar, click the **Circle Invalid Data** button to circle cells with invalid data.

Clear Validation Circles

When you're ready to hide the circles, display the **Formula Auditing** toolbar and click the **Clear Validation Circles** button.

Of course, it's frustrating if you want to enter data into a cell and, when a message box appears, telling you the data you tried to enter isn't acceptable, you aren't given the rules you need to follow. Excel lets you create messages that tell the user what values are expected before the data is entered and then, if the conditions aren't met, reiterate the conditions in a custom error message.

You can turn off data validation in a cell by displaying the **Settings** page of the **Data Validation** dialog box and clicking the **Clear All** button in the lower left corner of the dialog box.

In this exercise, you create a data validation rule limiting the credit line of The Garden Company customers to $2,500, add an input message mentioning the limitation, and then create an error message should someone enter a value greater than $2,500. After you've created your rule and messages, you test them.

OPEN: Validate from the *SBS\Access\UsingFilters* folder.

**1** Select cells K4 through K7.

**2** On the **Data** menu, click **Validation**.

The **Data Validation** dialog box appears with the **Settings** tab page in front.

**3** In the **Allow** box, click the down arrow and, from the list that appears, click **Whole Number**.

Boxes labeled **Minimum** and **Maximum** appear below the **Data** box.

**4** In the **Data** box, click the down arrow and, from the list that appears, click **less than or equal to**.

The **Minimum** box disappears.

**5** In the **Maximum** box, type **2500**.

**6** Clear the **Ignore blank** check box.

**7** Click the **Input Message** tab.

The **Input Message** tab page appears.

**8** In the **Title** box, type **Enter Limit**.

**9** In the **Input Message** box, type **Please enter the customer's credit limit, omitting** the dollar sign.

**10** Click the **Error Alert** tab page.

The **Error Alert** tab page appears.

**11** In the **Style** box, click the down arrow and, from the list that appears, choose **Stop**.

The icon that will appear in your message box changes to the **Stop** icon.

**12** In the **Title** box, type **Error**, and then click **OK**.

**13** Click cell K7.

A ScreenTip with the title *Enter Limit* and the text *Please enter the customer's credit limit, omitting the dollar sign* appears near cell K7.

**14** Type 2501, and press [Enter].

A stop box with the title **Error** and default text appears.

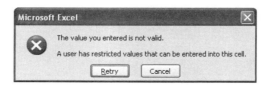

**Tip**   Leaving the **Error message** box blank causes Excel to use its default message: *The value you entered is not valid. A user has restricted values that can be entered into this cell.*

**15** Click **Cancel**.

The error box disappears.

**Important**   Clicking **Retry** lets you edit the bad value, while clicking **Cancel** deletes the entry.

**16** Click cell K7.

Cell K7 becomes the active cell, and the ScreenTip reappears.

**17** Type 2500, and press [Enter].

Excel accepts your input.

**18** On the **Tools** menu, point to **Formula Auditing**, and click **Show Formula Auditing Toolbar**.

The **Formula Auditing** toolbar appears.

Circle Invalid Data

**19** On the **Formula Auditing** toolbar, click the **Circle Invalid Data** button.

A red circle appears around the value in cell K4.

Clear Validation Circles

**20** On the **Formula Auditing** toolbar, click the **Clear Validation Circles** button.

The red circle around the value in cell K4 disappears.

**21** On the **Formula Auditing** toolbar, click the **Close** box.

The **Formula Auditing** toolbar disappears.

Save

**22** On the Standard toolbar, click the **Save** button.

CLOSE: Validate.

# Key Points

- A number of filters are defined in Excel—you may find the one you want already in place.

- Filtering an Excel worksheet based on values in a single column is easy to do, but you can create a custom filter to limit your data based on the values in more than one column as well.

- Don't forget that you can get a running total (or average, or any one of several other summary operations) for the values in a group of cells. Just select the cells and look on the status bar: the result will be there.

- Functions aren't set in stone when you create them. You can use the controls in the **Function** box to edit your functions.

- Use data validation techniques to improve the accuracy of data entered into your worksheets, and to identify data that doesn't meet the guidelines you set.

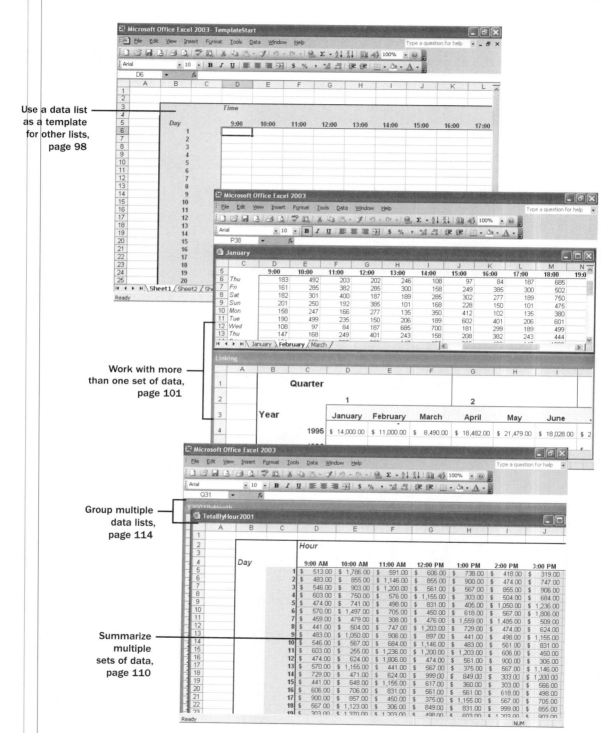

Use a data list as a template for other lists, page 98

Work with more than one set of data, page 101

Group multiple data lists, page 114

Summarize multiple sets of data, page 110

# Chapter 6 at a Glance

# 6 Combining Data from Multiple Sources

---

**In this chapter you will learn to:**

✔  **Use an existing data list as a template for other lists.**

✔  **Work with more than one set of data.**

✔  **Link to data in other workbooks.**

✔  **Summarize multiple sets of data.**

✔  **Group multiple data lists.**

---

Microsoft Excel gives you a wide range of tools with which to format, summarize, and present your data. Once you have created a workbook to hold data about a particular subject, you can create as many worksheets as you need to make that data easier to find within the workbook. For instance, you can create a workbook to store sales data for a year, with each worksheet representing a month in that year. To ensure that the workbook for every year has a similar appearance, you can create a workbook with the desired characteristics (such as more than the standard number of worksheets, custom worksheet formatting, or a particular color for the workbook's sheet tabs) and save it as a pattern for similar workbooks you create in the future. The benefit of ensuring that all of your sales data worksheets have the same layout is that you and your colleagues will immediately know where to look for specific totals. Also, when you create a summary worksheet, you will know in advance which cells to include in your calculations.

If you work with the same workbooks repeatedly, you can group those workbooks in a special file, called a *workspace*. When you open the workspace, Excel knows to open the files you included in that workspace.

A consequence of organizing your data into different workbooks and worksheets is that you need ways to manage, combine, and summarize data from more than one Excel document. You can always copy data from one worksheet to another, but if the original value were to change, that change would not be reflected in the cell range to which you copied the data. Rather than remember which cells you need to update when a value changes, you can create a link to the original cell. That way, Excel will update the value for you whenever you open the workbook. If multiple worksheets hold similar values, you can use links to summarize those values in a single worksheet.

In this chapter, you'll learn how to use a data list as a template for other lists, work with more than one set of data, link to data in other workbooks, summarize multiple sets of data, and group multiple data lists.

---

**See Also**   Do you need a quick refresher on the topics in this chapter? See the quick reference entries on pages xl–xlii.

---

**Important**   Before you can use the practice files in this chapter, be sure you install them from the book's companion CD-ROM to their default location. See "Using the Book's CD-ROM" on page xi for more information.

# Using a Data List as a Template for Other Lists

*Microsoft Office Specialist*

Once you have decided on the type of data you want to store in a workbook and what that workbook should look like, you will probably want to be able to create similar workbooks without adding all the formatting and formulas again. For example, you might have settled on a design for your monthly sales tracking workbook.

When you have settled on a design for your workbooks, you can save one of the workbooks as a *template*, or pattern, for similar workbooks you create in the future. You should remove any existing data from a workbook you save as a template, both to avoid data entry errors and to remove any confusion as to whether the workbook is a template. You can also remove any worksheets you and your colleagues won't need by right-clicking the tab of an unneeded worksheet and, from the shortcut menu that appears, clicking **Delete**.

If you want your template workbook to have more than the standard number of worksheets (such as 12 worksheets to track sales for a year, by month), you can add worksheets by right-clicking any sheet tab, clicking **Insert** from the shortcut menu that appears, and then, on the **General** page of the **Insert** dialog box, double-clicking the **Worksheet** icon.

To create a template from an existing workbook, you save the model workbook under the Template file type, which you can choose from the **Save as type** drop-down list in the **Save As** dialog box. If you ever want to change the template, you can open it like a standard workbook (that is, an Excel file with the .xls extension) and make your changes. When you have completed your work, resave the file normally—it will still be a template.

When you change the file type to *Template*, Excel changes the active directory to the default Microsoft Office 2003 templates directory. You need to save your template to this folder so that it will be available through the **Templates** dialog box. If you'd prefer to have Excel look in another directory for your templates, you can change the default directory Excel looks in when you start the program by opening the **Tools** menu, clicking **Options**, clicking the **General** tab, and typing the path of the directory in the **At startup, open all files in** box.

**Tip**   If you clear the **At startup, open all files in** box, Excel reverts to the default Templates directory.

Once you have saved a workbook as a template, you can use it as a model for new workbooks. To create a workbook from a template in Excel, you open the task pane from the **View** menu.

The **Templates** section of the **New Workbook** task pane has a list of any previously used templates as well as the **Templates Home Page**, **On my computer**, and **On my Web sites** options. Clicking **On my Web sites** will take you to the Web and let you search for templates on the Internet or your company's intranet, or on MSN. Clicking **On my computer** lists the templates available on your computer.

From the **Templates** dialog box, you can double-click the template you want to use as the model for your workbook. Excel will create a new workbook with the template's formatting and contents in place.

**Tip**   The default file type for files created with a template is workbook (.xls), not template (.xlt).

In this exercise, you create a template to track sales for a month at The Garden Company. You delete unneeded worksheets from the template, save the file with the Template file type, and then use your new template to create a workbook.

OPEN: TemplateStart from the *SBS\Excel\MultipleSources* folder.

**1**   On the tab bar, in the lower left corner of the workbook window, right-click the **Sheet2** tab and, from the shortcut menu that appears, click **Delete**.

The **Sheet2** worksheet disappears.

**2**   On the tab bar, in the lower left corner of the workbook window, right-click the **Sheet3** tab and, from the shortcut menu that appears, click **Delete**.

The **Sheet3** worksheet disappears.

**3**   On the **File** menu, click **Save As**.

The **Save As** dialog box appears.

**4**   Click the **Save as type** down arrow, and from the list that appears, click **Template (*.xlt)**.

The active directory changes to the default Office 2003 templates directory.

**5** In the **File name** box, delete the existing name and type MonthlySales.

**6** Click **Save**.

The **Save As** dialog box disappears, and Excel saves your document as a template.

**7** Click the template's **Close** button.

MonthlySales.xlt closes.

**8** On the **File** menu, click **MonthlySales**.

The MonthlySales template appears.

**9** Click the B column header.

**10** On the Formatting toolbar, click the **Center** button.

The contents of column B are centered.

**11** On the Standard toolbar, click the **Save** button.

Excel saves your changes.

**12** Click the template's **Close** button.

TemplateStart closes.

**13** On the **View** menu, click **Task Pane**. If necessary, click the Other Task Panes down arrow and select **New Workbook**.

The **New Workbook** task pane appears.

**14** In the **Templates** section of the task pane, click **On my computer**.

The **Templates** dialog box appears.

**15** In the **Templates** dialog box, double-click **MonthlySales.xlt**.

A new workbook named MonthlySales1.xls appears.

**16** On the Standard toolbar, click the **Save** button.

The **Save As** dialog box appears, with the default Templates directory as the active directory.

**17** Navigate to the MultipleSources exercise directory, and in the **File name** box, type December.

**18** Click **Save**.

Excel saves your workbook, and the **Save As** dialog box disappears.

Close

Save

Save

**19** On the **Tools** menu, click **Options**.

The **Options** dialog box appears.

**20** If necessary, click the **General** tab.

The **General** tab page appears.

**21** In the **At startup, open all files in** box, type C:\SBS\Excel\MultipleSources.

**22** Click **Cancel**.

The **Options** dialog box disappears without saving your changes.

**23** On the Standard toolbar, click the **Save** button.

Save

CLOSE: December.

# Working with More Than One Set of Data

An important part of managing your Excel data effectively is organizing it into workbooks by subject. For example, you can create a workbook to track sales for the new year or add a worksheet to a products workbook to maintain records of a new product category. When you store your data in more than one workbook, you need a way to work with multiple workbooks simultaneously. You can open more than one workbook at a time by accessing the **Open** dialog box multiple times, but you can also open more than one file from the **Open** dialog box at once.

In the **Open** dialog box, hold down the Ctrl key, click the files you want to open, and then click **Open**. For example, you might open the workbooks with the sales for the first three months in a year and compare the totals, both by day and by grand total.

**Tip** The only limit to the number of Excel files you can have open at a time is the amount of memory in your computer. Of course, the practical limit for most tasks is much lower and probably doesn't exceed four or five open files.

When you open more than one Excel workbook, the active workbook often hides the inactive workbooks on the screen. You can use the buttons on the taskbar to move from file to file, but you can also arrange the workbooks within the Excel window. For example, you can split the screen horizontally and show one workbook in each portion of the window, as in the following graphic.

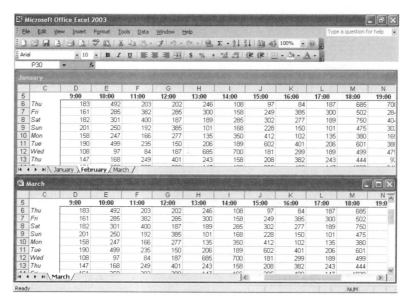

The problem with splitting the screen is that most of each workbook is hidden. You can arrange your workbooks within the Excel window so that most of the active workbook is shown but the others are easily accessible by clicking **Arrange** on the **Window** menu and, in the **Arrange Windows** dialog box, selecting the **Cascade** option. When you do, the windows will be arranged as in the following graphic.

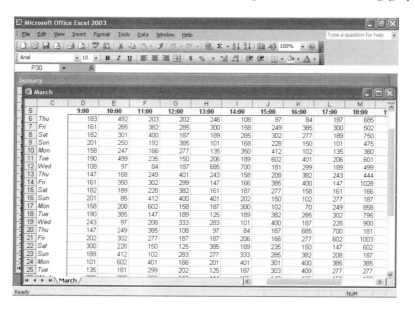

Another way you can work with more than one workbook is to copy a worksheet from another workbook to the current workbook. One circumstance in which you might consider copying worksheets to the current workbook would occur if you were to collect all monthly sales results for a year in one place. You can copy worksheets from another workbook by right-clicking the tab of the sheet you want to copy and, from the shortcut menu that appears, clicking **Move or Copy** to display the **Move or Copy** dialog box.

**Tip**   Selecting the **Create a copy** check box leaves the copied worksheet in its original workbook, while clearing the check box causes Excel to delete the worksheet from its original workbook.

Once the worksheets are in the target workbook, you can change their order to make the data easier to locate within the workbook. To change a worksheet's location in the workbook, you drag its sheet tab to the desired location on the tab bar. If you want a worksheet to stand out in a workbook, you can right-click its sheet tab and use the menu that appears to change the tab's color. At the other end of the spectrum, you can hide the active worksheet by opening the **Format** menu, pointing to **Sheet**, and clicking **Hide**. When you want to have the sheet show up in the workbook again, open the **Format** menu, point to **Sheet**, and click **Unhide**. Then, in the **Unhide** dialog box, click the sheet you want to display, and click **OK**.

In this exercise, you open multiple workbooks, change how the workbooks are displayed, insert two worksheets into a workbook, reorder the worksheets, hide one of the worksheets, and then change the tab color of one of the worksheets.

START: Microsoft Excel.

Open

1   On the Standard toolbar, click the **Open** button.

The **Open** dialog box appears.

2   Hold down the ⌃Ctrl key while you click **January.xls, February.xls**, and **March.xls**, and then click **Open**.

January.xls, February.xls, and March.xls open.

3   If necessary, on the **Window** menu, click **January.xls**.

January.xls becomes the active document.

**4**     On the **Window** menu, click **Arrange**.

The **Arrange Windows** dialog box appears.

**5**     Click the **Cascade** option button, and then click **OK**.

The windows of open Excel documents are cascaded within the Excel window.

**6**     Click the January.xls title bar.

**7**     On the **File** menu, click **Save As**.

The **Save As** dialog box appears.

**8**     In the **File name** box, type **FirstQuarter** and then click **Save**.

Excel saves the file under the name FirstQuarter.xls.

**9**     Click the February.xls title bar.

February.xls becomes the active document.

**10**     On the tab bar, right-click the **February** tab and then, from the shortcut menu that appears, click **Move or Copy**.

The **Move or Copy** dialog box appears.

**11**     Click the **To book** down arrow, and then, from the list that appears, click **FirstQuarter.xls**.

**12** In the **Before sheet** list, click (**move to end**).

**13** At the bottom of the **Move or Copy** dialog box, select the **Create a copy** check box.

**14** Click **OK**.

The February worksheet appears in FirstQuarter.xls. Cells D38 through O38 contain an error marker in the upper left corner of each cell.

| | C | D | E | F | G | H | I | J | K | L | M | N |
|---|---|---|---|---|---|---|---|---|---|---|---|---|
| 14 | Fri | 161 | 350 | 302 | 299 | 147 | 166 | 385 | 400 | 147 | 1028 | 2 |
| 15 | Sat | 182 | 189 | 228 | 382 | 161 | 187 | 277 | 158 | 161 | 166 | 3 |
| 16 | Sun | 201 | 85 | 412 | 400 | 401 | 202 | 150 | 102 | 277 | 187 | 2 |
| 17 | Mon | 158 | 208 | 602 | 158 | 187 | 300 | 102 | 70 | 249 | 858 | 4 |
| 18 | Tue | 190 | 385 | 147 | 189 | 125 | 189 | 382 | 285 | 302 | 795 | 6 |
| 19 | Wed | 243 | 97 | 208 | 333 | 283 | 101 | 400 | 187 | 228 | 900 | 1 |
| 20 | Thu | 147 | 249 | 385 | 108 | 97 | 84 | 187 | 685 | 700 | 181 | 2 |
| 21 | Fri | 202 | 302 | 277 | 187 | 187 | 206 | 166 | 277 | 602 | 1003 | 3 |
| 22 | Sat | 300 | 228 | 150 | 125 | 385 | 189 | 235 | 150 | 147 | 602 | 1 |
| 23 | Sun | 189 | 412 | 102 | 283 | 277 | 333 | 285 | 382 | 208 | 187 | 1 |
| 24 | Mon | 101 | 602 | 401 | 166 | 201 | 401 | 301 | 400 | 385 | 385 | 2 |
| 25 | Tue | 135 | 181 | 299 | 202 | 125 | 187 | 303 | 409 | 277 | 277 | 1 |
| 26 | Wed | 206 | 208 | 382 | 243 | 444 | 125 | 140 | 166 | 150 | 150 | 2 |
| 27 | Thu | 189 | 385 | 400 | 147 | 1028 | 283 | 249 | 235 | 102 | 102 | 3 |
| 28 | Fri | 161 | 302 | 357 | 158 | 247 | 166 | 302 | 140 | 247 | 401 | 1 |
| 29 | Sat | 182 | 228 | 166 | 102 | 277 | 187 | 499 | 249 | 499 | 299 | 2 |
| 30 | Sun | 201 | 412 | 235 | 192 | 208 | 385 | 475 | 302 | 285 | 382 | 1 |
| 31 | Mon | 158 | 602 | 140 | 166 | 385 | 277 | 380 | 165 | 168 | 400 | 2 |
| 32 | Tue | 158 | 333 | 249 | 235 | 277 | 150 | 299 | 147 | 166 | 158 | 3 |
| 33 | Wed | 190 | 279 | 302 | 140 | 150 | 102 | 189 | 158 | 247 | 166 | 2 |
| 34 | | | | | | | | | | | | |
| 35 | | | | | | | | | | | | |
| 36 | | | | | | | | | | | | |
| 37 | | | | | | | | | | | | |
| 38 | Total | 4984 | 8376 | 7655 | 6289 | 7697 | 6336 | 7985 | 7147 | 7097 | 12963 | 80 |

Error Options

**15** Select cells D38 through O38.

An **Error Options** button appears.

**Troubleshooting** The **Error Options** button appears because Excel asks whether the data in the cell above the top of the selected range should be included in the calculation. It's time data and shouldn't be included, so you can ignore the error message.

**16** Click the **Error Options** button, and then, from the shortcut menu that appears, click **Ignore Error**.

The error markers disappear from the selected cells.

**17** Click the March.xls title bar.

March.xls becomes the active document.

**18** On the tab bar, right-click the **March** tab and then, from the shortcut menu that appears, click **Move or Copy**.

The **Move or Copy** dialog box appears.

**19** Click the **To book** down arrow, and then, from the list that appears, click **FirstQuarter.xls**.

**20** In the **Before sheet** list, click **February**.

**21** At the bottom of the **Move or Copy** dialog box, select the **Create a copy** check box.

**22** Click **OK**.

The March worksheet appears in FirstQuarter.xls, to the left of the February tab. Cells D38 through O38 contain an error marker in the upper left corner of each cell.

**23** Select cells D38 through O38.

An **Error Options** button appears.

**24** Click the **Error Options** button, and then, from the shortcut menu that appears, click **Ignore Error**.

The error markers disappear from the selected cells.

**25** On the tab bar, drag the **February** tab to the left of the **March** tab. As you drag the **February** tab, a line will appear in the tab bar, marking the **February** tab's place.

The **February** tab moves to the left of the **March** tab.

**26** On the tab bar, click the **January** tab and then, on the **Format** menu, point to **Sheet**, and click **Hide**.

The January sheet disappears.

**27** On the tab bar, right-click the **March** tab, and then, from the shortcut menu that appears, click **Tab Color**.

The **Format Tab Color** dialog box appears.

**28** Click the light orange square, and then click **OK**.

Excel assigns the light orange color to the **March** tab.

**29** Click the **February** tab.

The February sheet is selected. Because the March sheet is in the background, the **March** tab turns light orange.

Save

**30** On the Standard toolbar, click the **Save** button.

Excel saves your changes.

CLOSE: FirstQuarter, February, and March.

# Linking to Data in Other Workbooks

Cutting and pasting data from one workbook to another is a quick and easy way to gather related data in one place, but there is a substantial limitation: if the data from the original cell changes, the change is not reflected in the cell to which the data was copied. In other words, cutting and pasting a cell's contents doesn't create a relationship between the original cell and the target cell.

You can ensure that the data in the target cell will reflect any changes in the original cell by creating a *link* between the two cells. Rather than enter a value into the target cell by typing or pasting, you create a type of formula that identifies the source from which Excel will derive the target cell's value.

To create a link between cells, open both the workbook with the cell from which you want to pull the value and the workbook with the target cell. Then click the target cell, and type an equal sign, signifying you want to create a formula. After you type the equal sign, activate the workbook with the cell from which you want to derive the value and then click that cell.

When you switch back to the workbook with the target cell, you will find that Excel has filled in the formula with a reference to the cell you clicked.

| IF | ▾ ✗ ✓ ƒₓ | =[TotalByHour2001.xls]Sheet1!$D$8 | | | | |
|---|---|---|---|---|---|---|
| | A | B | C | D | E | F |
| 1 | | | | | | |
| 2 | | | | | | |
| 3 | | =[TotalByHour2001.xls]Sheet1!$D$8| | | | |
| 4 | | | | | | |
| 5 | | | | | | |

The reference from this example, *=[TotalByHour2001.xls]Sheet1!$D$8*, gives three pieces of information: the workbook, the worksheet, and the cell you clicked in the worksheet. The first element of the reference, the name of the workbook, is enclosed in square brackets; the end of the second element is marked with an exclamation point; and the third element, the cell reference, has a dollar sign before both the row and the column identifiers. This type of reference is known as a *3-D reference*, reflecting the three dimensions (workbook, worksheet, and cell) that you need to point to a cell in another workbook.

**Note** For references to cells in the same workbook, the workbook information is omitted. Likewise, references to cells in the same worksheet don't use a worksheet identifier.

Whenever you open a workbook with a link to another document, Excel will try to update the information in linked cells. If the program can't find the source, such as when a workbook or worksheet is deleted or renamed, an alert box appears, indicating that there is a broken link. At that point, you can click the **Update** button and then the **Edit Links** button to open the **Edit Links** dialog box and find which link is broken. After you identify the broken link, you can close the **Edit Links** dialog box, click the cell containing the broken link, and create a new link to the desired data.

If you type a link yourself and you make an error, a #REF! error message will appear in the cell with the link. To fix the link, click the cell, delete its contents, and then either retype the link or create it with the point-and-click method described earlier in this section.

In this exercise, you create a link to another workbook, break the link, and then use the **Edit Links** dialog box to identify the broken link and the **Change Source** dialog box to fix the link.

START: Microsoft Excel.

Open

**1**     On the Standard toolbar, click the **Open** button.

      The **Open** dialog box appears.

**2**     Hold down the Ctrl key while you click the **Linking.xls** and **2001Q1.xls** files, and then click **Open**.

      Linking.xls and 2001Q1.xls open.

**3**     On the **Window** menu, click **Arrange**.

      The **Arrange Windows** dialog box appears.

**4**     Select the **Cascade** option button, and then click **OK**.

      The open Excel documents cascade in the Excel window.

**5**     In Linking.xls, click cell D10, and then type =.

**6**     Click the 2001Q1.xls title bar.

      The 2001Q1.xls file appears.

**7**     If necessary, click the **January** sheet tab.

**8**     Click cell Q38.

**9**    Click the Linking.xls title bar.

Linking.xls appears, with the formula *=[2001Q1.xls]January!$Q$38* in cell D10.

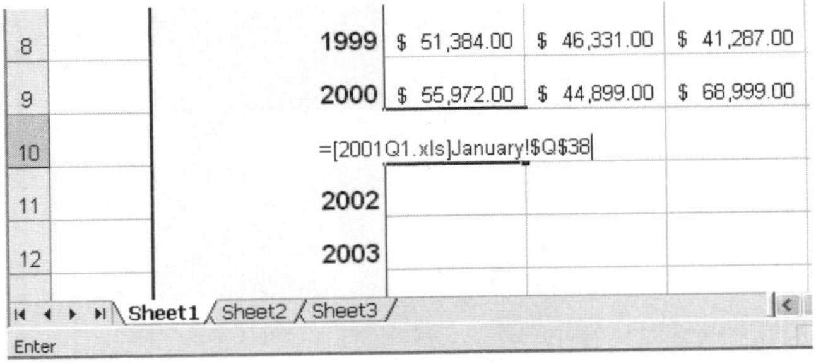

| 8 | | | 1999 | $ 51,384.00 | $ 46,331.00 | $ 41,287.00 |
|---|---|---|------|-------------|-------------|-------------|
| 9 | | | 2000 | $ 55,972.00 | $ 44,899.00 | $ 68,999.00 |
| 10 | | | =[2001Q1.xls]January!$Q$38 | | | |
| 11 | | | 2002 | | | |
| 12 | | | 2003 | | | |

|◄ ◄ ► ►|\ **Sheet1** / Sheet2 / Sheet3 /

Enter

**10**    Press ⏎.

The value *$97,925.00* appears in cell D10.

**11**    On the Standard toolbar, click the **Save** button.

Excel saves your changes.

**12**    Hold down the ⇧ key and, on the **File** menu, click **Close All**.

Linking.xls and 2001Q1.xls close.

**13**    On the Standard toolbar, click the **Open** button.

The **Open** dialog box appears.

**14**    Click **2001Q1.xls**, and then press ⌦. Confirm the deletion by clicking **Yes** in the dialog box that appears.

2001Q1.xls moves to the **Recycle Bin**.

**15**    Double-click **Linking.xls**.

Linking.xls opens, with an alert box asking whether you want to update the links in the workbook.

**16**    In the alert box, click **Update**.

The original alert box disappears, and a second alert box, with a message asking if you want to edit the broken link, appears.

Save

**17** Click **Edit Links**.

The **Edit Links** dialog box appears.

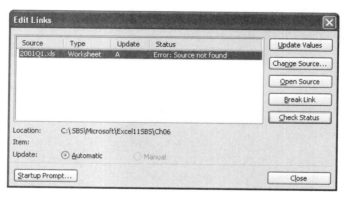

**18** Click **Change Source**.

The **Change Source** dialog box appears.

**19** Double-click **Y2001Q1.xls**.

The **Change Source** dialog box disappears, and the **Edit Links** dialog box reappears, with an indication that Y2001Q1.xls is a valid source for links.

**20** Click **Close**.

The **Edit Links** dialog box disappears, and *$97,925.00* appears in cell D10.

**21** Click cell D10.

*=[Y2001Q1.xls]January!$Q$38* appears in the formula bar.

**22** On the Standard toolbar, click the **Save** button.

Excel saves your changes.

CLOSE: Linking.

# Summarizing Multiple Sets of Data

*Microsoft Office Specialist*

When you create a series of worksheets that contain similar data, perhaps by using a template, you build a consistent set of workbooks where data is stored in a predictable place. For example, in the workbook template in the following graphic, sales for the hour 9:00 a.m. to 10:00 a.m. on the first day of the month are always stored in cell D6.

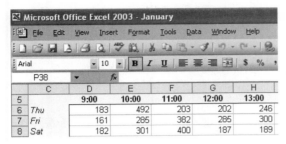

Using links to bring data from one worksheet to another gives you a great deal of power in combining data from several sources in a single spot. For example, you can create a worksheet that lists the total sales just for certain months of a year, use links to draw the values from the worksheets in which the sales were recorded, and then create a formula to perform calculations on the data. However, for large worksheets with hundreds of cells filled with data, creating links from every cell to cells in another worksheet is time-consuming. Also, to calculate a sum or an average for the data, you would need to include links to cells in every workbook.

Fortunately, there is an easier way to combine data from multiple worksheets in a single worksheet. This process, called *data consolidation*, lets you define ranges of cells from multiple worksheets and have Excel summarize the data. You define these ranges in the **Consolidate** dialog box.

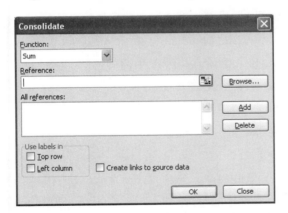

Once you have opened the dialog box, you move to the worksheet with the cells in the first range you want to include in your summary. When you select the cells, the 3-D reference for the cell range appears in the **Consolidate** dialog box.

Clicking **Add** stores the reference, while clicking **Delete** removes a range from the calculation. You can then choose the other cell ranges with data to include in the summary. Cells that are in the same relative position in the ranges will have their contents summarized together. So the cell in the upper left corner of one range will be added to the cell in the upper left corner of another range, even if those ranges are in different areas of the worksheet. After you choose the ranges to be used in your summary, you can choose the calculation to perform on the data (sum, average, and so on). When you're done selecting ranges to use in the calculation, click **OK** to have Excel summarize the data in your target worksheet.

**Important**    You can define only one data consolidation summary per workbook.

In this exercise, you define a series of ranges from two workbooks to be included in a data consolidation calculation. You then add the contents of the ranges and show the results in a worksheet.

START: Microsoft Excel.

Open

**1**    On the Standard toolbar, click the **Open** button.

The **Open** dialog box appears.

**2**    Hold down the [Ctrl] key while you click **Consolidate.xls** and **Y2001ByMonth.xls**, and then click **Open**.

Consolidate.xls and Y2001ByMonth.xls open.

**3**    If necessary, on the **Window** menu, click **Consolidate.xls**.

Consolidate.xls becomes the active document.

**4**    Click cell D5, and then, on the **Data** menu, click **Consolidate**.

The **Consolidate** dialog box appears.

**5**    On the **Window** menu, click **Y2001ByMonth.xls**.

Y2001ByMonth.xls becomes the active file.

**6**    If necessary, click the **January** sheet tab.

**7**    Click cell D6 and drag to cell O36.

As you drag, the **Consolidate** dialog box rolls up. When you release the mouse button, *[Y2001ByMonth.xls]January!$D$6:$O$36* appears in the **Reference** box of the **Consolidate** dialog box.

**8**    Click **Add** in the **Consolidate** dialog box.

*[Y2001ByMonth.xls]January!$D$6:$O$36* appears in the **All references** list of the **Consolidate** dialog box.

**9**    Click the **February** sheet tab.

Cells in the range D6:O36 are already selected. *[Y2001ByMonth.xls]February!$D$6:$O$36* appears in the **Reference** box of the **Consolidate** dialog box.

**10** Click **Add**.

*[Y2001ByMonth.xls]February!$D$6:$O$36* appears in the **All references** list of the **Consolidate** dialog box.

**11** Click the **March** sheet tab.

The range D6:O36 is already selected. *[Y2001ByMonth.xls]March!$D$6:$O$36* appears in the **Reference** box of the **Consolidate** dialog box.

**12** Click **Add**.

*[Y2001ByMonth.xls]March!$D$6:$O$36* appears in the **All references** list of the **Consolidate** dialog box.

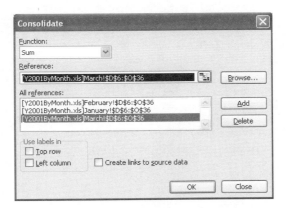

**13** On the **Window** menu, click **Consolidate.xls**.

Consolidate.xls becomes the active document.

**14** In the **Consolidate** dialog box, click **OK**.

The **Consolidate** dialog box disappears. The sums of the contents of the cells in the three worksheets named in the **Consolidate** dialog box appear in cells D5:O35.

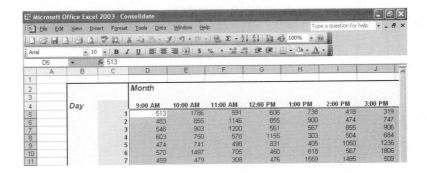

**15** On the Standard toolbar, click the **Save** button.

Save

Excel saves your changes.

CLOSE: Consolidate, Y2001ByMonth.

# Grouping Multiple Data Lists

*Microsoft
Office
Specialist*

When you work with Excel for a while, you'll find that you often work with a number of the same workbooks at a time. For instance, Catherine Turner, the owner of The Garden Company, might always pull up a yearly sales summary workbook and the sales figures for product categories offered by The Garden Company. She can open the workbooks together through the **Open** dialog box, but she can also group the files so that she has the option of opening them all simultaneously.

If you want to open a set of files simultaneously, you can define them as part of a workspace, which uses a single Excel file name to reference several workbooks instead of one. To define a workspace, you open the files you want to include and then open the **Save Workspace** dialog box.

When the **Save Workspace** dialog box is open, clicking **Save** saves references to the Excel files that are currently open. Whenever you open the workspace you create, all of the files that were open when you defined the workspace will appear. Including a file in a workspace doesn't remove it from general circulation; you can still open it by itself.

In this exercise, you save a workspace that consists of two workbooks, close the included files, and then test the workspace by opening it from the **Open** dialog box.

START: Microsoft Excel.

**1** On the Standard toolbar, click the **Open** button.

Open

The **Open** dialog box appears.

**2** Hold down the ⌃ key while you click the **Y2001ByMonth.xls** and **TotalByHour2001.xls** files, and then click **Open**.

Y2001ByMonth.xls and TotalByHour2001.xls appear.

**3** On the **File** menu, click **Save Workspace**.

The **Save Workspace** dialog box appears, with the file type in the **Save as type** box set to *Workspaces (*.xlw)*.

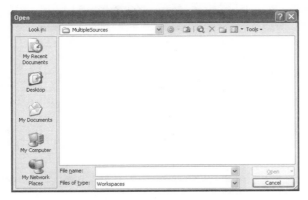

**4**   In the **File name** box, type **Y2001Summary** and then click **Save**.

Excel saves your workspace.

**5**   Hold down the `Shift` key and, on the **File** menu, click **Close All**.

Y2001ByMonth and TotalByHour2001close.

**6**   On the Standard toolbar, click the **Open** button.

The **Open** dialog box appears.

**7**   Double-click **Y2001Summary.xlw**.

The TotalByHour2001.xls and Y2001ByMonth.xls workbooks open.

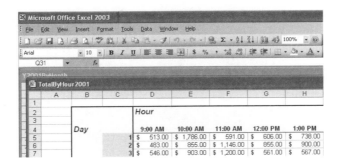

CLOSE: TotalByHour2001, Y2001ByMonth.

# Key Points

- If you create a lot of workbooks with the same layout and design, saving a workbook with the common elements (and no data) will take you much less time.

- You can change the default folder where Excel looks for templates, but you should do so only if you don't want anyone to create workbooks from other templates.

- When you work with several workbooks at once, you can change their arrangement on the Windows desktop to make it easier to move among them.

- Remember that you can close all open workbooks by holding down the [Shift] key and clicking **Close All** on the **File** menu.

- Worksheets aren't locked into place. You can move them within a workbook, copy or move them to another workbook, insert new ones, or hide them from view.

- When you want a worksheet to stand out, change the color of its sheet tab.

- You can use data in other worksheets or workbooks in your formulas. You make the link by clicking the cell, which creates a 3-D reference to that cell.

- If you always work on a group of workbooks at the same time, create a workspace so that you can open them all at once.

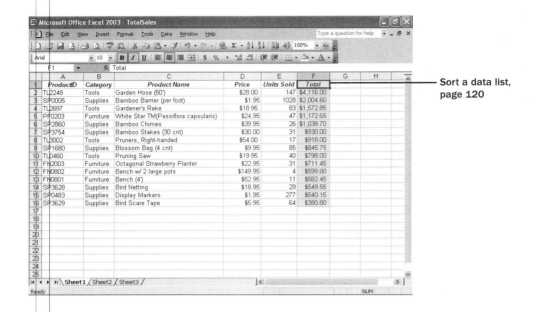

Sort a data list, page 120

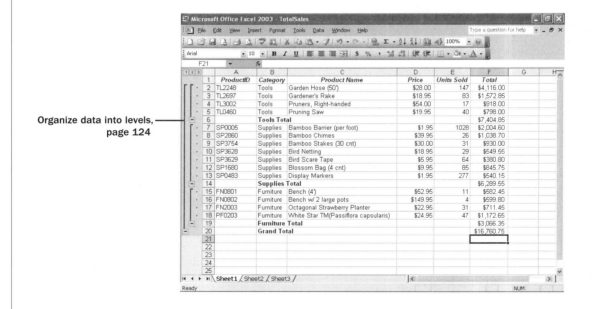

Organize data into levels, page 124

*Chapter 7 at a Glance*

# 7 Reordering and Summarizing Data

**In this chapter you will learn to:**

✔ Sort a data list.

✔ Organize data into levels.

Most of the time, when you enter data in a Microsoft Excel worksheet, you will enter it in chronological order. For instance, you would probably enter hourly sales data in a worksheet at the end of each day, starting with the first hour your store was open and moving to closing time. The data would naturally be displayed in the order in which you entered it, but that might not always be the best order to answer your questions. For instance, you might want to sort your data so that the top row in your worksheet shows the best sales day for the month, with subsequent rows displaying the remaining days of the month arranged by total sales. You can also sort based on the contents of more than one column. A good example would be sorting sales data by week, day, and then hour of the day.

Once you have sorted your data into the desired order, Excel lets you find partial totals, or *subtotals*, for groups of cells within a given range. Yes, you can create formulas to find the sum, average, or standard deviation of data in a cell range, but you can do the same thing much more quickly by having Excel calculate the total for cells with the same value in a column. If your worksheet held sales data for a list of products, you could calculate subtotals for each product category.

When you calculate subtotals in a worksheet, Excel creates an outline that marks the cell ranges used in each subtotal. For example, if the first 10 rows of a worksheet have furniture sales data and the second 10 rows have tool sales data, Excel will divide the rows into two units. You can use the markers on the worksheet to hide or display the rows used to calculate a subtotal; in this case, you can hide all of the rows with tool data, hide all of the rows with furniture data, hide both, or show both.

In this chapter, you'll learn how to sort your data using one or more criteria, calculate subtotals, and organize your data into levels.

**See Also** Do you need a quick refresher on the topics in this chapter? See the quick reference entries on pages xlii–xliii.

**Important** Before you can use the practice files in this chapter, be sure you install them from the book's companion CD-ROM to their default location. See "Using the Book's CD-ROM" on page xi for more information.

# Sorting a Data List

*Microsoft Office Specialist*

While Excel makes it easy to enter your business data and to manage it after you've saved it in a worksheet, it's rare that your data will answer every question you want to ask it. For example, you might want to discover which of your products has the highest total sales, which product has the next highest, and so on. You can find out that information by sorting your data.

When you *sort* data in a worksheet, you rearrange the worksheet rows based on the contents of cells in a particular column. Sorting a worksheet to find your highest-selling products in terms of units sold, for instance, might show the results displayed in the following graphic.

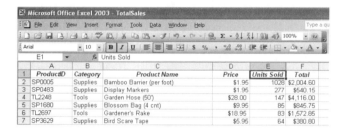

Sort Descending

You can sort a group of rows in a worksheet in a number of ways, but the first step is to identify the column that will provide the values by which the rows should be sorted. In the above graphic, you could find the highest sales totals by choosing the cells in the Total column and then clicking the **Sort Descending** toolbar button. Clicking the **Sort Descending** button has Excel put the row with the highest value in the Total column at the top of the worksheet and continue down to the lowest value.

Sort Ascending

If you wanted to sort the rows in the opposite order, from the lowest sales to the highest, you would select the cells in the Total column and then click the **Sort Ascending** toolbar button.

The **Sort Ascending** and **Sort Descending** toolbar buttons let you sort rows in a worksheet quickly, but you can use them only to sort the worksheet based on the contents of one column. For example, you might want to order the worksheet rows by product category and then by total so that you can see the highest-selling items in each category. You can sort rows in a worksheet by the contents of more than one column through the **Sort** dialog box, where you can pick up to three columns to use as sort criteria and choose whether to sort the rows in ascending or descending order.

The default setting for Excel is to sort numbers according to their values and to sort words in alphabetical order, but that pattern doesn't work for some sets of values. One example of where sorting a list of values in alphabetical order would yield incorrect results is with the months of the year. In an "alphabetical" calendar, April is the first month and September the last! Fortunately, Excel recognizes a number of special lists, such as days of the week and months of the year. You can have Excel sort the contents of a worksheet based on values in a known list; if needed, you can create your own list of values using the tools on the **Custom Lists** tab page of the **Options** dialog box.

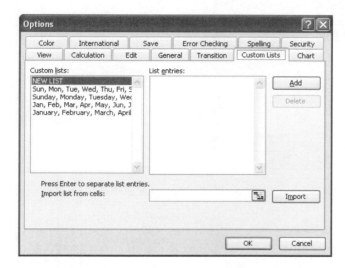

The default lists of weekdays in Excel both start with Sunday. If you keep your business records based on a Monday–Sunday week, you can create a new list with Monday as the first day and Sunday as the last.

**Important**   If you sort using a custom list, the custom list must be the primary sorting criterion.

In this exercise, you sort your worksheet using the **Sort Ascending** toolbar button, use the **Sort** dialog box to sort your worksheet based on the contents of more than one row, create a custom sort order, and then apply that custom sort order to your worksheet.

OPEN: Sorting from the *SBS\Excel\ReorderingAndSummarizing* folder.

**1**   If necessary, click the **Sales** tab to display the Sales worksheet.

**2**   Click cell A1 and drag to cell A32.

**3**   On the Standard toolbar, click the **Sort Ascending** button.

   The data in the selected range of cells is sorted in ascending order. Note that the first cell, which contains a data label, is not included in the sort.

**4** Click the **AllInfo** sheet tab.

The AllInfo worksheet appears.

**5** Click cell A1 and drag to cell D32.

**6** On the **Data** menu, click **Sort**.

The **Sort** dialog box appears.

**7** If necessary, click the **Sort by** down arrow and then, from the list that appears, click **Sales**.

*Sales* appears in the **Sort by** box.

**8** Click the **Then by** down arrow, and then, from the list that appears, click **Weekday**.

*Weekday* appears in the **Then by** box.

**9** Click **OK**.

The contents of the selected cells appear in sorted order.

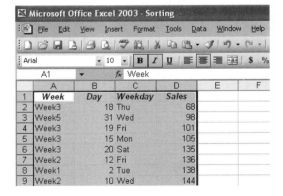

Undo

**10** On the Standard toolbar, click the **Undo** button.

The contents of the selected cells appear in their original order.

**11** Click cell G2 and drag to cell G8.

**12** On the **Tools** menu, click **Options**.

The **Options** dialog box appears.

**13** Click the **Custom Lists** tab.

The **Custom Lists** tab page appears, with *$G$2:$G$8* in the **Import list from cells** box.

**14** Click **Import**.

The items in the cells appear in the **List entries** list, while the series appears in the **Custom lists** list.

**15** Click **OK**.

The **Options** dialog box closes.

**16** Click cell A1 and drag to cell D32.

**17** On the **Data** menu, click **Sort**.

The **Sort** dialog box appears.

**18** Click the **Sort by** down arrow, and then, from the list that appears, click **Weekday**.

*Weekday* appears in the **Sort by** box.

**19** Click the **Options** button.

The **Sort Options** dialog box appears.

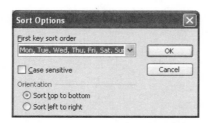

**20** Click the **First key sort order** down arrow, and then, from the list that appears, click **Mon, Tue, Wed, Thu, Fri, Sat, Sun**.

*Mon, Tue, Wed, Thu, Fri, Sat, Sun* appears in the **First key sort order** box.

**21** Click **OK**.

The **Sort Options** dialog box disappears.

22 Click the **Then by** down arrow, and then, from the list that appears, click **Sales**.

*Sales* appears in the **Then by** box.

23 Click **OK**.

The selected data appears in sorted order.

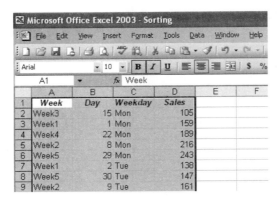

24 On the Standard toolbar, click the **Save** button to save your changes.

CLOSE: Sorting.

# Organizing Data into Levels

*Microsoft Office Specialist*

After you have sorted the rows in an Excel worksheet or entered the data in such a way that it doesn't need to be sorted, you can have Excel calculate subtotals, or totals for a portion of the data. In a worksheet with sales data for three different product categories, for example, you can sort the products by category, select all of the cells that contain data, and then open the **Subtotal** dialog box.

In the **Subtotal** dialog box, you can choose the column on which to base your subtotals (such as every change of value in the Week column), the summary calculation you want to perform, and the column or columns with values to be summarized. In the worksheet in the preceding graphic, for example, you could also calculate subtotals for the number of units sold in each category. After you define your subtotals, they appear in your worksheet.

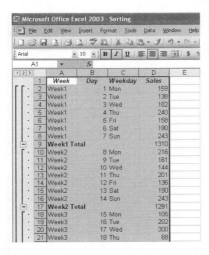

As the graphic shows, when you add subtotals to a worksheet, Excel also defines groups based on the rows used to calculate a subtotal. The groupings form an outline of your worksheet based on the criteria you used to create the subtotals. In the above example, all of the rows with furniture products are in one group, rows with tools are in another, and so on. The outline section at the left of your worksheet holds controls you can use to hide or display groups of rows in your worksheet.

There are three types of controls in the outline section: **Hide Detail** buttons, **Show Detail** buttons, and level buttons.

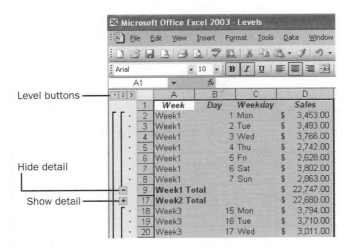

Hide Detail

The **Hide Detail** button beside a group can be clicked to hide the rows in that group. In the previous graphic, clicking the **Hide Detail** button next to row 9 would hide rows 2 through 8 but leave the row holding the subtotal for that group, row 9, visible.

Show Detail

When you hide a group of rows, the button next to the group changes to a **Show Detail** button. Clicking a group's **Show Detail** button restores the rows in the group to the worksheet.

Level

The level buttons comprise the other set of buttons in the outline section of a worksheet with subtotals. Each button represents a level of organization in a worksheet; clicking a level button hides all levels of detail below that of the button you clicked. The following table identifies the three levels of organization in the previous graphic.

| Level | Description |
| --- | --- |
| 1 | The grand total |
| 2 | Subtotals for each group |
| 3 | Individual rows in the worksheet |

Level 2

Clicking the **Level 2** button in the worksheet shown in the previous illustration would hide the rows with data on the sales of individual products but would leave the row with the grand total (Level 1) and all rows with the subtotals for each product (Level 2) visible in the worksheet.

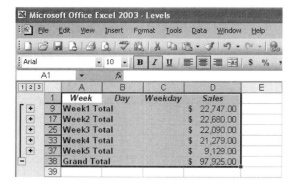

If you like, you can add levels of detail to the outline Excel creates. For instance, you might want to be able to hide sales of bamboo barrier, bamboo chimes, and bamboo stakes (which you know sell well) to see how other products sell in comparison. To create a new outline group within an existing group, select the rows you want to group and then open the **Data** menu, point to **Group and Outline**, and click **Group**. Excel will create a new group on a new level.

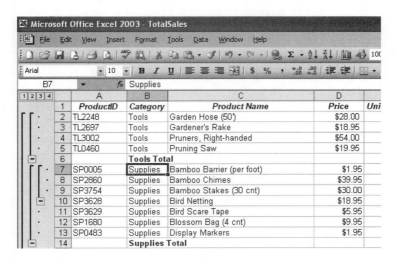

You can remove a group by selecting the rows in the group and clicking **Ungroup** from the same submenu.

**Tip** If you want to remove all subtotals from a worksheet, open the **Subtotal** dialog box and click the **Remove All** button.

In this exercise, you add subtotals to a worksheet and then use the outline that appears to show and hide different groups of data in your worksheet.

**OPEN:** Levels from the *SBS\Excel\ReorderingAndSummarizing* folder.

**1** Click the row head of row 1 and drag to the row head of row 32.

Rows 1 through 32 are highlighted.

**2** On the **Data** menu, click **Subtotals**.

The **Subtotal** dialog box appears, with the default options to add a subtotal at every change in the Week column, to return the sum of the values in the subtotaled rows, and to add a row with the subtotal of values in the Sales column below the final selected row.

**3** Click **OK**.

The **Subtotal** dialog box disappears. In Levels.xls, new rows appear with subtotals for sales during each week represented in the worksheet. The new rows are numbered 9, 17, 25, 33, and 37. A row with the grand total of all rows also appears; that row is row 38. A new section with outline bars and group-level indicators appears to the left of column A.

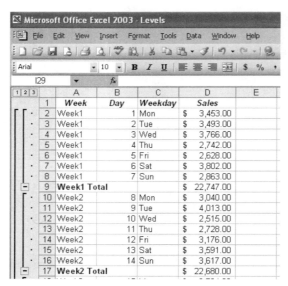

**4**     Click the row head of row 2 and drag to the row head of row 6.

Rows 2 through 6 are highlighted.

**5**     On the **Data** menu, point to **Group and Outline**, and then click **Group**.

Rows 2 through 6 are made into a new group. An outline bar appears on a new level in the outline section, and a corresponding **Level 4** button appears at the top of the outline section.

**6**     In the outline section, click the **Hide Detail** button next to row 7.

Rows 2 through 6 are hidden, and the **Hide Detail** button you clicked changes to a **Show Detail** button.

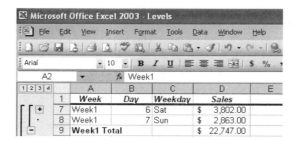

**7**     In the outline section, click the **Show Detail** button next to row 7.

Rows 2 through 6 reappear.

**8**     In the outline section, click the **Level 1** button.

All rows except row 1, with the column headings, and row 38, with the grand total, are hidden.

| 2 |
| Level 2 |

**9** In the outline section, click the **Level 2** button.

The rows with the subtotal for each week appear.

| 3 |
| Level 3 |

**10** In the outline section, click the **Level 3** button.

All rows except rows 2 through 6 appear.

| 4 |
| Level 4 |

**11** In the outline section, click the **Level 4** button.

Rows 2 through 6 reappear.

**12** On the Standard toolbar, click the **Save** button to save your work.

CLOSE: Sorting.

# Key Points

■ You can rearrange the data in a worksheet quickly by clicking either the **Sort Ascending** or **Sort Descending** toolbar button.

■ Don't forget that you can sort the rows in a worksheet using orders other than alphabetical or numerical. For example, you can sort a series of days based on their order in the week.

■ If none of the existing custom sort orders (days, weekdays, and so on) meet your needs, you can create your own custom sort order.

■ You can divide the data in your worksheet into levels, and find a subtotal for each level.

■ Creating subtotals lets you show or hide groups of data in your worksheets.

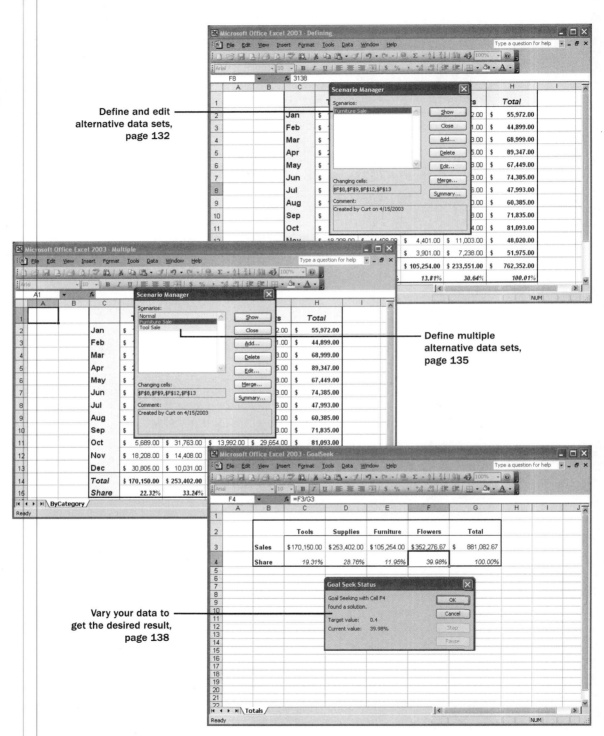

Define and edit
alternative data sets,
page 132

Define multiple
alternative data sets,
page 135

Vary your data to
get the desired result,
page 138

*Chapter 8 at a Glance*

# 8 Analyzing Alternative Data Sets

**In this chapter you will learn to:**

✔ Define and edit an alternative data set.

✔ Define multiple alternative data sets.

✔ Vary your data to get a desired result.

✔ Use the Solver to find solutions to multivariate problems.

✔ Describe your data using the Analysis ToolPak.

When you store data in a Microsoft Excel workbook, you can use that data, either by itself or as part of a calculation, to discover important information about your business. When you track total sales on a time basis, you can find your best and worst sales periods and correlate them with outside events. For businesses like The Garden Company, sales of all products pick up during the early spring as gardeners get ready for the coming year. During the winter holidays, tool sales pick up as customers purchase gifts for friends and family members who garden.

The data in your worksheets is great for asking, "What happened?" but is less useful for asking "what if" questions, such as, "How would our total revenue be affected if we increased furniture sales by 20 percent?" You can always save an alternative version of a workbook and create formulas that calculate the effects of your changes, but you can do the same thing in your workbook by defining one or more alternative data sets and switching between the original data and the new sets you create.

Excel also provides the tools to determine the inputs that would be required for a formula to produce a given result. For example, the owner of The Garden Company could find out to what level tool sales would need to rise for that category to account for 25 percent of total sales.

In this chapter, you'll learn how to define alternative data sets and determine the necessary inputs to make a calculation produce a particular result.

---

**See Also** Do you need a quick refresher on the topics in this chapter? See the quick reference entries on pages xliii–xlvi.

**Important** Before you can use the practice files in this chapter, be sure you install them from the book's companion CD-ROM to their default location. See "Using the Book's CD-ROM" on page xi for more information.

# Defining and Editing Alternative Data Sets

*Microsoft Office Specialist*

When you save data in an Excel worksheet, you create a record that reflects the characteristics of an event or object. That data could represent an hour of sales on a particular day, the price of an item you just began offering for sale, or the percentage of total sales accounted for by a category of products. Once the data is in place, you can create formulas to generate totals, find averages, and sort the rows in a worksheet based on the contents of one or more columns. However, if you want to perform *what-if analysis*, or explore the impact that changes in your data would have on any of the calculations in your workbooks, you will need to change your data.

The problem of working with data that reflects an event or item is that changing any data to affect a calculation runs the risk of destroying the original data if you accidentally save your changes. You can avoid ruining your original data by creating a duplicate workbook and making your changes to it, but you can also create alternative data sets, or *scenarios*, within an existing workbook.

When you create a scenario, you give Excel alternative values for a list of cells in a worksheet. You can add, delete, and edit scenarios using the **Scenario Manager**.

Clicking the **Add** button causes the **Add Scenario** dialog box to appear.

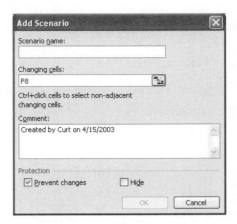

From within this dialog box, you can identify the cells that will hold alternative values, and after you click **OK**, a new dialog box with spaces for you to enter the new values will appear.

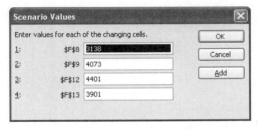

Clicking **OK** returns you to the **Scenario Manager** dialog box. From there, clicking the **Show** button will replace the values in the original worksheet with the alternative values you just defined. Any formulas using cells with changed values will recalculate their results. You can then remove the scenario by clicking the **Undo** button on the Standard toolbar.

**Warning**   If you save and close a workbook while a scenario is in effect, those values will become the default values for the cells changed by the scenario! You should strongly consider creating a scenario that contains the original values of the cells you change.

In this exercise, you create a scenario to measure the projected impact of a furniture sale on total revenue for The Garden Company.

OPEN: Defining from the *SBS\Excel\AnalyzingAlternativeDataSets* folder.

**1**   If necessary, click cell A1.

**2**   On the **Tools** menu, click **Scenarios**.

The **Scenario Manager** dialog box appears.

**3** Click **Add**.

The **Add Scenario** dialog box appears.

**4** In the **Scenario name** box, type Furniture Sale.

Collapse
Dialog

**5** At the right edge of the **Changing cells** box, click the **Collapse Dialog** button.

The **Add Scenario** dialog box collapses, and its title bar changes to *Add Scenario - Changing Cells*.

**6** Delete the contents of the **Add Scenario** dialog box, and then hold down [Ctrl] while you click cells F8, F9, F12, and F13.

*$F$8,$F$9,$F$12,$F$13* appears in the **Changing cells** box.

Expand Dialog

**7** At the right edge of the **Changing cells** box, click the **Expand Dialog** button.

The **Edit Scenario** dialog box appears.

**8** Click **OK**.

The **Edit Scenario** dialog box disappears, and the **Scenario Values** dialog box appears.

**9** In the **1: $F$8** box, type 5000.

**10** In the **2: $F$9** box, type 5750.

**11** In the **3: $F$12** box, type 6000.

**12** In the **4: $F$13** box, type 5000.

**13** Click **OK**.

The **Scenario Manager** dialog box reappears.

**14** Click **Show**.

The contents of your worksheet change to reflect the values in your scenario.

**15** Click **Close**.

The **Scenario Manager** dialog box closes.

**16** On the Standard toolbar, click the **Undo** button to revert to the original numbers in the worksheet.

**17** On the Standard toolbar, click the **Save** button to save your changes.

CLOSE: Defining.

# Defining Multiple Alternative Data Sets

*Microsoft Office Specialist*

One great feature of Excel scenarios is that you're not limited to creating one alternative data set—you can create as many as you like and switch among them at will with the **Scenario Manager**. To change from one scenario to another in the **Scenario Manager**, click the name of the scenario to which you want to change and then click the **Show** button. The values you defined as part of that scenario will appear in your worksheet, and Excel will update any calculations involving the changed cells.

**Tip**   If you apply a scenario to a worksheet and then apply another scenario to the same worksheet, both sets of changes will appear. If the second scenario changes a cell changed by the first scenario, the cell will reflect the value in the second scenario.

Changing from one scenario to another gives you an overview of how the scenarios affect your calculations, but Excel also gives you a way to view the results of all of your scenarios in a single worksheet. To create a worksheet in your current workbook that summarizes the changes caused by your scenarios, open the **Scenario Manager** and then click the **Summary** button. When you do, the **Scenario Summary** dialog box appears.

Collapse Dialog

From within the **Scenario Summary** dialog box, you can choose the type of summary worksheet you want to create and the cells you want to appear in the summary worksheet. To choose the cells to appear in the summary, click the **Collapse Dialog** button in the **Result cells** box, select the cells you want to appear, and then expand the dialog box. After you verify that the range in the **Result cells** box represents the cells you want included on the summary sheet, click **OK** to create the new worksheet.

It's a good idea to create an "undo" scenario named *Normal* with the original values of every cell changed in other scenarios. For example, if you create a scenario named *No rain* that changes the sales figures in three cells, your *Normal* scenario will restore those cells to their original values. That way, even if you accidentally modify your worksheet, you can apply the *Normal* scenario and won't have to reconstruct the worksheet from scratch.

**Tip**   Each scenario can change a maximum of 32 cells, so you might need to create more than one scenario to restore a worksheet.

In this exercise, you create scenarios to represent projected revenue increases from two sales, view the two scenarios, and then summarize the scenario results in a new worksheet.

OPEN: Multiple from the *SBS\Excel\AnalyzingAlternativeDataSets* folder.

**1**   If necessary, click cell A1.

**2**   On the **Tools** menu, click **Scenarios**.

The **Scenario Manager** dialog box appears.

**3**   Click **Add**.

The **Add Scenario** dialog box appears, with A1 in the **Changing cells** box.

**4**   In the **Scenario name** box, type Furniture Sale.

**5**   In the **Changing cells** box, click the **Collapse Dialog** button.

The **Add Scenario** dialog box collapses, and its title bar changes to *Add Scenario - Changing Cells*.

**6**   Delete the contents of the **Add Scenario** dialog box, and then hold down ⌃ while you click cells F8, F9, F12, and F13.

*$F$8,$F$9,$F$12,$F$13* appears in the **Changing cells** box.

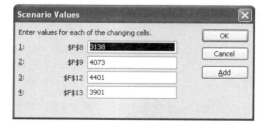

**7**   At the right edge of the **Changing cells** box, click the **Expand Dialog** button.

Expand Dialog

The **Edit Scenario** dialog box appears.

**8**   Click **OK**.

The **Edit Scenario** dialog box disappears, and the **Scenario Values** dialog box appears.

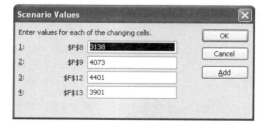

**9**   In the **1: $F$8** box, type 5400.

**10**   In the **2: $F$9** box, type 5850.

**11**   In the **3: $F$12** box, type 6300.

**12**    In the **4: $F$13** box, type 7000.

**13**    Click **OK**.

     The **Scenario Values** dialog box disappears, and the **Scenario Manager** dialog box appears.

**14**    Click **Add**.

     The **Add Scenario** dialog box appears.

**15**    In the **Scenario name** box, type Tool Sale.

**16**    In the **Changing cells** box, click the **Collapse Dialog** button.

     The **Add Scenario** dialog box collapses, and its title bar changes to *Add Scenario - Changing Cells*.

**17**    Delete the contents of the **Add Scenario** dialog box, click cell D7, and drag to cell D11.

     *$D$7:$D$11* appears in the **Changing cells** box.

**18**    At the right edge of the **Changing cells** box, click the **Expand Dialog** button.

     The **Edit Scenario** dialog box appears.

**19**    Click **OK**.

     The **Edit Scenario** dialog box disappears, and the **Scenario Values** dialog box appears.

**20**    In the **1: $D$7** box, type 8500.

**21**    In the **2: $D$8** box, type 9000.

**22**    In the **3: $D$9** box, type 12000.

**23**    In the **4: $D$10** box, type 7500.

**24**    In the **5: $D$11** box, type 7500.

**25**    Click **OK**.

     The **Scenario Manager** dialog box appears.

**26**    Click **Summary**.

     The **Scenario Summary** dialog box appears.

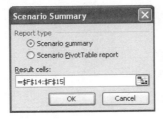

**27** In the **Result cells** box, click the **Collapse Dialog** button.

The **Scenario Summary** dialog box is minimized.

**28** Click cell C14 and drag to cell H15.

*=$C$14:$H$15* appears in the **Result cells** box.

**29** In the **Result cells** box, click the **Expand Dialog** button.

The **Scenario Summary** dialog box is maximized.

**30** Click **OK**.

Excel adds a new worksheet named *Scenario Summary* to your workbook and displays that worksheet.

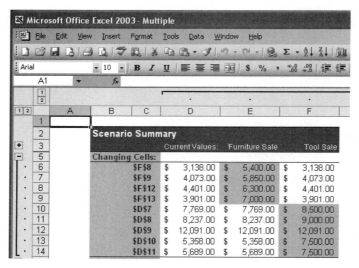

**31** On the Standard toolbar, click the **Save** button to save your work.

CLOSE: Multiple.

# Varying Your Data to Get a Desired Result

An important aspect of running a business is knowing how every department and product is performing, both in absolute terms and in relation to other departments or products in the company. Just as you might want to reward your employees for maintaining a perfect safety record and keeping down your insurance rates, you would also want to stop carrying products you are unable to sell.

When you plan how you want to grow your business, you should have specific goals in mind for each department or product category. For example, Catherine Turner, the owner of The Garden Company, might have the goal of increasing the total revenue generated from flower sales by 10 percent a year. Finding the sales amount that represents the 10 percent increase is simple, but expressing goals in other ways can make finding the solution more challenging. Rather than grow flower sales by 10 percent a year, Catherine might want to increase the sales so that flower sales represent 40 percent of the total sales for The Garden Company.

As an example, consider the following worksheet, which holds sales figures for the four categories of products offered by The Garden Company and uses those figures to calculate both total sales and the share each category has of that total.

| | | Tools | Supplies | Furniture | Flowers | Total |
|---|---|---|---|---|---|---|
| Sales | | $170,150.00 | $253,402.00 | $105,254.00 | $233,551.00 | $ 762,357.00 |
| Share | | 22.32% | 33.24% | 13.81% | 30.64% | 100.00% |

**Important** In this worksheet, the values in the Share row are displayed as percentages, but the underlying values are decimals. For example, *0.3064* is represented as *30.64%*.

While it would certainly be possible to figure the sales target that would make flower sales represent 40 percent of the total, there is an easier way to do it in Excel: *Goal Seek*. To use Goal Seek, you choose **Goal Seek** from the **Tools** menu to open the **Goal Seek** dialog box.

In the **Set cell** box, you identify the cell with the target value; in this case, that would be cell F4, which has the percentage of sales accounted for by the Flowers category. The **To value** box has the target value (*.4*, which is equivalent to *40%*), and the **By changing cell** box identifies the cell with the value Excel should change to generate the target value of *40%* in cell F4. In this example, the cell to be changed is F3.

Clicking **OK** tells Excel to find a solution for the goal you set. When Excel finishes its work, the new values appear in the designated cells and the **Goal Seek Status** dialog box appears.

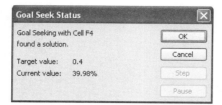

**Tip** Goal Seek finds the closest solution it can without exceeding the target value. In this case, the closest percentage it could find was *39.98%*.

In this exercise, you use Goal Seek to determine how much total revenue from tool sales would be required to make the Tools category account for 25 percent of total sales for The Garden Company.

OPEN: GoalSeek from the *SBS\Excel\AnalyzingAlternativeDataSets* folder.

**1** Click cell C4.

**2** On the **Tools** menu, click **Goal Seek**.

The **Goal Seek** dialog box appears with *C4* in the **Set cell** box.

**3** In the **To value** box, type **.25**.

**Tip** You type *.25*, not *25*, because cells C4:G4 are formatted to show percentages. With the Percentage format, *.25* is displayed as *25%*.

**4** In the **By changing cell** box, type **C3**.

**5** Click **OK**.

The **Goal Seek Status** dialog box appears, announcing that Excel has found a solution. The new values appear in your worksheet.

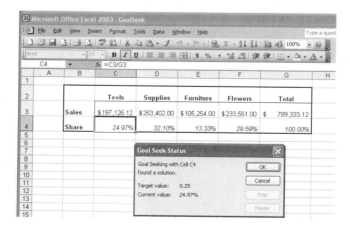

**6**  Click **OK**.

The **Goal Seek Status** dialog box disappears.

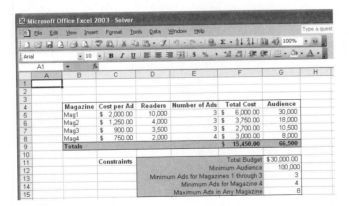
Undo

**7**  On the Standard toolbar, click the **Undo** button.

The contents of the cells in your workbook revert to their original values.

**8**  On the Standard toolbar, click the **Save** button to save your changes.

CLOSE: GoalSeek.

# Finding Optimal Solutions with Solver

**Microsoft Office Specialist**

GoalSeek is a great tool for finding out how much you need to change a single input to generate a desired result from a formula, but it's of no help if you want to find the best mix of several inputs. For example, Catherine Turner might want to advertise in four regional magazines to drive customers to The Garden Company's Web site, but she might not know the best mix of ads to place among the publications. She asked the publishers for ad pricing and readership numbers, which are reflected in the spreadsheet shown below, along with the minimum number of ads per publication (three) and the minimum number of times she would like the ad to be seen (100,000). Because Catherine is a contributing editor to the fourth magazine, she does want to take out at least four ads in that publication despite its relatively low readership. The goal of the ad campaign is for your ads to be seen as many times as possible without spending more than your $30,000 budget.

| | Magazine | Cost per Ad | Readers | Number of Ads | Total Cost | Audience |
|---|---|---|---|---|---|---|
| 5 | Mag1 | $ 2,000.00 | 10,000 | 3 | $ 6,000.00 | 30,000 |
| 6 | Mag2 | $ 1,250.00 | 4,000 | 3 | $ 3,750.00 | 18,000 |
| 7 | Mag3 | $ 900.00 | 3,500 | 3 | $ 2,700.00 | 10,500 |
| 8 | Mag4 | $ 750.00 | 2,000 | 4 | $ 3,000.00 | 8,000 |
| 9 | **Totals** | | | | $ 15,450.00 | 66,500 |

| | Constraints | |
|---|---|---|
| 11 | Total Budget | $30,000.00 |
| 12 | Minimum Audience | 100,000 |
| 13 | Minimum Ads for Magazines 1 through 3 | 3 |
| 14 | Minimum Ads for Magazine 4 | 4 |
| 15 | Maximum Ads in Any Magazine | 8 |

**Tip**  It helps to spell out every aspect of your problem so that you'll be able to identify the cells you want Solver to use in its calculations.

If you performed a complete installation when you installed Excel on your system, you will see the **Solver** item on the **Tools** menu. If not, you will need to install the

Solver *Add-In*. To do so, on the **Tools** menu, click **Add-Ins** to display the **Add-Ins** dialog box. Select the **Solver Add-in** check box, and click **OK** to install Solver.

**Note**    You might be prompted for your Microsoft Office 2003 installation CD-ROM. If you are, put the CD-ROM in your CD-ROM drive and click OK.

After the installation is complete, open the **Tools** menu and click **Solver** to display the **Solver Parameters** dialog box.

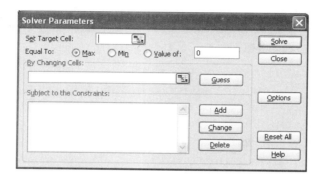

The first step in setting up your Solver problem is to identify the cell that reflects the results of changing the other cells in the worksheet. To identify that cell, click in the **Set Target Cell** box, click the target cell, and then select the option button representing whether you want to minimize the cell's value, maximize the cell's value, or make the cell take on a specific value. Next you click in the **By Changing Cells** box and select the cells Solver should vary to change the value in the target cell. Finally, you set the limits for the values Solver can use by clicking **Add** to display the **Add Constraint** dialog box.

You add constraints to the Solver problem by selecting the cells to which you want to apply the constraint, selecting the comparison operation (less than or equal to, greater than or equal to, requiring the value to be an integer, and so on) by clicking the down arrow in the middle box, clicking in the **Constraint** box, and selecting the cell with the value of the constraint. You could also type a value in the **Constraint** box, but referring to a cell makes it possible for you to change the constraint without opening Solver.

**Tip**    After you run Solver, you can use the controls in the **Solver Results** dialog box, save the results as changes to your worksheet, or create a scenario based on the changed data.

In this exercise, you use Solver to determine the best mix of ads given the following constraints:

■    You want to maximize the number of people who see the ads.

■    You must buy at least three ads in three magazines, and at least four in the fourth.

■    You can buy no more than eight ads in any one magazine.

■    You must reach at least 100,000 people.

■    Your ad budget is $30,000.

OPEN: Solver from the *SBS\Excel\AnalyzingAlternativeDataSets* folder.

**1**    On the **Tools** menu, if the **Solver** item doesn't appear, click **Add-Ins**.

The **Add-Ins** dialog box appears.

**2**    Select the **Solver Add-in** check box, and click **OK**.

**Note**    Insert your Office 2003 CD-ROM in your computer's CD-ROM drive if prompted to do so.

**3**    On the **Tools** menu, click **Solver**.

The **Solver** dialog box appears.

**4**    Click in the **Set Target Cell** box, and then click cell G9.

*$G$9* appears in the **Set Target Cell** box.

**5**    Select the **Max** option button.

**6**    Click in the **By Changing Cells** box, and select cells E5:E8.

*$E$5:$E$8* appears in the **By Changing Cells** box.

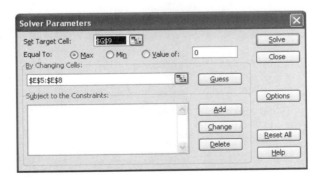

**7**    Click **Add**.

The **Add Constraint** dialog box appears.

**8**    Click cell F9.

*$F$9* appears in the **Cell Reference** box.

**9**    Click in the **Constraint** box, and then click cell G11.

*$G$11* appears in the **Constraint** box.

**10**    Click **Add**.

The constraint is added to the Solver problem, and the **Add Constraint** dialog box clears for the next constraint.

**11**    Click cell G9.

*$G$9* appears in the **Cell Reference** box.

**12**    Click the down arrow in the middle box, and select **>=**.

**13**    Click in the **Constraint** box, and then click cell G12.

*$G$12* appears in the **Constraint** box.

**14**    Click **Add**.

The constraint is added to the Solver problem, and the **Add Constraint** dialog box clears for the next constraint.

**15**    Select cells E5:E7.

*$E$5:$E$7* appears in the **Cell Reference** box.

**16**    Click the down arrow in the middle box, and select **>=**.

**17**    Click in the **Constraint** box, and then click cell G13.

*$G$13* appears in the **Constraint** box.

**18**    Click **Add**.

The constraint is added to the Solver problem, and the **Add Constraint** dialog box clears for the next constraint.

**19**    Click cell E8.

*$E$8* appears in the **Cell Reference** box.

**20**    Click the down arrow in the middle box, and select **>=**.

**21**    Click in the **Constraint** box, and then click cell G14.

*$G$14* appears in the **Constraint** box.

**22**    Click **Add**.

The constraint is added to the Solver problem, and the **Add Constraint** dialog box clears for the next constraint.

**23** Select cells E5:E8.

*$E$5:$E$8* appears in the **Cell Reference** box.

**24** Click in the **Constraint** box, and then click cell G15.

*$G$15* appears in the **Constraint** box.

**25** Click **Add**.

The constraint is added to the Solver problem, and the **Add Constraint** dialog box clears for the next constraint.

**26** Select cells E5:E8.

*$E$5:$E$8* appears in the **Cell Reference** box.

**27** Click the down arrow in the middle box, and select **int**.

**28** Click **OK**.

The constraint is added to the Solver problem, and the **Add Constraint** dialog box disappears.

**29** Click **Solve**.

The **Solver Results** dialog box appears, indicating Solver found a solution. The result is displayed in the body of the worksheet.

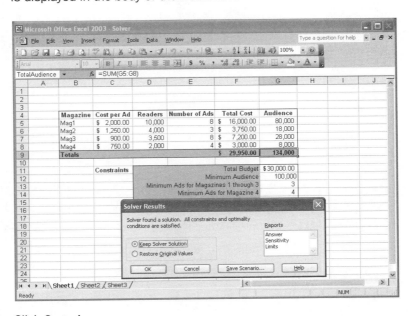

**30** Click **Cancel**.

The **Solver Results** dialog box disappears.

31    Click **Close**. If you are asked if you want to save your changes, click **No**.

The **Solver** dialog box disappears.

CLOSE: Solver.

# Analyzing Data with Descriptive Statistics

*Microsoft Office Specialist*

Experienced business people can tell a lot about numbers just by looking at them to see if they "look right"—that is, the sales figures are about where they're supposed to be for a particular hour, day, or month; the average seems about right; and sales have increased from year to year. When you need more than an off-the-cuff assessment, though, you can use the tools in the Analysis ToolPak, another Excel Add-In.

If you performed a complete installation when you installed Excel on your system, you will see the **Data Analysis** item on the **Tools** menu. If not, you will need to install the Analysis ToolPak. To do so, on the **Tools** menu, click **Add-Ins** to display the **Add-Ins** dialog box. Select the **Analysis ToolPak** check box, and click **OK** to install the **Analysis ToolPak**.

**Note**    You might be prompted for your Office 2003 installation CD-ROM. If you are, put the CD-ROM in your CD-ROM drive and click OK.

After the installation is complete, open the **Tools** menu and click **Data Analysis** to display the **Data Analysis** dialog box.

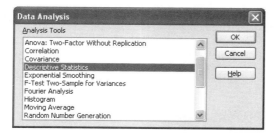

You then click the item representing the type of data analysis you want to perform, click **OK**, and use the controls in the resulting dialog box to analyze your data.

In this exercise, you will use the Analysis ToolPak to generate descriptive statistics of sales data.

OPEN: Descriptive from the *SBS\Excel\AnalyzingAlternativeDataSets* folder.

1    On the **Tools** menu, if the **Data Analysis** item doesn't appear, click **Add-Ins**.

The **Add-Ins** dialog box appears.

2    Select the **Analysis ToolPak** check box, and click **OK**.

**Note** Insert your Office 2003 CD-ROM in your computer's CD-ROM drive if prompted to do so.

**3** On the **Tools** menu, click **Data Analysis**.

The **Data Analysis** dialog box appears.

**4** Click **Descriptive Statistics**, and click **OK**.

The **Descriptive Statistics** dialog box appears.

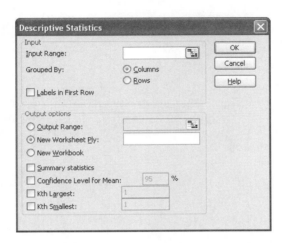

Collapse
Dialog

**5** Click the **Collapse Dialog** button at the right edge of the **Input Range** box.

The **Descriptive Statistics** dialog box collapses.

**6** Select cells D38 to O38.

*$D$38:$O$38* appears in the **Input Range** box.

Expand Dialog

**7** Click the **Expand Dialog** button at the right edge of the **Input Range** box.

The **Descriptive Statistics** dialog box expands.

**8** Select the **Rows** option button.

**9** Select the **New Worksheets Ply** option button.

**10** Select the **Summary Statistics** check box.

**11** Click **OK**.

The **Descriptive Statistics** dialog box disappears, and a new worksheet with statistics describing your data appears in your workbook.

**12** On the Standard toolbar, click the **Save** button to save your changes.

CLOSE: Descriptive.

# Key Points

- Scenarios let you describe many potential business cases within a single workbook.

- It's usually a good idea to create a "normal" scenario that lets you reset your worksheet.

- Remember that you can change up to 32 cells in a scenario, but no more.

- You can summarize your scenarios on a new worksheet to compare how each scenario approaches the data.

- Use Goal Seek to determine what value you need in a single cell to generate the desired result from a formula.

- If you want to vary the values in more than one cell to find the optimal mix of inputs for a calculation, use the Solver Add-In.

- Advanced statistical tools are available in the Analysis ToolPak—use them to go over your data thoroughly.

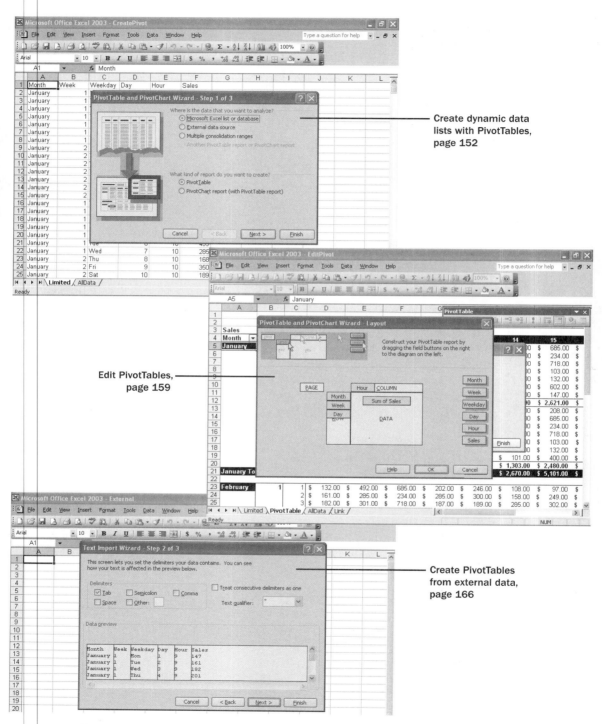

Create dynamic data lists with PivotTables, page 152

Edit PivotTables, page 159

Create PivotTables from external data, page 166

# Chapter 9 at a Glance

# 9 Creating Dynamic Lists with PivotTables

**In this chapter you will learn to:**

✔ Create dynamic data lists with PivotTables.

✔ Edit PivotTables.

✔ Create PivotTables from external data.

An important consideration when you create your Microsoft Excel worksheets is how you want the data to appear when you show it to your colleagues. You can change the formatting of your data to emphasize the contents of specific cells, sort and filter your worksheets based on the contents of specific columns, or hide rows containing data that isn't relevant to the point you're trying to make.

One limitation of the standard Excel worksheet is that you can't change how the data is organized on the page. For example, in a worksheet in which each column represents an hour in the day, each row represents a day in a month, and the body of the worksheet contains the total sales for every hourly period of the month, you can't easily change the worksheet so that it displays only sales on Tuesdays during the afternoon.

An Excel tool lets you create worksheets that can be sorted, filtered, and rearranged dynamically to emphasize different aspects of your data. That tool is the *PivotTable*.

In this chapter, you'll learn how to create and edit PivotTables from an existing worksheet, and how to create a PivotTable with data imported from a text file.

**See Also** Do you need a quick refresher on the topics in this chapter? See the quick reference entries on pages xlvi–xlviii.

 **Important** Before you can use the practice files in this chapter, be sure you install them from the book's companion CD-ROM to their default location. See "Using the Book's CD-ROM" on page xi for more information.

# Creating Dynamic Lists with PivotTables

Excel worksheets let you gather and present important data, but the standard worksheet can't be changed from its original configuration easily. As an example, consider the worksheet in the following graphic.

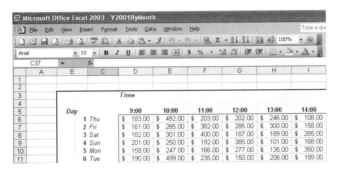

This worksheet records hourly sales for The Garden Company. The data in the worksheet is organized so that each row represents a day of sales, while the columns in the body of the worksheet represent an hour of each day. When presented in this arrangement, the monthly sales totals for an hourly period (calculated at the bottom of the worksheet) and the daily sales totals (calculated at the right edge of the worksheet) are given equal billing: neither set of totals stands out.

Such a neutral presentation of your data is versatile, but it has limitations. First, while you can use sorting and filtering to restrict the rows or columns shown, it's difficult to change the worksheet's organization. For example, in a standard worksheet you can't reorganize the contents of your worksheet so that the hours are assigned to the rows and the days to the columns.

You can use an Excel tool to reorganize and redisplay your data dynamically. You can create a PivotTable, or dynamic worksheet, that lets you reorganize and filter your data on the fly. For instance, you can create a PivotTable with the same layout as the worksheet shown above and then change the PivotTable layout to have the rows represent the month, week, and day and the columns represent hours in a day, as shown in the following graphic.

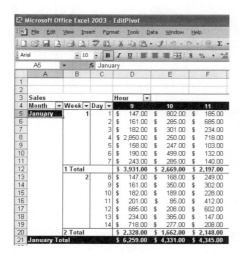

To create a PivotTable, you must have your data collected in a list in which every row represents a cell in the body of the finished PivotTable. The following graphic shows the first few lines of the list used to create the PivotTable just shown.

|   | A | B | C | D | E | F |
|---|---|---|---|---|---|---|
| 1 | Month | Week | Weekday | Day | Hour | Sales |
| 2 | January | 1 | Mon | 1 | 9 | 147 |
| 3 | January | 1 | Tue | 2 | 9 | 161 |
| 4 | January | 1 | Wed | 3 | 9 | 182 |
| 5 | January | 1 | Thu | 4 | 9 | 201 |
| 6 | January | 1 | Fri | 5 | 9 | 158 |
| 7 | January | 1 | Sat | 6 | 9 | 190 |
| 8 | January | 1 | Sun | 7 | 9 | 243 |
| 9 | January | 2 | Mon | 8 | 9 | 147 |

Notice that every line of the list holds the Month, Week, Weekday, Day, Hour, and Sales for every hour in the month. Excel needs that data when it creates the PivotTable so that it can maintain relationships among the data. If you want to filter your Pivot-Table so that it shows all sales from 5:00 p.m. to 8:00 p.m. on Thursdays in January, Excel must be able to identify January 11 as a Thursday and find the entries in the list representing sales for the hours beginning at 5:00 p.m., 6:00 p.m., and 7:00 p.m.

Once you have created a list, you can click any cell in that list, open the **Data** menu, and click **PivotTable and PivotChart Report** to launch the **PivotTable and PivotChart Wizard**.

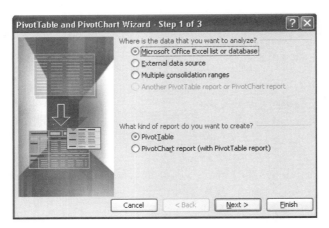

On this wizard page, you identify the data source for your PivotTable and whether you want to create a PivotTable by itself or a PivotTable and a PivotChart. Clicking **Next** accepts the default choices and moves you to the second wizard screen.

Collapse
Dialog

On this screen, you verify that the wizard has correctly identified the cells with the data for your PivotTable. If not, you can click the **Collapse Dialog** button in the **Range** box, select the cells that contain your data, and then expand the dialog box to continue. Once the proper cell range is listed in the **Range** box, click **Next** to move to the final wizard screen.

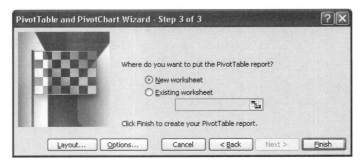

This wizard screen asks whether you want to create your PivotTable in a new or an existing worksheet. Because the data lists used to create PivotTables are usually quite long, it is often best to create the PivotTable in a new worksheet. Clicking **Finish**

closes the wizard; creates a new worksheet in your workbook; and adds a PivotTable, the **PivotTable** toolbar, and the **Pivot Table Field List** dialog box to that worksheet.

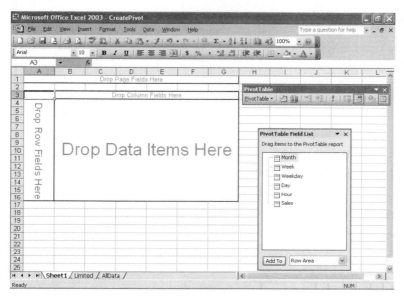

To assign a *field*, or column in a data list, to an area of the PivotTable, you drag the field head to the desired area on the PivotTable outline. For example, you can drag the **Week** field head to the **Drop Row Fields Here** box, drag the **Day** field head to the **Drop Row Fields Here** box, drag the **Hour** field head to the **Drop Column Fields Here** box, and then drag the **Sales** field head to the **Drop Data Items Here** box to populate the body of the PivotTable with data. After you drop a field head in the **Drop Data Items Here** box, the PivotTable fills with data.

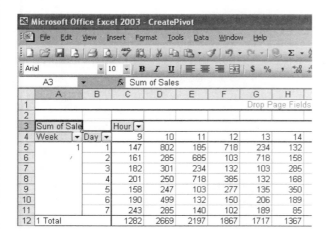

**Tip** You can also move a field head to an area of the PivotTable by clicking the field head, clicking the **Add To** down arrow in the **Pivot Table Field List** dialog box, clicking the area to which you want to move the field, and then clicking the **Add To** button in the **Pivot Table Field List** dialog box.

Note that the order in which you enter the fields in the row and column areas affects how the data in the PivotTable is grouped. In the preceding example, the rows show all of the days in the first week before showing all of the days in the second week, while the columns show all of the hours in a business day at The Garden Company. You can change how the data in the PivotTable is grouped by moving the **Hour** field head to the left of the **Week** field head in the **Drop Row Fields Here** box. Doing so would cause Excel to group the data in the PivotTable as shown in the following graphic.

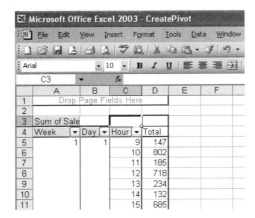

**Tip** The **Drop Page Fields Here** box is used to filter the contents of the worksheet based on the values in a column from the original data list. You'll work with the Page area in the next section of this chapter.

Once you have created a PivotTable, you can change the formatting of its cells as in any other Excel worksheet. Because the data in the sample PivotTable is sales data, you can apply the Currency style to those cells by selecting them and then clicking the **Currency Style** button on the Formatting toolbar. You can also distinguish cells with headings, subtotals, and totals by formatting the contents of those cells in bold type, italics, or a larger type size.

Although you can apply your own formats to a PivotTable, Excel comes with a set of *AutoFormats*, or predefined formats that you can apply to your PivotTable. To view the AutoFormats available in Excel and apply one to your PivotTable, click any cell in the PivotTable, and then, on the **PivotTable** toolbar, click the **Format Report** button to display the **AutoFormat** dialog box.

$ 

Currency Style

To assign an AutoFormat to a PivotTable, pick the AutoFormat you like the best from the list in the **AutoFormat** dialog box, and then click **OK**.

**Tip** To return a PivotTable to its default formatting, choose the **PivotTable Classic** Auto-Format, which can be found at the bottom of the list in the **AutoFormat** dialog box.

In this exercise, you create a PivotTable in a new worksheet, arrange its data, format the cells in the body of the PivotTable, and then apply an AutoFormat to the PivotTable.

OPEN: CreatePivot from the *SBS\Excel\PivotTable* folder.

**1** Click cell A1, and then, on the **Data** menu, click **PivotTable and PivotChart Report**.

The **PivotTable and PivotChart Wizard** appears with the **Microsoft Excel list or database** option button selected in the top pane, identifying your worksheet as the data source, and the **PivotTable** option button selected in the bottom pane, indicating that you want to create a PivotTable only.

**2** Click **Next** to move to the next page of the wizard.

The next page of the wizard appears, with the range *$A$1:$F$169* in the **Range** box.

**3** Click **Next** to move to the next page of the wizard.

The final page of the wizard appears, with the **New worksheet** option button selected, which tells the wizard to create a new worksheet to hold the PivotTable.

**4** Click **Finish**.

The wizard closes, and the **PivotTable** toolbar, the **PivotTable Field List** dialog box, and your new PivotTable appear in a new worksheet.

**5** From the **PivotTable Field List** dialog box, drag **Month** to the **Drop Row Fields Here** box.

*Month* appears in the **Drop Row Fields Here** box.

**6** From the **PivotTable Field List** dialog box, drag **Week** to the right edge of the **Drop Row Fields Here** box.

**Tip** A large gray insertion point will appear to the right of the **Month** field head when the mouse pointer is in the correct position.

*Week* appears to the right of *Month* in the **Drop Row Fields Here** box.

**7** From the **PivotTable Field List** dialog box, drag **Day** to the **Drop Row Fields Here** box and drop it to the right of the **Week** field head.

The PivotTable is updated to reflect the added field.

**8** From the **PivotTable Field List** dialog box, drag **Hour** to the **Drop Column Fields Here** box.

The PivotTable is updated to reflect the added field.

**9** From the **PivotTable Field List** dialog box, drag **Sales** to the **Drop Data Items Here** box.

The PivotTable is updated to reflect the added field.

| | A | B | C | D | E | F | G | H |
|---|---|---|---|---|---|---|---|---|
| 1 | | | | | | | | Drop Page |
| 2 | | | | | | | | |
| 3 | Sum of Sale | | | Hour | | | | |
| 4 | Month | Week | Day | 9 | 10 | 11 | 12 | 13 |
| 5 | January | 1 | 1 | 147 | 802 | 185 | 718 | 234 |
| 6 | | | 2 | 161 | 285 | 685 | 103 | 718 |
| 7 | | | 3 | 182 | 301 | 234 | 132 | 103 |
| 8 | | | 4 | 201 | 250 | 718 | 385 | 132 |
| 9 | | | 5 | 158 | 247 | 103 | 277 | 135 |
| 10 | | | 6 | 190 | 499 | 132 | 150 | 206 |
| 11 | | | 7 | 243 | 285 | 140 | 102 | 189 |
| 12 | | 1 Total | | 1282 | 2669 | 2197 | 1867 | 1717 |

Hide Field List

**10** On the **PivotTable** toolbar, click the **Hide Field List** button to hide the **PivotTable Field List** dialog box.

Format Report

**11** On the **PivotTable** toolbar, click the **Format Report** button.

The **AutoFormat** dialog box appears.

**12** Scroll down and click the **Table 1** format, and then click **OK**.

Excel applies the AutoFormat to your PivotTable.

**13** Select cells in the range D5:P22, and then, on the Formatting toolbar, click the **Currency Style** button.

Excel applies the Currency style to the selected cells.

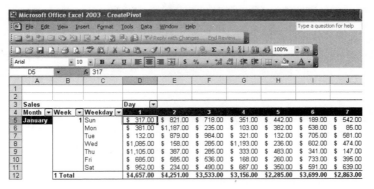

**14** On the Standard toolbar, click the **Save** button to save your work.

CLOSE: CreatePivot.

# Editing PivotTables

After you have created a PivotTable, you can edit it to control how your data is displayed. As an example, consider the following PivotTable.

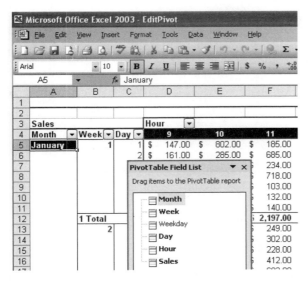

In this example, two fields require editing: **Month** and **Weekday**. Because all of the data in the list used to create the PivotTable is from the month of January, no information is imparted by including the **Month** field. The unused **Weekday** field, however, can be used to limit the data shown in the body of the PivotTable to sales occurring on one weekday, such as Wednesday.

**Tip**    Fields used in the PivotTable appear bold in the **Pivot Table Field List** dialog box, while fields not used in the PivotTable appear in normal type.

Show Field List

To open a PivotTable for editing, you click any cell in the PivotTable and then, if necessary, display the fields available for the PivotTable by clicking the **Show Field List** button on the **PivotTable** toolbar.

While the **PivotTable Field List** dialog box is open, you can drag any field name from the dialog box to the active PivotTable. Dragging a field name to the **Drop Page Fields Here** box doesn't change how the data in your PivotTable is arranged, but it does let you filter your PivotTable based on the contents of the field. As an example, consider the following graphic, in which the **Weekday** field has been added to the **Drop Page Fields Here** box and its down arrow clicked.

Clicking a field head's down arrow displays a list of values in the field (in this case, the days of the week). Clicking any of these values and then clicking **OK** limits the data shown in the PivotTable to data gathered on the selected weekday.

To remove a filter from a PivotTable, click the down arrow of the field head used to filter the PivotTable, click **(All)**, and then click **OK**.

You can filter a PivotTable based on the contents of fields in either the **Drop Row Fields Here** or the **Drop Column Fields Here** box as well. To do so, click the down arrow of the field head holding the values with which you want to filter the Pivot-Table, and then clear the check box next to any value you don't want displayed. To limit the hours shown to the range of 9:00 a.m. to 11:00 a.m., for example, you would click the **Hour** down arrow and then clear the check boxes next to every entry in the list except *9*, *10*, and *11*.

Another way to modify the contents of your PivotTable is to *pivot* the table by changing the arrangement of field heads while the PivotTable is open. To pivot a Pivot-Table, you drag a field head to a new position in the PivotTable. For example, in the following graphic, the PivotTable rows are grouped by week and then by day, while the columns are grouped by hour.

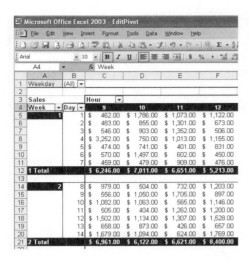

To pivot the PivotTable, drag the **Hour** field head to the right of the **Day** field head in the **Drop Row Fields Here** box. When you release the mouse button, Excel updates the PivotTable to reflect the new organization. You can also drag field heads from the **Drop Row Fields Here** box to the **Drop Column Fields Here** box, and vice versa, to reorganize your data.

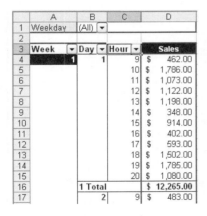

**Tip**    When you drag a field name over an area where the field can be dropped, a large gray insertion point will appear in the PivotTable, indicating where the field name you are dragging will be dropped when you release the mouse button.

If you have trouble dropping field names at the right place in your PivotTable, you can use the **Layout** screen of the **PivotTable and PivotChart Wizard** to help you. To open the **Layout** screen, click any cell in the PivotTable and then, on the **PivotTable** toolbar, click **PivotTable** and then click **PivotTable Wizard** to display the final page of the **PivotTable and PivotChart Wizard**.

In this screen, click the **Layout** button to display a slightly friendlier version of the PivotTable template.

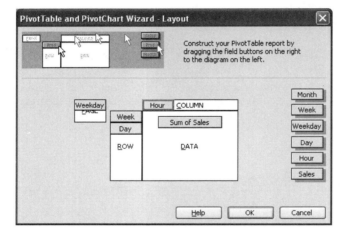

Refresh
External Data

One nice aspect of PivotTables is that you can update them to reflect any changes in the data list used to create them. For example, the general manager of The Garden Company might have received a large phone order from a client and, rather than routing it through a cash register at the retail store, instead added the total to the company's books directly. Updating the PivotTable's data list to reflect the sale will change the values in the PivotTable, but you don't need to re-create the PivotTable to account for the change. Instead, you can click any cell in the PivotTable and then, on the **PivotTable** toolbar, click the **Refresh External Data** button to have Excel reexamine the data list and update the PivotTable.

Another way to manipulate the contents of a PivotTable is to show or hide its detail rows. For example, the PivotTable in the following graphic displays its rows organized by month, then by week, and then by day.

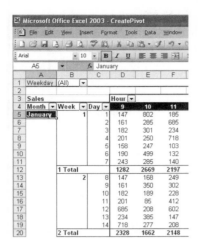

Double-clicking cell A5, which holds the *January* value for the **Month** field, hides the detail of all sales in January, leaving only the Total row for the month.

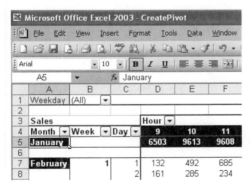

To show the detail rows for the month of January, double-click cell A5 again.

In versions prior to Excel 2002, you couldn't create a link to a cell in a PivotTable. Now you are able to create a link from a cell in another workbook to a cell in your PivotTable. To create a link, you click the cell you want to link to your PivotTable, type an equal sign, and then click the cell in the PivotTable with the data you want linked. When you click the PivotTable cell, a *GETPIVOTDATA* formula appears in the formula bar of the worksheet with the PivotTable. When you press ⌨Enter⌨, the contents of the PivotTable cell will appear in the linked cell.

In this exercise, you add a field to a PivotTable, filter the contents of a PivotTable, change a PivotTable's layout, refresh PivotTable data, show and hide PivotTable detail, and create a link to a PivotTable field.

OPEN: EditPivot from the *SBS\Excel\PivotTable* folder.

**1** If necessary, click the **PivotTable** sheet tab on the tab bar to display the PivotTable worksheet.

**2** If necessary, right-click the Standard toolbar, and then, from the shortcut menu that appears, click **PivotTable** to show the **PivotTable** toolbar.

**3** Click any cell in the PivotTable, and then, on the **PivotTable** toolbar, click the **Show Field List** button.

The **PivotTable Field List** dialog box appears.

**4** From the **PivotTable Field List** dialog box, drag the **Weekday** field to the **Drop Page Fields Here** box.

The **Weekday** field head appears in the **Drop Page Fields Here** box.

**5** On the **PivotTable** toolbar, click the **Hide Field List** button.

The **PivotTable Field List** dialog box disappears.

Hide Field List

**6** Drag the **PivotTable** toolbar to the top of the workbook window.

The **PivotTable** toolbar docks below the Standard toolbar.

**7** Click the **Weekday** down arrow, click **Mon**, and then click **OK**.

Excel filters the PivotTable so that only data representing sales on Mondays appears in the PivotTable.

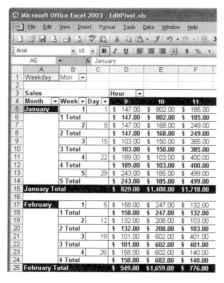

**8** Click the **Weekday** down arrow, click **(All)**, and then click **OK**.

The PivotTable displays data from all weekdays.

**9**  Click the **Week** down arrow, and clear the check boxes next to *3*, *4*, and *5*. Click **OK** to apply the filter.

Excel filters the PivotTable so that only data representing sales during the first two weeks of a month appears in the PivotTable.

**10**  Click the **Week** down arrow, and select the **(Show All)** check box. Click **OK** to apply the filter.

The PivotTable displays data from all weeks.

**11**  On the **PivotTable** toolbar, click **PivotTable** and then click **PivotTable Wizard**.

The **PivotTable and PivotChart Wizard** appears.

**12**  Click **Layout**.

The **Layout** page of the **PivotTable and PivotChart Wizard** appears.

**13**  Drag **Hour** from the **Column** box to the **Page** box.

**14**  Drag **Weekday** from the **Page** box to the **Column** box, and click **OK**.

The **Layout** page disappears.

**15**  Click **Finish**.

Your PivotTable changes to reflect the new layout.

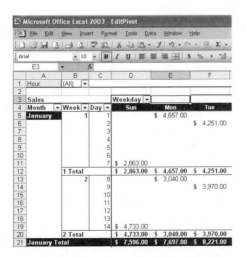

**16**  Drag the **Hour** field head to the **Drop Column Fields Here** box.

Your PivotTable changes in response to the pivot.

**17**  Drag the **Weekday** field head to the **Drop Page Fields Here** box, positioned in row 1.

Your PivotTable changes in response to the pivot.

**18** On the tab bar, click the **AllData** sheet tab to display the AllData worksheet.

**19** Click cell F5, type 2850, and then press ⏎Enter.

**20** On the tab bar, click the **PivotTable** sheet tab to display the PivotTable worksheet.

**21** On the **PivotTable** toolbar, click the **Refresh External Data** button.

Excel updates the data in your PivotTable to reflect the change in the source data list.

**22** Double-click cell A5.

The detail rows of the January section of the PivotTable are hidden, leaving only the January Total data displayed.

**23** Double-click cell A5 again.

The detail rows of the January section of the PivotTable are unhidden.

**24** On the tab bar, click the **Link** sheet tab to move to the Link worksheet.

**25** Click cell C5, type =, and then, on the tab bar, click the **PivotTable** sheet tab.

The PivotTable worksheet appears.

**26** Click cell P115.

*=GETPIVOTDATA("Sales",PivotTable!$A$3)* appears in the formula bar.

**27** Press ⏎Enter.

Excel switches back to the Link worksheet, and *$330,896.00*, the value in the cell linked to, appears in cell C5.

**Tip** Cell C5 had the Currency style applied to it when the worksheet was created. If cell C5 were formatted with the General style, the value would be displayed as 330896.

**28** On the Standard toolbar, click the **Save** button to save your work.

CLOSE: EditPivot.

# Creating PivotTables from External Data

*Microsoft Office Specialist*

While most of the time you will create PivotTables from data stored in Excel worksheets, you can also bring data from outside sources into Excel. For example, you might need to work with data created in another spreadsheet program with a file format that Excel can't read directly. Fortunately, you can transfer worksheets from one program to another by exporting the data from the original program into a text file, which Excel then translates into a worksheet.

Spreadsheet programs store data in cells, so the goal of representing spreadsheet data in a text file is to indicate where the contents of one cell end and those of the next cell begin. The character that marks the end of a cell is a delimiter, in that it marks the end (or "limit") of a cell. The most common cell delimiter is the comma, so the delimited sequence *15, 18, 24, 28* would represent data in four cells. The problem with using commas to delimit financial data is that larger values, such as *52,802*, can be written with commas as thousands markers. To avoid confusion when importing a text file, the most commonly used delimiter for financial data is the Tab character.

To import data from a text file, you open the **Data** menu, point to **Import External Data**, and then click **Import Data** to open the **Select Data Source** dialog box.

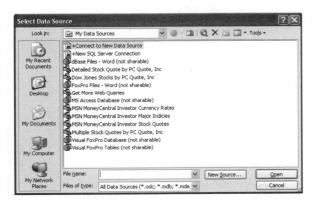

From within the **Select Data Source** dialog box, you navigate to the directory with the text file you want to import. Double-clicking the file launches the **Text Import Wizard**.

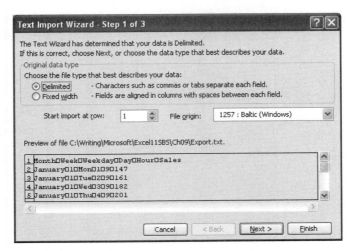

The first page of the **Text Import Wizard** lets you indicate whether the data file you are importing is delimited or fixed-width; fixed-width means that each cell value will fall within a specific position in the file. Clicking **Next** to accept the default choice,

**Delimited** (which Excel assigns after examining the data source you selected), advances you to the next wizard screen.

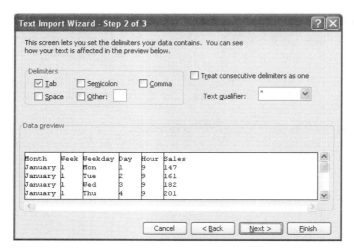

This screen lets you choose the delimiter for the file (in this case, Excel detected tabs in the file and selected the **Tab** check box for you) and gives you a preview of what the text file will look like when imported. Clicking **Next** advances you to the final wizard screen.

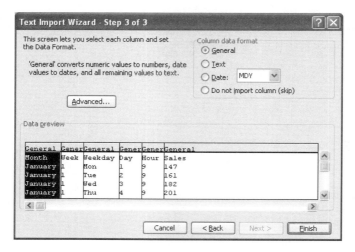

This screen lets you change the data type and formatting of the columns in your data list. Because you will assign formats and AutoFormats after you create the PivotTable from the data, you can click **Finish** to import the data into your worksheet. Once the data is in Excel, you can work with it normally.

In this exercise, you import a data list into Excel from a text file and then create a PivotTable based on that list.

OPEN: External from the *SBS\Excel\PivotTable* folder.

**1**   On the **Data** menu, point to **Import External Data** and then click **Import Data**.

The **Select Data Source** dialog box appears.

**2**   Navigate to the PivotTable directory, and double-click **Export.txt**.

The **Text Import Wizard** appears, with the **Delimited** option button selected, *1* in the **Start import at row** box, and a preview of the file's contents in the **Preview** box.

**3**   Click **Next**.

The second page of the **Text Import Wizard** appears. In the **Delimiters** pane, the **Tab** check box is selected. A preview of your data as it will appear when imported is visible in the **Data Preview** box.

**4**   Click **Next**.

The next screen of the **Text Import Wizard** appears. The data type for each column is set to General.

**5**   Click **Finish** to accept the values and data types as assigned by the wizard.

The **Import Data** dialog box appears with the **Existing worksheet** option button selected and *=$A$1* in the **Existing worksheet** box.

**6**   Click **OK** to paste the imported data into the active worksheet, beginning at cell A1.

The data appears in your workbook, and the **External Data** toolbar appears.

Close

**7**   Click the **Close** button to hide the **External Data** toolbar.

**8**   Click cell A1, and then, on the **Data** menu, click **PivotTable and PivotChart Report**.

The **PivotTable and PivotChart Wizard** appears with the **Microsoft Excel list or database** option button selected in the top pane, identifying your worksheet as the data source, and the **PivotTable** option button selected in the bottom pane, indicating that you want to create a PivotTable only.

**9**   Click **Next** to move to the next page of the wizard.

The next page of the wizard appears, with the range *$A$1:$F$169* in the **Range** box.

**10** Click **Next** to move to the next page of the wizard.

The final page of the **PivotTable and PivotChart Wizard** appears, with the **New worksheet** option button selected, which tells the wizard to create a new worksheet to hold the PivotTable.

**11** Click **Finish**.

The wizard closes, and the **PivotTable** toolbar, the **PivotTable Field List** dialog box, and your new PivotTable appear in a new worksheet.

**12** From the **PivotTable Field List** dialog box, drag **Week** to the **Drop Row Fields Here** box.

*Week* appears in the **Drop Row Fields Here** box.

**13** From the **PivotTable Field List** dialog box, drag **Day** to the **Drop Row Fields Here** box and drop it to the right of the **Week** field head.

**Tip**   A large gray insertion point will appear to the right of the **Week** field head when the mouse pointer is in the correct position.

The PivotTable is updated to reflect the added field.

**14** From the **PivotTable Field List** dialog box, drag **Hour** to the **Drop Column Fields Here** box.

The PivotTable is updated to reflect the added field.

**15** From the **PivotTable Field List** dialog box, drag **Sales** to the **Drop Data Items Here** box.

The PivotTable is updated to reflect the added field.

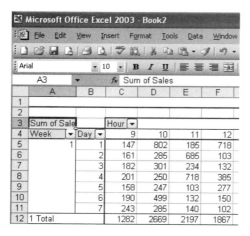

**16** On the Standard toolbar, click the **Save** button to save your work.

Save

**CLOSE:** External.

# Key Points

- A PivotTable is a versatile tool you can use to rearrange your data dynamically, letting you emphasize different aspects of your data without creating new worksheets.

- PivotTable data must be formatted as a list.

- There are several AutoFormats available for PivotTables; you'll probably find one you like.

- The PivotTable wizard walks you through the creation process, but be sure you add the field that will provide the data for the body of your PivotTable last.

- Just as you can limit the data shown in a static worksheet, you can use filters to limit the data shown in a PivotTable.

- If you have data in a compatible format, such as a text file, you can import that data into Excel and create a PivotTable from it.

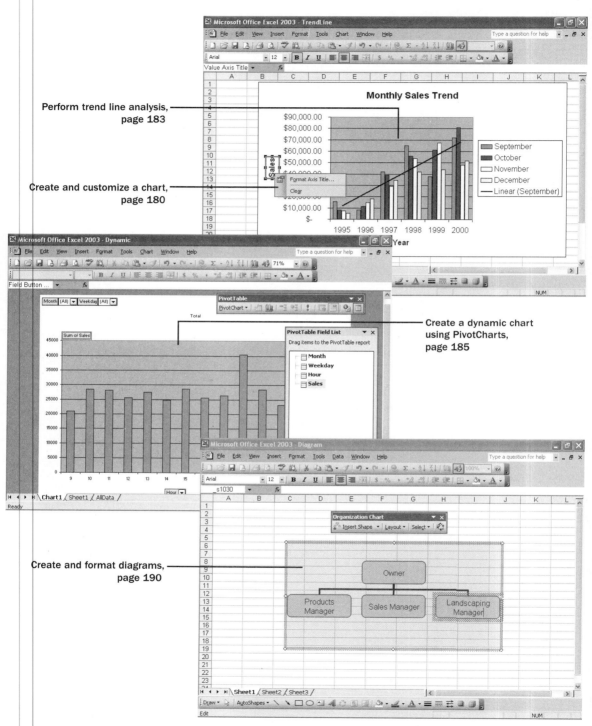

Perform trend line analysis, page 183

Create and customize a chart, page 180

Create a dynamic chart using PivotCharts, page 185

Create and format diagrams, page 190

*Chapter 10 at a Glance*

# 10 Creating Charts

**In this chapter you will learn to:**

✔ Create and customize a chart.

✔ Perform trend line analysis.

✔ Create a dynamic chart using PivotCharts.

✔ Create diagrams to illustrate relationships and processes.

When you enter data into a Microsoft Excel worksheet, you create a record of important events, whether they are individual sales, sales for an hour of a day, or the price of a product. What a list of values in cells can't communicate easily, however, are the overall trends in the data. The best way to communicate trends in a large collection of data is through *charts* and *graphs*, which summarize data visually.

You have a great deal of control over your charts' appearance—you can change the color of any chart element, modify a chart's type to better summarize the underlying data, and change the display properties of text and numbers in a chart. If the data in the worksheet used to create a chart represents a progression through time, such as sales over a number of months, you can have Excel extrapolate future sales and add a *trend line* to the graph representing that prediction.

Just as you can create PivotTables to reorganize a data list dynamically, you can create a *PivotChart* that reflects the contents and organization of the associated Pivot-Table. You can also create diagrams, such as organizational charts, that are useful in many organizations.

In this chapter, you'll learn how to create a chart and customize its elements, find trends in your overall data, create dynamic charts, and create and format diagrams.

---

**See Also** Do you need a quick refresher on the topics in this chapter? See the quick reference entries on pages xlviii–li.

---

**Important** Before you can use the practice files in this chapter, be sure you install them from the book's companion CD-ROM to their default location. See "Using the Book's CD-ROM" on page xi for more information.

# Creating a Chart

Chart Wizard

To present your Excel data graphically, you select the cells you want to represent graphically and then click the **Chart Wizard** button on the Standard toolbar to launch the **Chart Wizard**.

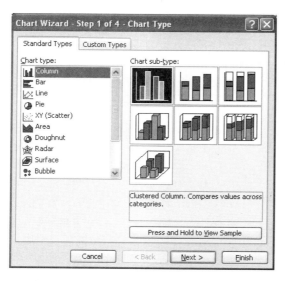

*Microsoft Office Specialist*

On the first page of the **Chart Wizard**, you choose the type and subtype of chart you want to create. When you click a chart type, the subtypes for that type appear in the **Chart sub-type** section, and the default subtype is selected, with a description of it appearing in the description box. You can go beyond those descriptions and get a preview of how your data would appear in a specific chart subtype by selecting the subtype and using the **Press and Hold to View Sample** button. When you've selected the type and subtype for your chart, click **Next** to move to the next wizard page.

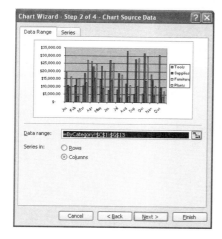

On this wizard page, you ensure that the **Data range** box has the reference for the cells to be used to create the chart, and you tell the wizard whether the data to be used to create the chart is arranged in columns or rows.

**Tip**   Excel does a good job of guessing whether the cells are arranged in columns or rows, but you should check the preview of the chart that appears in the wizard and select the other option button if necessary.

Once you have ensured that the correct cells and their arrangement have been selected, you can click the **Series** tab to name the data series, or set of values used to define the contents of the chart.

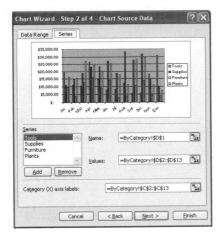

The cell range used to create this chart has the data labels included, so the correct labels appear in the wizard. You should verify that the series labels and ranges are indeed correct and then click **Next**.

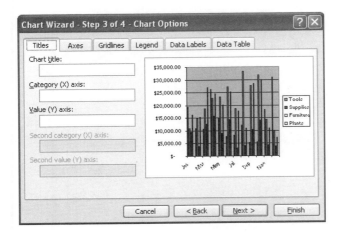

This wizard page lets you set the appearance of your chart, such as by adding a chart title and labels for both the horizontal (X) and vertical (Y) axes. After you type a label or a title in a box, the preview of the chart will change to reflect that addition. The other tab pages available on this wizard screen let you change the appearance of the chart, such as by adding gridlines to reflect changes in value, changing the position of or hiding the legend, or labeling the columns or points on your chart. When you're satisfied with the chart's appearance, click **Next** to move to the final **Chart Wizard** page.

On this wizard page, you can choose to create your chart on a new page by selecting the **As new sheet** option button or as part of an existing worksheet. The name of the worksheet with the data used to create the chart appears in the **As object in** box, but you can choose another worksheet by clicking the down arrow at the right edge of the **As object in** box and clicking the name of another worksheet from the list that appears. If you plan to use the chart as an independent exhibit, or if you are printing the entire contents of the worksheet on a single page and the chart would obscure the underlying data, you can create the chart in a new worksheet. If you want the chart to be associated with its data whenever you or your colleagues open the worksheet with the data, or if you want to group all charts you create in a single worksheet, you should create the chart in an existing worksheet. When you click **Finish**, the chart appears in the selected worksheet.

As with most other objects in an Excel worksheet, you can customize the chart's appearance. For example, you can resize the chart by dragging one of the sizing handles at the edges of the chart. You can also change the chart's fill effect, or background, by opening the **Format Chart Area** dialog box. To open that dialog box, you right-click the chart's Chart Area (where the body of the chart appears) and then choose **Format Chart Area** from the shortcut menu that appears.

You can change the chart's background color by clicking any of the color squares on the palette in the **Area** section of the dialog box. To change the chart's fill effect, click the **Fill Effects** button.

You can use the controls in the **Fill Effects** dialog box to choose the color scheme, texture, pattern, or picture to serve as the background for the active chart.

In this exercise, you create a chart using the **Chart Wizard**, resize the chart, customize the chart's appearance, and then change the chart's fill effect.

**OPEN:** CreateChart from the *SBS\Excel\Charts* folder.

**1** Select cells C1:G13, and then, on the Standard toolbar, click the **Chart Wizard** button.

The **Chart Wizard** appears.

**2** If necessary, in the **Chart type** list, click **Column** and then, in the **Chart sub-type** section, click the first subtype.

**3** Click **Next** to move to the next wizard page.

The next wizard page appears.

**4** If necessary, select the **Series** tab. Verify that the **Category (X) axis labels** box specifies the months of the year (=*ByCategory!$C$2:$C$13*) and that the four series are named *Tools*, *Supplies*, *Furniture*, and *Plants*.

**5** Click **Next**.

The next wizard page appears.

**6** In the **Chart title** box, type Monthly Sales by Category and then press Tab .

The chart preview is updated to reflect the new chart title.

**7** In the **Category (X) axis** box, type Month and then press Tab .

The chart preview is updated to reflect the value in the **Category (X) axis** box.

**8** In the **Value (Y) axis** box, type Sales and then click **Next**.

The next wizard page appears.

**9** Click **Finish** to accept the default choice to create the chart as part of the ByCategory worksheet.

The chart and the **Chart** toolbar appear in the ByCategory worksheet.

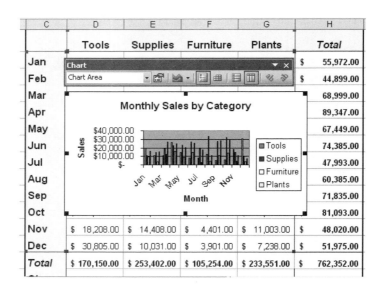

|  | Tools | Supplies | Furniture | Plants | Total |
|---|---|---|---|---|---|
| Jan |  |  |  |  | $ 55,972.00 |
| Feb |  |  |  |  | $ 44,899.00 |
| Mar |  |  |  |  | 68,999.00 |
| Apr |  |  |  |  | 89,347.00 |
| May |  |  |  |  | 67,449.00 |
| Jun |  |  |  |  | 74,385.00 |
| Jul |  |  |  |  | 47,993.00 |
| Aug |  |  |  |  | 60,385.00 |
| Sep |  |  |  |  | 71,835.00 |
| Oct |  |  |  |  | 81,093.00 |
| Nov | $ 18,208.00 | $ 14,408.00 | $ 4,401.00 | $ 11,003.00 | $ 48,020.00 |
| Dec | $ 30,805.00 | $ 10,031.00 | $ 3,901.00 | $ 7,238.00 | 51,975.00 |
| Total | $ 170,150.00 | $ 253,402.00 | $ 105,254.00 | $ 233,551.00 | 762,352.00 |

**Note** Notice that the cells with the chart data are outlined in blue, the cells with the series names are outlined in green, and the cells with the categories are outlined in purple.

**10** Drag the chart until it covers approximately cells C17:G30.

**11** Grab the sizing handle at the lower right corner of the chart, and drag it to the lower right corner of cell H33.

The chart becomes larger, giving you more room to add other information in the chart.

**12** Right-click anywhere in the **Chart Area** of the chart, and then, from the shortcut menu that appears, click **Format Chart Area**.

The **Format Chart Area** dialog box appears.

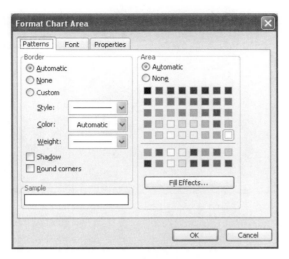

**13** In the **Border** section of the dialog box, select the **Custom** option button.

**14** Click the **Weight** down arrow, and then, from the list that appears, click the item at the bottom of the list.

**15** Select the **Shadow** check box.

**16** In the **Area** section, click the **Fill Effects** button.

The **Fill Effects** dialog box appears.

**17** Click the **Texture** tab to display the **Texture** tab page.

**18** Click the texture in the upper left corner of the **Texture** section.

**Newsprint** appears in the text box below the samples, and a preview of the Newsprint texture appears in the Sample pane, in the lower right corner of the dialog box.

**19** Click **OK**.

The **Format Chart Area** dialog box reappears.

**20** Click **OK**.

The **Format Chart Area** dialog box disappears, and the chart takes on the characteristics you applied to it.

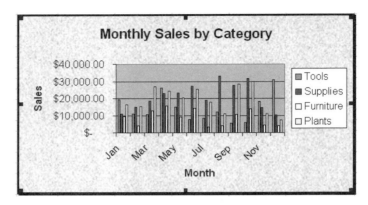

**21** On the Standard toolbar, click the **Save** button to save your work.

CLOSE: CreateChart.

# Customizing Chart Labels and Numbers

*Microsoft Office Specialist*

After you create a chart, you can customize its elements to conform to a particular color scheme, fill effect, or border pattern. You can also change the appearance of the labels and numbers in your chart.

To change the display characteristics of a chart label, double-click the label to open a formatting dialog box. You can use the controls in the dialog box to format the label.

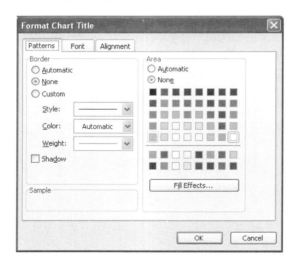

**Tip** If you want to change the text of a label, click the label to activate it and then click in the box that appears around the label. When you're done editing the text, click outside the box around the label.

You can also change the display characteristics of the format used to display numeric values in your charts. For example, the sales values on the vertical axis of the chart in the following graphic are formatted with the Accounting format.

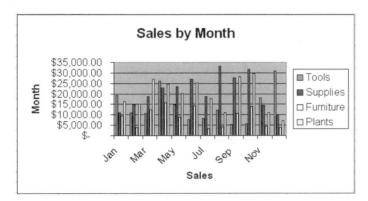

The default setting for the Accounting format has a thousands separator, a currency symbol, and two digits to the right of the decimal point. In the chart above, the vertical axis measures sales in $5,000 increments, so the digits to the right of the decimal point are superfluous. You can change the format of the numbers displayed on the vertical axis by double-clicking the axis and then clicking the **Number** tab in the dialog box that appears.

To change the number of digits to the right of the decimal point, type the new number in the **Decimal places** box. When you click **OK**, the chart will change to reflect your choice.

In this exercise, you create a line graph, change the formatting of the chart title, and then change the display characteristics of the numbers on the chart's vertical axis.

**OPEN: Customize from the *SBS\Excel\Charts* folder.**

Chart Wizard

**1** Select the cells in the range C1:G13, and then, on the Standard toolbar, click the **Chart Wizard** button.

The **Chart type** page of the **Chart Wizard** appears.

**2** In the **Chart type** list, click **Line** and then click **Next**.

The next **Chart Wizard** page appears.

**3** Click **Next** to move to the next wizard page.

**4** In the **Chart title** box, type Sales by Month and then press [Tab].

*Sales by Month* appears as the chart title in the preview box.

**5** In the **Category (X) axis** box, type **Month** and then press ⌧.

*Month* appears as the Category (X) axis label.

**6** In the **Value (Y) axis** box, type **Sales** and then press ⏎.

The next wizard page appears.

**7** Click **Finish**.

The chart appears in the active worksheet.

**8** Drag the chart so that it covers cells in the range C17:G30.

**9** Double-click **Sales by Month**.

The **Format Chart Title** dialog box appears.

**10** Click the **Font** tab.

The **Font** tab page appears.

**11** In the **Size** box, click **14** and then click **OK**.

The chart title appears in 14-point type.

**12** Double-click the **Value (Y)** axis area of the chart.

The **Format Axis** dialog box appears.

**13** If necessary, click the **Number** tab to display the **Number** tab page.

**14** In the **Decimal places** box, type **0** and then click **OK**.

The values on the Value (Y) axis appear with the formatting changes applied.

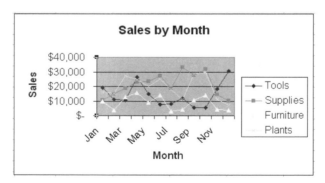

**15** On the Standard toolbar, click the **Save** button to save your changes.

CLOSE: Customize.

# Finding Trends in Your Data

*Microsoft
Office
Specialist*

You can use the data in Excel workbooks to discover how your business has performed in the past, but you can also have Excel make its best guess as to future sales if the current trend continues. As an example, consider the following graph for The Garden Company.

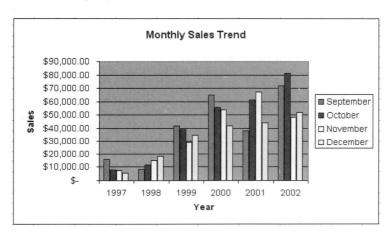

This graph shows the September to December sales totals for the years 1997 through 2002. The total for each month has grown from 1997 to 2002, but the growth hasn't been uniform, so guessing how much sales would increasce if the overall trend continued would require math you might not know.

Fortunately, Excel knows that math. To have Excel project future sales for one of the data series in the chart, right-click the first column for that data series and then, from the shortcut menu that appears, click **Add Trendline** to open the **Add Trendline** dialog box.

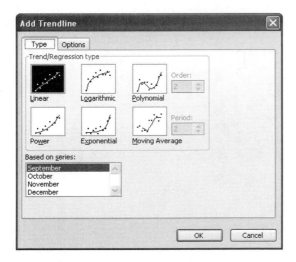

The **Type** tab page of the **Add Trendline** dialog box lets you choose the data distribution that Excel should expect when it makes its projection. The right choice for most business data is Linear—the other distributions (such as Exponential, Logarithmic, and Polynomial) are used for scientific and operations research applications.

**Tip**   Basically, if you don't know which distribution to choose, choose Linear.

After you pick the distribution type, click the **Options** tab to display the **Options** tab page.

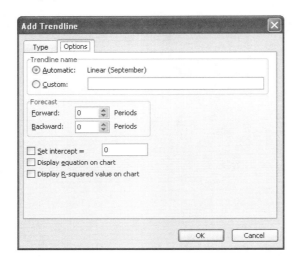

The horizontal axis of the chart used in this example shows sales by year from 1997 to 2002. To tell Excel how far in the future to look, you type a number in the **Forecast** section's **Forward** box. In this case, to look ahead two years you would type **2** in the **Forward** box and then click **OK** to add the trend line to the chart.

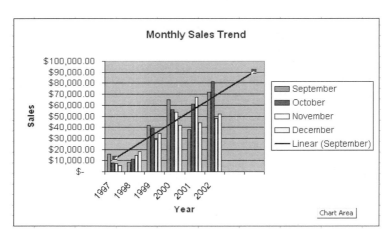

As with other chart elements, you can double-click the trend line to open a formatting dialog box.

In this exercise, you add a trend line to a chart.

OPEN: TrendLine from the *SBS\Excel\Charts* folder.

**1** If necessary, on the tab bar, click the **Trends** tab.

The Trends worksheet appears.

**2** In the embedded chart, right-click the **September** column above the **1995** label and then, from the shortcut menu that appears, click **Add Trendline**.

The **Type** tab page of the **Add Trendline** dialog box appears.

**3** If necessary, in the **Trend/Regression type** section, click **Linear**.

**4** Click the **Options** tab.

The **Options** tab page appears.

**5** In the **Forecast** section, type **2** in the **Forward** box and then click **OK**.

The **Add Trendline** dialog box disappears, and the trend line you created appears on the chart.

**6** On the Standard toolbar, click the **Save** button to save your work.

CLOSE: TrendLine.

# Creating a Dynamic Chart Using PivotCharts

*Microsoft Office Specialist*

Just as you can create tables that you can reorganize on the fly to emphasize different aspects of the data in a list, you can also create dynamic charts, or PivotCharts, to reflect the contents and organization of a PivotTable.

You can create a PivotChart in two ways: by clicking a cell in an existing PivotTable and then clicking the **Chart Wizard** button on the Standard toolbar, or by selecting the appropriate option button on the last page of the **PivotTable and PivotChart Wizard**.

Chart Wizard

The first method of creating a PivotChart is fairly straightforward. In a worksheet with an existing PivotTable, click a cell in the PivotTable and then click the **Chart Wizard** button. When you do, a PivotChart appears in a new worksheet.

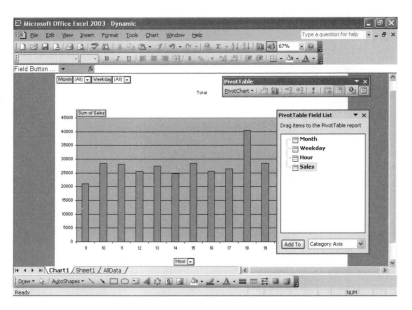

**Refresh Data**

Any changes to the PivotTable on which the PivotChart is based will be reflected in the PivotChart. For example, if the data in an underlying data list changes, clicking the **Refresh Data** button on the **PivotTable** toolbar will change the PivotChart to reflect the new data. Also, you could filter the contents of the PivotTable shown here by clicking the **Weekday** down arrow, clicking **Wed** from the list that appears, and then clicking **OK**. The PivotTable will then show sales on Wednesdays. The PivotChart will also reflect the filter.

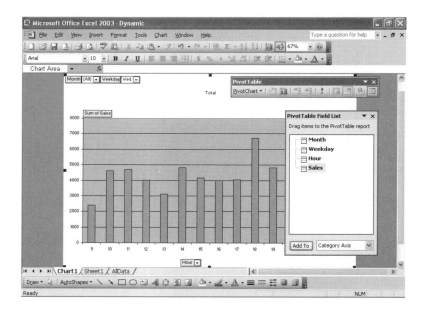

The PivotChart has controls with which you can filter the data in the PivotChart and PivotTable. Clicking the **Weekday** down arrow, clicking **(All)** from the list that appears, and then clicking **OK** will restore the PivotChart to its original configuration.

Once you have created a PivotChart, you can save it as a chart type that will be available in the **Chart Wizard**. To save the PivotChart as a user-defined chart type, click the chart, and on the **Chart** menu, click **Chart Type** to display the **Chart Type** dialog box. Once the **Chart Type** dialog box appears, click the **Custom Types** tab.

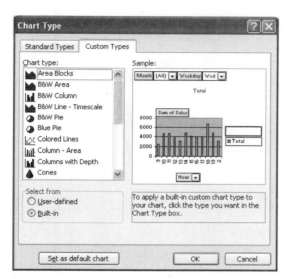

On the **Custom Types** tab page, click the **User-defined** option button in the **Select From** section to display the available user-defined chart types. The list of types in the **Chart type** list has one entry: **Default**. To add a new type, click the **Add** button.

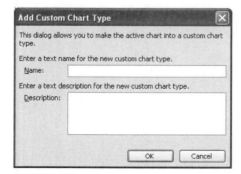

Type a name and a description for the new type, and then click **OK**. The new chart type will appear in the **Chart Type** dialog box.

If you ever want to change the chart type of an existing chart, you can do so by opening the **Chart Type** dialog box and clicking a new type for the chart. When you click **OK**, your data will be represented by the new chart.

**Caution**   If your data is of the wrong type to be represented by the chart type you select, an error message will appear.

In this exercise, you create a PivotTable and associated PivotChart, change the under-lying data and update the PivotChart to reflect that change, save the PivotChart as a custom chart type, and then change the PivotChart's type.

OPEN: Dynamic from the *SBS\Excel\Charts* folder.

1   Click cell A1, and then on the **Data** menu, click **PivotTable and PivotChart Report**.

    The first page of the **PivotTable and PivotChart Wizard** appears.

2   Select the **PivotChart report (with PivotTable report)** option button, and then click **Next**.

    The next wizard page appears with *$A$1:$D$1117* in the **Range** box.

3   Click **Next**.

    The final wizard page appears.

4   Be sure that the **New worksheet** option button is selected, and then click **Finish**.

    Two new worksheets appear in the active workbook, one with the new PivotTable and the other with the new PivotChart. The worksheet with the PivotChart is active and has the **PivotTable Field List** dialog box and the **PivotTable** toolbar displayed.

5   From the **PivotTable Field List** dialog box, drag the **Hour** field to the **Drop Category Fields Here** box.

    The PivotChart changes to reflect the assignment.

6   From the **PivotTable Field List** dialog box, drag the **Month** field to the **Drop Page Fields Here** box.

    The PivotChart changes to reflect the assignment.

7   From the **PivotTable Field List** dialog box, drag the **Weekday** field to the right of the **Month** field head in the **Drop Page Fields Here** box.

    The PivotChart changes to reflect the assignment.

8   From the **PivotTable Field List** dialog box, drag the **Sales** field to the **Drop Data Items Here** box.

The body of the PivotChart fills with data from the **Sales** field, organized by the contents of the **Hour** field.

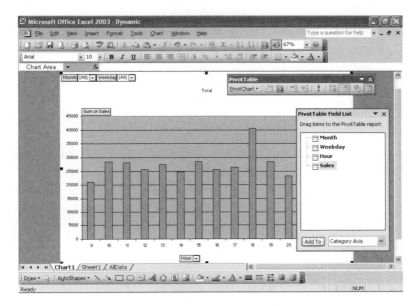

Close

9    In the **PivotTable Field List** dialog box, click the **Close** button.

The **PivotTable Field List** dialog box disappears.

10   On the tab bar, in the lower left corner of the workbook, click the **AllData** sheet tab.

The AllData worksheet appears.

11   In cell D9, type 4140.

12   On the tab bar, click the **Chart1** sheet tab.

The Chart1 worksheet appears.

13   On the **PivotTable** toolbar, click the **Refresh Data** button.

The bar representing total sales for hour 9 changes to reflect the new total.

14   On the **Chart** menu, click **Chart Type**.

The **Chart Type** dialog box appears.

15   If necessary, click the **Custom Types** tab to display the **Custom Types** tab page.

16   In the **Select from** section, select the **User-defined** option button and then click **Add**.

The **Add Custom Chart Type** dialog box appears.

17   In the **Name** box, type Sales PivotChart.

**18**    In the **Description** box, type PivotChart created with Month, Weekday, Hour, and Sales fields and then click **OK**.

The **Add Custom Chart Type** dialog box disappears, and the new chart type appears in the **Chart Type** dialog box.

**19**    Click the **Standard Types** tab.

The **Standard Types** tab page of the **Chart Type** dialog box appears.

**20**    In the **Chart type** list, click **Area** and then click **OK**.

The chart changes to reflect its new type.

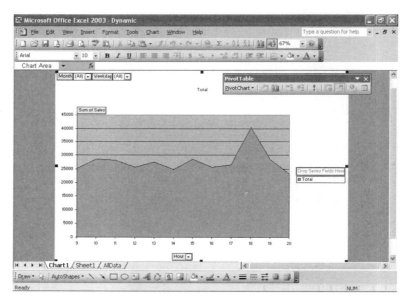

**21**    On the Standard toolbar, click the **Save** button to save your work.

Save

CLOSE: Dynamic.

# Creating Diagrams

*Microsoft Office Specialist*

The Garden Company is a frequent destination for school field trips because of its wide variety of plants, so Catherine would like to make up some diagrams showing how recycling and weather cycles relate to her business and the kids. Excel has just the tool she needs to create those diagrams: the **Diagram Gallery** dialog box, which you can display by opening the **Insert** menu and clicking **Diagram**.

---

**See Also** For more information on adding pictures from existing files to your worksheets, see "Adding a Graphic to a Document" on page 34.

---

Clicking one of the buttons in the **Diagram Gallery** dialog box selects the type of diagram the button represents and causes a description of the diagram type to appear in the bottom pane of the dialog box. The following table lists the six types of diagrams you can create using the **Diagram Gallery** dialog box.

| Diagram | Description |
| --- | --- |
| Organization chart | Used to show hierarchical relationships, such as within a company. |
| Cycle diagram | Used to show a process with a continuous cycle. |
| Radial diagram | Used to show the relationships of a core element. |
| Pyramid diagram | Used to show foundation-based relationships, such as a series of skills. |
| Venn diagram | Used to show the areas of overlap among sets of items. |
| Target diagram | Used to show steps toward a goal. |

After you click the button representing the type of diagram you want to create, clicking **OK** will add the diagram to your worksheet. You can then edit the elements of the diagram using the controls on the Formatting toolbar as well as on the Format menu. In fact, when one of the elements in a diagram is selected, there will be a **Format AutoShape** item on the **Format** menu; clicking it displays the **Format AutoShape** dialog box.

**Note** If you have selected the text in an AutoShape, only the **Font** tab of the **Format AutoShape** dialog box will be available.

You can use the controls in the **Format AutoShape** dialog box to change any of the attributes of the diagram, including fill color, borders, and text properties.

In this exercise, you create an organization chart, fill in the shapes, add a shape, change the layout of the diagram without changing the information it embodies, and change the formatting of one of the diagram elements.

OPEN: Diagram from the *SBS\Excel\Charts* folder.

**1** On the Insert menu, click **Diagram**.

The **Diagram Gallery** dialog box appears.

**2** Click the **Organization Chart** button at the top left of the dialog box, and click **OK**.

The **Diagram Gallery** dialog box disappears, a diagram appears on the active worksheet, and the **Organization Chart** toolbar appears.

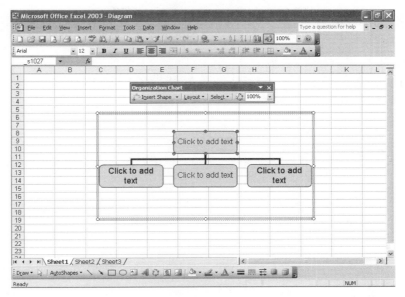

**3**   Click in the top shape in the organization chart, type Owner, and click a blank space in the organization chart.

*Owner* appears in the top shape.

**4**   Click the shape at the left of the second row, type Products Manager, and click a blank space in the organization chart.

*Products Manager* appears in the leftmost shape on the second row of the organization chart.

**5**   Click the shape in the center of the second row, type Sales Manager, and click a blank space in the organization chart.

*Sales Manager* appears in the center shape on the second row of the organization chart.

**6**   Click the shape at the right of the second row, type Landscaping Manager, and click a blank space in the organization chart.

*Landscaping Manager* appears in the rightmost shape on the second row of the organization chart.

**7** Click the **Products Manager** shape.

**8** On the **Organization Chart** toolbar, click the **Insert Shape** down arrow, and click **Subordinate**.

A shape appears below the **Products Manager** shape.

**9** Click the new shape, type Warehouse, and click a blank space in the organization chart.

**10** Click the **Owner** shape.

**11** On the **Organization Chart** toolbar, click the **Layout** down arrow, and click **Right Hanging**.

The shapes one level below the **Owner** shape change to a right-hanging arrangement.

**12** Click the **Products Manager** shape.

**13** On the **Organization Chart** toolbar, click the **Layout** down arrow, and click **Right Hanging**.

The shape one level below the **Products Manager** shape changes to a right-hanging arrangement.

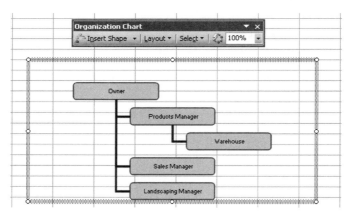

**14** Click the border of the **Owner** shape.

**15** On the **Format** menu, click **AutoShape**.

The **Format AutoShape** dialog box appears.

**16** If necessary, click the **Font** tab, and then, in the **Font Style** list, click **Bold**.

**17** Click **OK**.

The contents of the **Owner** shape appear in bold type.

**18** On the Standard toolbar, click the **Save** button to save your work.

Save

CLOSE: Diagram.

# Key Points

■ You can use charts to summarize large sets of data in an easy-to-follow visual format.

■ You're not stuck with the chart you create; if you want to change it, you can.

■ Adding chart labels and a legend makes your chart much easier to follow.

■ If your chart data represents a series of events over time (such as monthly or yearly sales), you can use trendline analysis to extrapolate future events based on the past data.

■ A PivotChart lets you rearrange your chart on the fly, emphasizing different aspects of the same data without having to create a new chart for each view.

■ Excel lets you create and modify common business and organizational diagrams, such as organization charts and process diagrams, quickly.

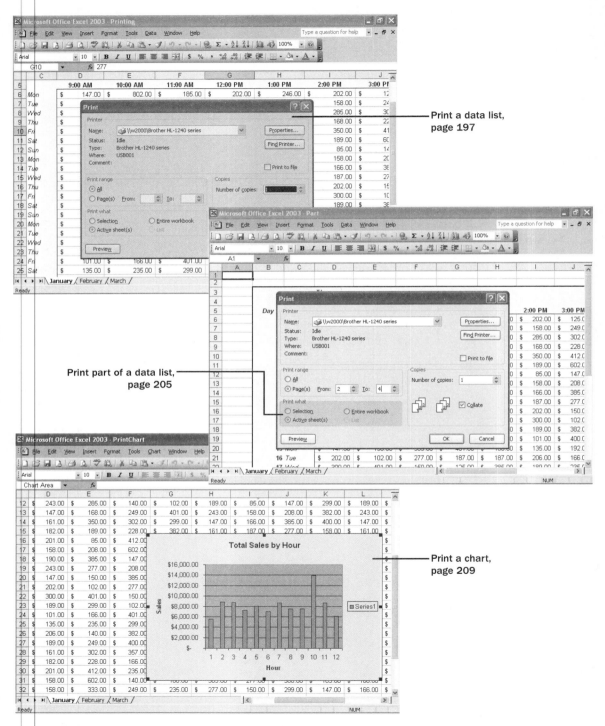

Print a data list,
page 197

Print part of a data list,
page 205

Print a chart,
page 209

*Chapter 11 at a Glance*

# 11 Printing

**In this chapter you will learn to:**

✔  Print data lists.

✔  Print part of a data list.

✔  Print a chart.

Excel gives you a wide range of tools to create and manipulate your data lists. By using filters, by sorting, and by creating PivotTables and charts, you can change your worksheets so that they convey the greatest possible amount of information. Once you have configured your worksheet so that it shows your data to best advantage, you can print your Excel documents to use in a presentation or include in a report. You can choose to print all or part of any of your worksheets, change how your data and charts appear on the printed page, and even suppress any error messages that might appear in your worksheets.

In this chapter, you'll learn how to print all or part of a data list and how to print charts.

**See Also**  Do you need a quick refresher on the topics in this chapter? See the quick reference entries on pages li–liv.

**Important**  Before you can use the practice files in this chapter, be sure you install them from the book's companion CD-ROM to their default location. See "Using the Book's CD-ROM" on page xi for more information.

## Printing Data Lists

Microsoft
Office
Specialist

One of the most important considerations in creating a paper copy of an Excel document is determining how you want your data to appear on the printed page. For example, you can decide how far from the edge of the page you want your data to start, change the order in which Excel prints the pages in your worksheet, and even change where Excel ends one printed page and begins the next.

Print

**Tip**  If you want to print the active worksheet without changing any settings, click the **Print** button on the Standard toolbar.

## Preview a Worksheet Before Printing

Print Preview

You can view your Excel worksheet as it would be printed by clicking the **Print Preview** button on the Standard toolbar. When you do, Excel displays the active worksheet in the Print Preview window.

When the Print Preview window opens, it shows the active worksheet as it would be printed with its current settings. In the lower left corner of the Print Preview window, Excel indicates how many pages the worksheet will require when printed and the number of the page you are viewing.

**Tip** You can view the next printed page by pressing the [Page Down] key; to move to the previous page, press the [Page Up] key.

## Change Your Printer Setup

While you have your worksheet open in the Print Preview window, you can use the buttons at the top of the window to change how your worksheet will appear when printed. Clicking the **Setup** button, for example, opens the **Page Setup** dialog box.

**Important** Any page setup or other changes you make to a worksheet are confined to that worksheet.

You can use the controls in the **Page Setup** dialog box to change the orientation of the printed page between portrait mode, which has the short edge of the paper at the top, and landscape mode, which has the long edge of the paper at the top. Clicking the **Margins** tab displays a tab page with controls for changing the amount of space to be left at the edges of the paper (and the amount of space dedicated to headers and footers) when Excel prints your worksheet.

**Important** The remaining controls on the **Page** tab are discussed in the next section of this chapter, "Printing Part of a Data List."

You can also change the margins allotted to each area of your worksheet in the Print Preview window. When you click the **Margins** button, Excel draws lines on your worksheet to indicate where the sections of your document begin and end. To change a margin, you just drag its line to the desired position.

**Tip** When you drag a margin to a new position, the distance from the margin to the nearest edge appears in the lower left corner of the Print Preview window.

## Zoom In on Part of a Page

While you are viewing a worksheet in the Print Preview window, you can view the details of any section of the worksheet by clicking the **Zoom** button. Clicking the

**Zoom** button doubles the size of the document in the window; clicking it again returns the document to its normal display size.

## Change the Page Breaks in a Worksheet

Another way you can change how your worksheet will appear on the printed page is to change where Excel assigns its page breaks, or the point where Excel prints all subsequent data on a new sheet of paper. You can do that indirectly by changing a worksheet's margins, but you can do it directly by displaying your document in Page Break Preview mode. To display your worksheet in Page Break Preview mode from the Print Preview window, click the **Page Break Preview** button.

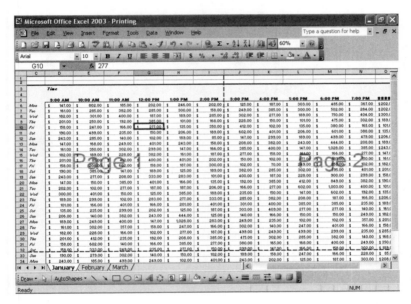

The blue lines in the window represent the page breaks. To move a page break, you drag the line representing the break to its new position. Excel will change the worksheet's properties so that the area you defined will be printed on a single page. You exit Page Break Preview mode by clicking **Normal** on the **View** menu.

**Tip**    You can view your worksheet in Page Break Preview mode at any time by clicking **Page Break Preview** on the **View** menu.

## Change the Page Printing Order for a Worksheet

When you view a document in Page Break Preview mode, Excel indicates the order in which the pages will be printed with light gray words on the worksheet pages. (These indicators appear only in Page Break Preview mode; they won't show up when the document is printed.) You can change the order in which the pages are printed by clicking the **Setup** button and opening the **Page Setup** dialog box to the **Sheet** page.

On the **Sheet** page, selecting the **Over, then down** option button will change the order in which the worksheets will be printed from the default **Down, then over**. You might want to change the order in which your worksheets are printed to keep certain information together on consecutive printed pages. For example, suppose you have a worksheet that holds hourly sales information; the columns represent hours of the day, and the rows represent days of the month. If you want to print out consecutive days for each hour, you use **Down, then over**, as shown in the following graphic. Pages 1 and 2 let you see the 9:00 a.m. to 2:00 p.m. sales for the entire month, pages 3 and 4 let you see the 3:00 p.m. to 7:00 p.m. sales for the entire month, and so on.

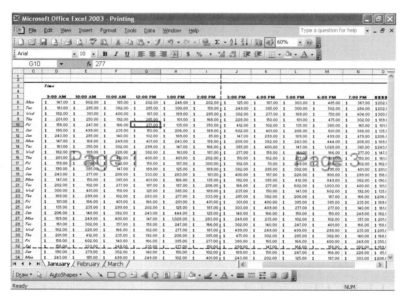

As the next graphic shows, changing the print order to **Over, then down** prints consecutive hours for each day. Pages 1 and 2 let you see the 9:00 a.m. to 7:00 p.m. sales for the first 24 days of the month, and pages 3 and 4 let you see the 9:00 a.m. to 7:00 p.m. sales for the last 7 days of the month.

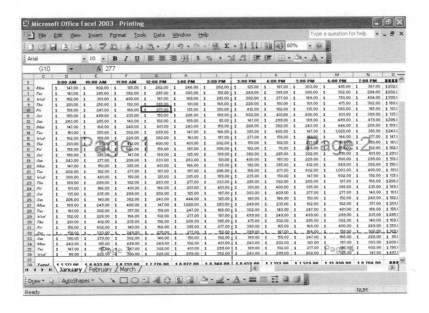

## Suppress Errors in a Worksheet

A helpful option on the **Sheet** tab page of the **Page Setup** dialog box is the **Cell errors as** box, which lets you select how Excel will print any errors in your worksheet. You can print the error as it normally appears in the worksheet, print a blank cell in place of the error, or choose one of two other indicators that are not standard Excel error messages.

Once you have prepared your worksheet for printing, you can print it by opening the **Print** dialog box. In the **Print** dialog box, you can choose the pages of the worksheet you want to print. To print every page in the worksheet, select the **All** option button in the **Print range** section and then click **OK**. To print every worksheet in the active workbook, select the **Entire workbook** option button in the **Print what** section.

## Print Nonadjacent Sheets from a Workbook

If you want to print more than one worksheet from the active workbook, but not every worksheet in the workbook, you can select the worksheets to print from the tab bar. To select the worksheets to print, hold down the Ctrl key while you click the sheet tabs of the worksheets you want to print and then click the **Print** toolbar button.

**Note** The worksheets you select for printing do not need to be next to one another in the workbook.

In this exercise, you preview a worksheet before printing, change your printer setup, change the document's margins, zoom in on part of a page, preview and change your worksheet's page breaks, change the page printing order for a worksheet, suppress errors in a worksheet, and then print nonadjacent worksheets in your workbook.

OPEN: Printing from the *SBS\Excel\Printing* folder.

**1** If necessary, click the **January** sheet tab.

**2** On the Standard toolbar, click the **Print Preview** button.

The worksheet appears in preview mode.

**3** Click **Setup**.

The **Page Setup** dialog box appears.

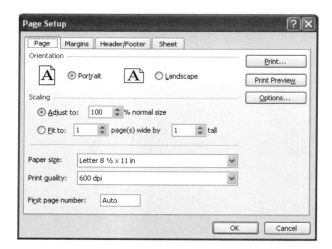

**4** Click the **Zoom** button.

Excel increases the display size of the document.

**5** Click the **Zoom** button.

Excel decreases the display size of the document.

**6** In the **Orientation** section of the **Page** tab, select the **Landscape** option button and then click **OK**.

The **Page Setup** dialog box closes, and the active worksheet reappears in preview mode.

**7**    Click **Margins**.

Margin lines appear on your worksheet.

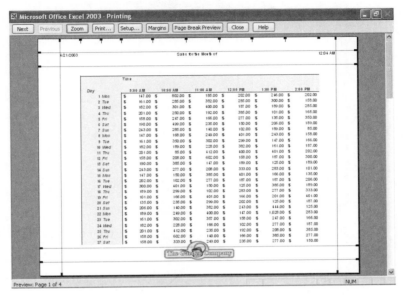

**8**    Move the mouse pointer over the second margin line from the bottom, and then, when the mouse pointer changes to a vertical double-headed arrow, drag the margin line until it is above the logo.

Excel adjusts the margins to reflect your change.

**9**    Click **Page Break Preview**.

**10**    If a message box appears, click **OK** to close it.

The Print Preview window closes. The active worksheet appears, with the page breaks indicated by blue lines and the printing order of the worksheet sections indicated by gray text on the background of the pages.

**11**    Drag the page break line on the border of columns I and J to the border of columns G and H.

Excel repaginates your document to reflect the new page break position.

**12**    On the **View** menu, click **Normal**.

Excel changes the document view from Page Break Preview mode to Normal.

**13**    On the **File** menu, click **Page Setup**.

The **Page Setup** dialog box appears.

**14** Click the **Sheet** tab.

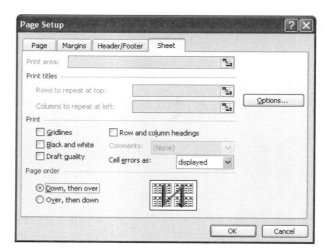

**15** In the **Page order** section, select the **Over, then down** option button.

The graphic in the **Page order** section changes to reflect your choice.

**16** In the **Print** section, click the **Cell errors as** box and then, from the list that appears, click **<blank>**.

**17** Click the **Page** tab.

**18** If necessary, select the **Adjust to** option button and then, in the **Adjust to** box, type **100**.

**Note** The **Adjust to** value might have changed from *100%* to *78%* when you moved the page break earlier in this exercise.

**19** Click **OK**.

The **Page Setup** dialog box closes.

**20** Hold down the ⌃ key while you click the **March** tab on the tab bar.

The January and March worksheets are now active.

**21** On the **File** menu, click **Print**.

The **Print** dialog box appears.

**22** In the **Print what** section, ensure that the **Active sheet(s)** option button is selected.

**23** Click **OK** to print the selected worksheets, or click **Cancel** to avoid printing the selected worksheets.

**24** On the Standard toolbar, click the **Save** button to save your changes.

**CLOSE:** Printing.

# Printing Part of a Data List

*Microsoft
Office
Specialist*

Excel gives you a great deal of control over what your worksheets look like when you print them, but you also have a lot of control over what parts of your worksheets will be printed. For example, you can use the **Print** dialog box to choose which pages of a multipage worksheet you want to print.

Selecting the **Page(s)** option button in the **Print range** section of the dialog box lets you fill in the page numbers you want to print in the **From** and **To** boxes.

**Tip**   You can use the Page Break Preview window to determine which pages you want to print, and if the pages aren't in an order you like, you can use the controls on the **Sheet** tab page of the **Page Setup** dialog box to change the order in which they will be printed.

Another way you can modify how a worksheet will be printed is to have Excel fit the entire worksheet on a specified number of pages. For example, you can have Excel resize a worksheet so that it will fit on a single printed page. Fitting a worksheet onto a single page is a handy tool when you need to add a sales or other summary to a report and don't want to spread important information across more than one page.

To have Excel fit a worksheet on a set number of pages, you open the **Page Setup** dialog box to the **Page** tab and select the **Fit to** option button. The default selection is to fit the worksheet to a print area one page high by one page wide, but you can type different values in the boxes to change the total pages on which the worksheet will be printed.

If you want to print a portion of a worksheet rather than the entire worksheet, you can define the area or areas you want to have printed. To identify the area of the worksheet you want to print, select the cells with the data you want to print, and on the **File** menu, point to **Print Area**, and then click **Set Print Area**. Excel marks the area with a dotted line around the border of the selected cells and will print only the cells you selected. To remove the selection, open the same submenu and click **Clear Print Area**.

**Tip**   You can include noncontiguous groups of cells in the area to be printed by holding down the ⌗ key as you select the cells.

Once you have defined a print area, you can use the **Page Setup** dialog box to position the print area on the page. Specifically, you can have Excel center the print area on the page by selecting the **Horizontally** and **Vertically** check boxes on the **Margins** tab page.

Another option at your disposal when printing an Excel worksheet is to hide specific rows or columns during the printing. For example, if a salesperson were giving a presentation on how different product lines sold at The Garden Company, he or she might want to show every row in a worksheet except the totals by category, saving that information for the next slide.

You can hide rows or columns by selecting the rows or columns, and then on the **Format** menu, pointing to **Row** or **Column**, and then clicking **Hide**. The rows or columns will be hidden until you point to **Row** or **Column** on the **Format** menu and click **Unhide**, but they are still there! They would be erased only if you selected the rows or columns and then clicked **Delete** on the **Edit** menu.

If the contents of a worksheet will take up more than one printed page, you can have Excel repeat one or more rows at the top of the page or columns at the left of the page. For example, if you wanted to print a lengthy data list containing the mailing addresses of customers signed up to receive your company's monthly newsletter, you could repeat the column headings Name, Address, City, and so forth at the top of the page. To repeat rows at the top of each printed page, on the **File** menu, click **Page Setup**. In the **Page Setup** dialog box, click the **Sheet** tab to move to the **Sheet** tab page.

Collapse
Dialog

On the **Sheet** tab page, you can use the controls in the **Print titles** section of the dialog box to select the rows or columns to repeat. To choose rows to repeat at the top of the page, click the **Collapse Dialog** button next to the **Rows to repeat at top** box, select the rows, and then click the **Expand Dialog** button. The rows you selected appear in the **Rows to repeat at top** box.

Expand Dialog

Similarly, to have a set of columns appear at the left of every printed page, click the **Collapse Dialog** button next to the **Columns to repeat at left** box, select the columns, and then click the **Expand Dialog** button. When you're done, click **OK** to accept the settings.

A final feature that comes in handy when you print Excel worksheets is Intelliprint, which prevents any blank pages from being printed at the end of a document. The end result is that you don't need to set a print area manually unless you want to print a subset of the data in your worksheet, or if you want to print blank pages after the rest of your data.

In this exercise, you print selected pages from a multipage worksheet, print an entire worksheet on a single page, define a print area and center it on a page, hide rows for printing, and then unhide the rows.

OPEN: Part from the *SBS\Excel\Printing* folder.

**1**   If necessary, click the **January** tab.

**2**   On the **File** menu, click **Print**.

   The **Print** dialog box appears.

**3**   In the **Print range** section, select the **Page(s)** option button.

**4**   In the **From** box, type 2 .

**5**   In the **To** box, type 3 .

**6**    Click **OK** to print pages 2 and 3 of the worksheet.

**Important**    If your computer is not connected to a printer, click **Cancel**.

**7**    On the **File** menu, click **Page Setup**.

The **Page Setup** dialog box appears.

**8**    If necessary, click the **Page** tab.

**9**    In the **Scaling** section, select the **Fit to** option button and then, if necessary, type 1 in both the **page(s) wide by** and **tall** boxes.

**10**    Click **OK**.

Excel resizes your worksheet so that it will fit on one printed page.

**11**    Click cell A1 and drag to cell G12.

**12**    On the **File** menu, point to **Print Area**, and then click **Set Print Area**.

A dotted line appears on the borders of the cells defined as the print area.

| | A | B | C | D | E | F | G |
|---|---|---|---|---|---|---|---|
| 1 | | | | | | | |
| 2 | | | | | | | |
| 3 | | | | *Time* | | | |
| 4 | | | | | | | |
| 5 | | *Day* | | 9:00 AM | 10:00 AM | 11:00 AM | 12:00 PM |
| 6 | | | 1 *Mon* | $  147.00 | $  802.00 | $  185.00 | $  202.00 |
| 7 | | | 2 *Tue* | $  161.00 | $  285.00 | $  382.00 | $  285.00 |
| 8 | | | 3 *Wed* | $  182.00 | $  301.00 | $  400.00 | $  187.00 |
| 9 | | | 4 *Thu* | $  201.00 | $  250.00 | $  192.00 | $  385.00 |
| 10 | | | 5 *Fri* | $  158.00 | $  247.00 | $  166.00 | $  277.00 |
| 11 | | | 6 *Sat* | $  190.00 | $  499.00 | $  235.00 | $  150.00 |
| 12 | | | 7 *Sun* | $  243.00 | $  285.00 | $  140.00 | $  102.00 |

Print Preview

**13**    On the Standard toolbar, click the **Print Preview** button.

A preview of the selected print area appears.

**14**    Click the **Setup** button.

The **Page Setup** dialog box appears.

**15**    Click the **Margins** tab to display the **Margins** tab page.

**16**    In the **Center on page** section, select the **Horizontally** check box and the **Vertically** check box.

**17** Click **OK**.

The Print Preview window reappears, with the selected print area centered on the page.

**18** In the Print Preview window, click **Close**.

The Print Preview window closes.

**19** On the **File** menu, point to **Print Area** and then click **Clear Print Area**.

Excel removes the print area you defined earlier.

**20** Select columns D through G, and then, on the **Format** menu, point to **Column** and then click **Hide**.

Columns D through G are hidden.

**21** On the Standard toolbar, click the **Print Preview** button.

A preview of your worksheet as it will be printed appears.

**22** In the Print Preview window, click **Close**.

**23** On the **Format** menu, point to **Column** and then click **Unhide**.

The hidden columns reappear.

**24** On the Standard toolbar, click the **Save** button to save your work.

CLOSE: Part.

# Printing a Chart

*Microsoft
Office
Specialist*

Charts, which are graphic representations of your Excel data, let you communicate lots of information with a picture. Depending on your data and the type of chart you make, you can show trends across time, indicate the revenue share for various departments in a company for a month, or project future sales using trend line analysis. Once you have created a chart, you can print it to include in a report or use in a presentation.

If you embed a chart in a worksheet, however, the chart will probably obscure some of your data unless you move the chart to a second page in the worksheet. That's one way to handle printing a chart or the underlying worksheet, but there are other ways that don't involve changing the layout of your worksheets.

You can print a worksheet without printing an embedded chart by setting the chart's properties so that it remains hidden when the worksheet in which the chart is embedded is printed. You can find this option, which is directly analogous to hiding rows or columns when you print a worksheet, by opening the **Format Chart Area** dialog box to the **Properties** tab page.

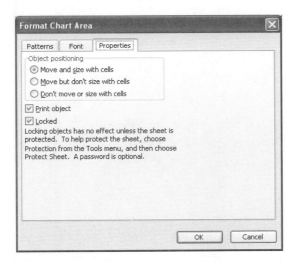

Selecting the **Print object** check box causes Excel to print the chart when the worksheet is printed, while clearing the check box hides the chart.

To print a chart, click the chart and then on the **File** menu, click **Print** to display the **Print** dialog box. In the **Print what** section, the **Selected Chart** option button is the only one available. If you were to click anywhere on the worksheet outside the chart, the **Print what** section would appear with the **Active sheet(s)** option button selected, meaning that the chart and underlying worksheet would be printed as they appear on the screen.

When you print a chart by itself, the default behavior is to resize the chart so that it takes up an entire printed page. If you want to print the chart at its actual size, such as when a full-page slide would be too large for your projection equipment, you can do so by opening the **Page Setup** dialog box to the **Chart** tab page. Selecting the **Custom** option button in the **Printed chart size** section tells Excel to print the chart at its actual size.

**Tip** You can resize a chart by selecting it in the workbook window and dragging one of the corner handles until the outline of the chart is the desired size.

In this exercise, you print a chart by itself, print the underlying worksheet without the chart, and then use the **Chart** tab of the **Page Setup** dialog box to set the chart's properties so that it is printed at its actual size.

OPEN: PrintChart from the *SBS\Excel\Printing* folder.

**1** Click the chart, and then, on the **File** menu, click **Print**.

The **Print** dialog box appears.

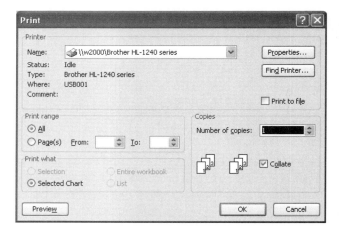

**2** In the **Print what** section, ensure that the **Selected Chart** option button is selected.

**3** Click **OK** to print your chart, or click **Cancel** to continue without printing.

The **Print** dialog box disappears. If you printed the chart, notice that the chart expanded to fit the entire page.

**4** Right-click the **Chart Area** of the chart, and then, from the shortcut menu that appears, click **Format Chart Area**.

The **Format Chart Area** dialog box appears.

**5** Click the **Properties** tab.

The **Properties** tab page appears.

**6**   Clear the **Print object** check box, and then click **OK**.

The **Format Chart Area** dialog box disappears.

Print

**7**   Click any spot on the worksheet and, if your computer is connected to a printer, on the Standard toolbar, click the **Print** button.

**Important**   If your computer is not connected to a printer, continue to the next step without printing.

Excel prints the worksheet without the chart.

**8**   Right-click the **Chart Area** of the chart, and then, from the shortcut menu that appears, click **Format Chart Area**.

The **Format Chart Area** dialog box appears.

**9**   Click the **Properties** tab.

The **Properties** tab page appears.

**10**   Select the **Print object** check box, and then click **OK**.

**11**   On the Standard toolbar, click the **Print Preview** button.

Print Preview

The Print Preview window appears. Notice that the chart has been resized to fit the entire page.

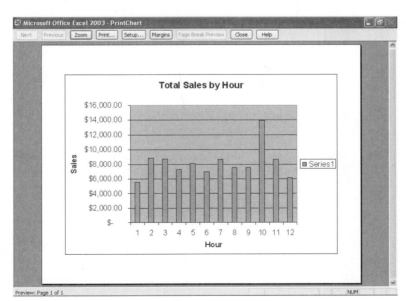

**12** Click the **Setup** button.

The **Page Setup** dialog box appears.

**13** Click the **Chart** tab.

The **Chart** tab page appears.

**14** Select the **Custom** option button, and then click **OK**.

The Print Preview window reappears, with the chart shown at its original size.

**15** Click **Print**.

The **Print** dialog box appears.

**16** Click **OK** to print your chart, or click **Cancel** to continue without printing.

The worksheet with the chart reappears.

**17** On the Standard toolbar, click the **Save** button to save your work.

CLOSE: PrintChart.

# Key Points

■ Excel gives you complete control over how your worksheets appear on the printed page. Don't be afraid to experiment until you find a look you like.

■ Use **Print Preview** to see what your worksheet will look like on paper before you print, especially if you're using an expensive color printer.

■ You can preview where the page breaks will fall when you print a worksheet and change them if you so desire.

■ Don't forget that you can have Excel avoid printing error codes! Be sure to use your power wisely.

■ You can choose either to print or not print hidden rows and columns, and repeat rows or columns in a printed worksheet.

■ When you print a worksheet that contains a chart, you can print the chart so it fills up an entire sheet of paper, print the chart at its actual size, or print the worksheet without the chart.

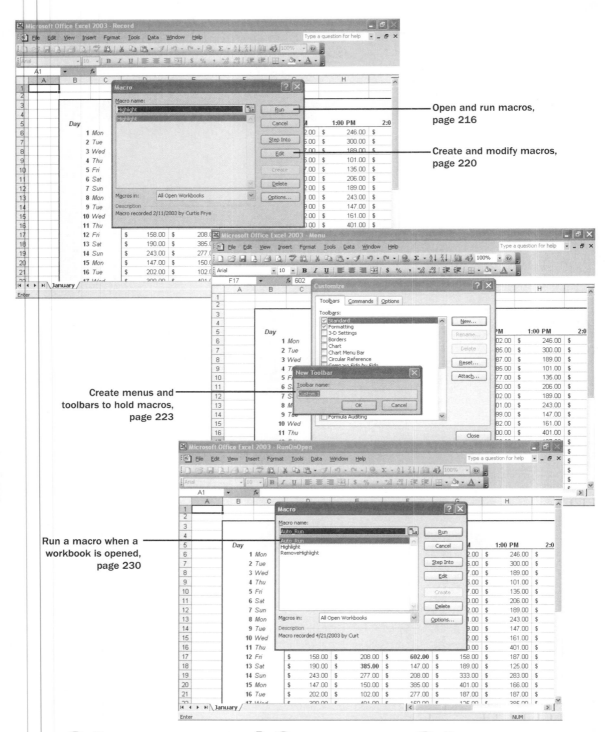

Open and run macros,
page 216

Create and modify macros,
page 220

Create menus and
toolbars to hold macros,
page 223

Run a macro when a
workbook is opened,
page 230

*Chapter 12 at a Glance*

# 12 Automating Repetitive Tasks with Macros

**In this chapter you will learn to:**

✔ Open and run macros.

✔ Create and modify macros.

✔ Create toolbars and menus to hold macros.

✔ Run a macro when a workbook is opened.

Many tasks you perform in Microsoft Excel, such as entering sales data for a particular day or adding formulas to a worksheet, either are done once or, like changing the format of a cell range, can be repeated quickly using available tools in Excel. However, you will often perform one or two tasks frequently that require a lot of steps to accomplish. For example, you might have a number of cells in a worksheet that contain important data you use quite often in presentations to your colleagues.

Rather than go through a lengthy series of steps to highlight the cells with the important information, you can create a *macro*, or series of recorded actions, to perform the steps for you. Once you have created a macro, you can run, edit, or delete it as needed.

Under the standard Excel interface, you run and edit macros using the items on the **Tools** menu. You can make your macros easier to access by creating new toolbars or menus with buttons or menu items to which you can assign macros. If you run a macro to highlight specific cells in a worksheet every time you show that worksheet to a colleague, you can save time by adding a toolbar button that runs a macro to highlight the cells for you.

Another handy feature of Excel macros is that you can create macros that run when a workbook is opened. For example, you might want to ensure that no cells in a worksheet are highlighted when the worksheet opens. You can create a macro that removes any special formatting from your worksheet cells when its workbook opens, allowing you to emphasize the data you want as you present the information to your colleagues.

In this chapter, you'll learn how to open, run, create, and modify macros; create toolbars and menus to hold macros; define macro security settings; and run a macro when a workbook is opened.

---

**See Also**   Do you need a quick refresher on the topics in this chapter? See the quick reference entries on pages liv–lvii.

---

**Important**   Before you can use the practice files in this chapter, be sure you install them from the book's companion CD-ROM to their default location. See "Using the Book's CD-ROM" on page xi for more information.

# Introducing Macros

After you have worked with your Excel documents for a while, you will probably discover some series of actions you perform repeatedly. While many of these actions, such as saving your changes or printing, can be accomplished quickly, some sequences involve many steps and take time to accomplish by hand. For example, you might want to highlight a number of cells in a worksheet to emphasize an aspect of your data. Rather than highlight the cells by hand every time you present your findings, you can create a macro, or series of automated actions, to do the highlighting for you.

*Microsoft*
*Office*
*Specialist*

The best way to get an idea of how macros work is to examine an existing macro. To do that, on the **Tools** menu, point to **Macro**, and click **Macros** to open the **Macro** dialog box. You can also open the **Macro** dialog box by pressing [Alt]+[F8].

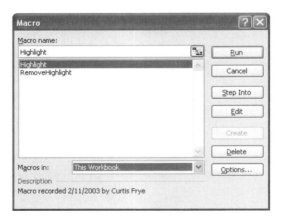

**Note**   In the **Macro** dialog box, you can display the macros available in other workbooks by clicking the **Macros in** box and selecting a workbook by name or by selecting **All Open Workbooks**, which will display every macro in any open workbook. If you select either of those choices, the macro names displayed will include the name of the workbook in which the macro is stored. Clicking **This Workbook** displays the macros in the active workbook.

If you have trouble running macros in your workbooks because of your security settings, you can change the settings by opening the **Tools** menu, pointing to **Macros**, and clicking **Security**. On the page that appears, click the **Medium** option button and then click **OK.**

Choosing the **Medium** macro security level means a dialog box asking if you want to enable macros will appear whenever you start to open a workbook that contains macros. Clicking **Enable Macros** will allow you to run the macros in the workbook, clicking **Disable Macros** will prevent the macros from being run, and clicking **Cancel** will prevent the workbook from being opened. The **High** setting means Excel will enable only digitally signed macros from trusted sources, while the **Low** setting means Excel will automatically enable any macros, regardless of the source.

**Warning**    Because it is possible to write macros that act as viruses, potentially causing harm to your computer and spreading copies of themselves to other computers, you should never choose the **Low** security setting, even if you have virus checking software installed on your computer.

The **Macro** dialog box has a list of macros in your workbook. To view the code behind a macro, you click the macro's name and then click **Edit**.

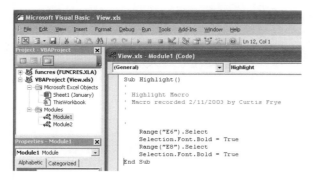

Excel macros are recorded using the Visual Basic for Applications programming language (VBA). The preceding graphic shows the code for a macro that highlights cell E6, changes the cell's formatting to bold, and then repeats the process for cell E8. After introductory information about the macro (its name and when it was created), the first line of the macro identifies the cell range to be selected (in this case, cell E6). After the cell is selected, the next line of the macro changes the formatting of the selected cell to bold, which has the same result as clicking a cell and then clicking the **Bold** button on the Formatting toolbar. The next two lines of the macro repeat the process for cell E8.

To see how the macro works, you can open the **Macro** dialog box, click the name of the macro you want to examine, and then click **Step Into**. The Microsoft Visual Basic Editor appears, with a highlight around the instruction that will be executed next. To execute an instruction, you press [F8]. The highlight moves to the next instruction, and your worksheet changes to reflect the action that resulted from executing the preceding instruction.

Effect of previous instruction

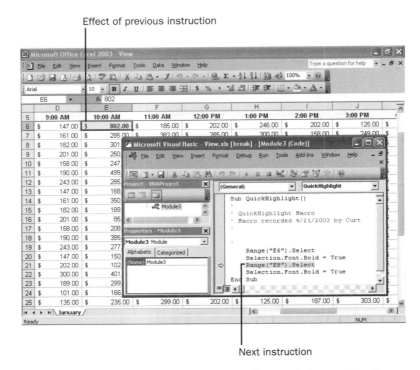

Next instruction

You can run a macro without stopping after each instruction by opening the **Macro** dialog box, clicking the macro to run, and then clicking **Run**. Usually you'll run the macro this way; after all, the point of using macros is to save time.

In this exercise, you examine a macro in the Microsoft Visual Basic Editor, move through the macro one step at a time, and then run the macro without stopping.

START: Microsoft Excel.

**1** On the **Tools** menu, point to **Macro** and then click **Security**.

The **Security** dialog box appears.

**2** Select the **Medium** option button and click **OK**.

The **Security** dialog box disappears.

**3** On the **File** menu, click **Open**, navigate to the *SBS\Excel\Macros* folder, click **View**, and click **Open**. If necessary, click **Enable Macros** to open the workbook.

**4** On the **Tools** menu, point to **Macro** and then click **Macros**.

The **Macro** dialog box appears.

**5** In the **Macro name** section, click **Highlight** and then click **Edit**.

The Microsoft Visual Basic Editor opens, with the code for the **Highlight** macro displayed in the Module1 (Code) window.

**6** Click the Visual Basic Editor **Close** button.

The Microsoft Visual Basic Editor closes, and View.xls reappears.

**7** On the **Tools** menu, point to **Macro** and then click **Macros**.

The **Macro** dialog box appears.

**8** In the **Macro name** section, click **Highlight** and then click **Step Into**.

The Microsoft Visual Basic Editor opens, with the first line of the macro highlighted.

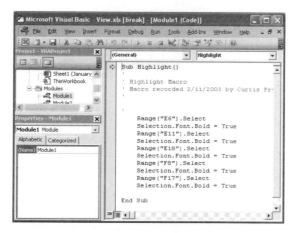

**9** Right-click the taskbar, and then, from the shortcut menu that appears, click **Tile Windows Vertically**.

The Excel and Microsoft Visual Basic Editor windows appear.

**10** Click the Microsoft Visual Basic Editor title bar, and then press F8.

In the Microsoft Visual Basic Editor, the next step in the macro is highlighted.

**11** Press F8.

In the Microsoft Visual Basic Editor, the next step in the macro is highlighted. In the Excel window, cell E6 is highlighted.

**12** Press ⒡.

In the Microsoft Visual Basic Editor, the next step in the macro is highlighted. In the Excel window, the value in cell E6 appears in bold.

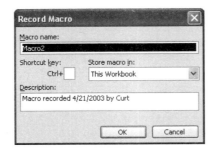

**13** In the Microsoft Visual Basic Editor, click the **Close** button. Click **OK** to close the dialog box that appears.

Close

The editor closes.

**14** On the **Tools** menu, point to **Macro** and then click **Macros**.

The **Macro** dialog box appears.

**15** If necessary, in the **Macro name** section, click **Highlight**.

**16** Click **Run**.

The **Macro** dialog box disappears, and Excel runs the macro. The contents of cells E6, E11, E18, F8, and F17 appear in bold type.

**17** On the Standard toolbar, click the **Save** button to save your work.

Save

CLOSE: View.

# Creating and Modifying Macros

The first step in creating a macro is to plan every step of the process you want to automate. Computers today are quite fast, so adding an extra step that doesn't affect the outcome of a process won't slow you down noticeably, but leaving out a step means you will need to rerecord a macro.

Microsoft
Office
Specialist

Once you have planned your process, you can create a macro by pointing to **Macro** on the **Tools** menu and then clicking **Record New Macro**. When you do, the **Record Macro** dialog box appears.

After you type the name of your macro in the **Macro name** box, click **OK**. The **Record Macro** dialog box disappears, and the **Stop Recording** toolbar appears.

Stop Recording

You can now perform the actions you want Excel to repeat later; when you're done, click the **Stop Recording** button. The **Stop Recording** toolbar disappears, and your macro is added to the list of macros available in your workbook.

To modify an existing macro, you can open it in the Microsoft Visual Basic Editor and add to or change the macro's instructions. If you're not sure how to write the necessary VBA code, you can simply delete the macro and rerecord it. To delete a macro, you open the **Macro** dialog box, click the macro you want to delete, and then click **Delete**.

In this exercise, you record a macro that removes the bold formatting from four cells and then modify the macro to remove the bold formatting from a fifth cell.

OPEN: Record from the *SBS\Excel\Macros* folder.

1   If a warning dialog box appears, click **Enable Macros**.

2   On the **Tools** menu, point to **Macro** and then click **Record New Macro**.

    The **Record Macro** dialog box appears.

3   In the **Macro name** box, delete the existing name, and then type RemoveHighlight.

4   Click **OK**.

    The **Stop Recording** toolbar appears.

Bold

5   Click cell E6, and then, on the Formatting toolbar, click the **Bold** button.

6   Click cell E11, and then, on the Formatting toolbar, click the **Bold** button.

7   Click cell E18, and then, on the Formatting toolbar, click the **Bold** button.

8   Click cell F8, and then, on the Formatting toolbar, click the **Bold** button.

9   On the **Stop Recording** toolbar, click the **Stop Recording** button.

    The **Stop Recording** toolbar disappears.

10  On the **Tools** menu, point to **Macro** and then click **Macros**.

    The **Macro** dialog box appears.

11  In the **Macro name** section, click **RemoveHighlight** and then click **Edit**.

    The Microsoft Visual Basic Editor appears.

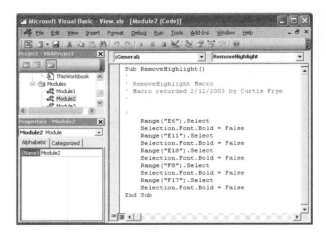

**12** Click at the end of the line just above *End Sub*, press ⌈Enter⌉, and type
Range("F17").Select.

This macro statement selects cell F17.

**Tip** To get more information about Visual Basic for Applications, type **VBA** in the
**Ask A Question** box on the Standard toolbar and click **Get Help for Visual Basic for
Applications** from the list of help topics that appears.

**13** Type Selection.Font.Bold = False, and then press ⌈Enter⌉.

This macro statement removes bold formatting from the selected cell (F17).

**14** On the Standard toolbar, click the **Save** button to save your change.

**15** Click the **Close** button of the Microsoft Visual Basic window.

The Microsoft Visual Basic Editor disappears, and Record.xls appears.

**16** On the **Tools** menu, point to **Macro** and then click **Macros**.

The **Macro** dialog box appears.

**17** Click **Highlight**, and then click **Run**.

The contents of cells E6, E11, E18, F8, and F17 appear in bold type.

**18** On the **Tools** menu, point to **Macro** and then click **Macros**.

The **Macro** dialog box appears.

**19** Click **RemoveHighlight**, and then click **Run**.

The contents of cells E6, E11, E18, F8, and F17 appear in regular type.

**20** On the Standard toolbar, click the **Save** button to save your changes.

CLOSE: Record.

# Creating a Toolbar to Hold Macros

Although you can run any of your macros from the **Macro** dialog box, the ability to run a macro by clicking a toolbar button makes your worksheets much easier to use, especially for colleagues with relatively little experience using Excel. To create a toolbar to host your macros, on the **Tools** menu, click **Customize** to open the **Customize** dialog box.

**Important**   The **Customize** dialog box must be open for you to be able to change any of your toolbars or menus.

To create a toolbar in the **Customize** dialog box, you display the **Toolbars** tab page and then click **New**. The **New Toolbar** dialog box appears; type a name for your new toolbar in the space provided, and then click **OK**. Your new toolbar appears next to the **Customize** dialog box.

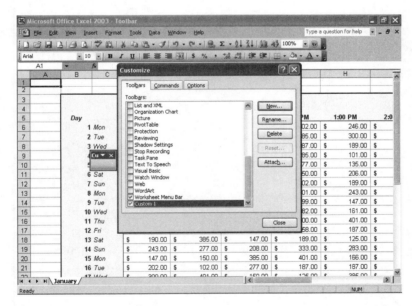

Once you have created the new toolbar, you can assign your macros to it. To do so, you display the **Commands** tab page of the **Customize** dialog box.

On the **Commands** tab page, you pick **Macros** from the list of options in the **Categories** list. Two items will appear in the **Commands** list: **Custom Menu Item** and **Custom Button**. To add a button to your new toolbar, drag the **Custom Button** item to the toolbar.

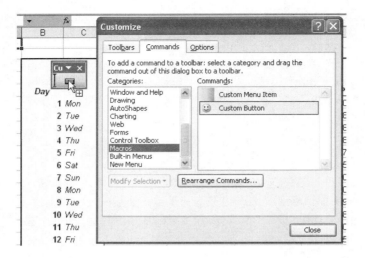

**Tip** When your button is over a place where it can be dropped, the indicator at the lower right of your mouse pointer changes to a plus sign.

After you have added the button to your toolbar, you can assign the macro that the button will run by right-clicking the button and then, from the shortcut menu that appears, clicking **Assign Macro**. The **Assign Macro** dialog box appears; click the macro you want to run when the toolbar button is clicked, and then click **OK**.

After you create a toolbar, Excel will display it whenever you open the workbook in which it was created. If you want, you can hide your toolbar so that only you and colleagues who know the toolbar exists can use it. Right-clicking any toolbar shows a shortcut menu with the names of toolbars available in the active workbook—toolbars currently displayed have a check mark next to their name. To hide a toolbar, click its name to remove the check mark. You can always redisplay the toolbar by right-clicking any toolbar and clicking the toolbar's name from the list that appears.

If you remove the macros you've created from your workbook, or if you don't want to make the macros available on a toolbar, you can delete the toolbar from the **Customize** dialog box. To do so, click the toolbar you want to delete in the **Toolbars** list and then click **Delete**.

**Warning** Be careful! You can delete any **Excel** toolbar. If you accidentally delete a toolbar from the default set, you will have to reinstall Excel to restore it.

If you like, you can customize the button you use to represent your macro. To change the appearance of a toolbar button, you open the **Customize** dialog box, right-click the button you want to change, and then, from the shortcut menu that appears, point to **Change Button Image** to display a set of images you can use for your button.

In this exercise, you create a toolbar to hold your macro, create a button to represent the macro on the toolbar, run the macro from the toolbar, and then delete the toolbar.

**OPEN: Toolbar from the *SBS\Excel\Macros* folder.**

**1**   If a warning dialog box appears, click **Enable Macros**.

**2**   On the **Tools** menu, click **Customize**.

The **Customize** dialog box appears.

**3**   If necessary, click the **Toolbars** tab to display the **Toolbars** tab page.

**4**   Click **New**.

The **New Toolbar** dialog box appears.

**5**   In the **Toolbar name** box, type Custom Macros and then click **OK**.

A new toolbar named Custom Macros appears in the workbook window; the toolbar is also listed in the **Toolbars** list of the **Customize** dialog box.

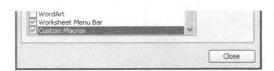

**6**   In the **Customize** dialog box, click the **Commands** tab.

The **Commands** tab page appears.

**7**   In the **Categories** list, click **Macros**.

The **Commands** list changes to reflect your choice.

**8**   Drag the **Custom Button** command to the **Custom Macros** toolbar.

The **Custom** button appears on the **Custom Macros** toolbar.

**9**   On the **Custom Macros** toolbar, right-click the **Custom** button and then, from the shortcut menu that appears, click **Name**.

The text next to the **Name** menu item is highlighted.

**10**   Type Highlight, and then press ⌷Enter⌷.

The menu disappears, and your button is now named Highlight.

**11**   On the **Custom Macros** toolbar, right-click the **Highlight** button, point to **Change button image** on the shortcut menu that appears, and then click the **Up Arrow** button image.

The **Highlight** button image changes to an up arrow.

**12** On the **Custom Macros** toolbar, right-click the **Highlight** button and then, from the shortcut menu that appears, click **Assign Macro**.

The **Assign Macro** dialog box appears.

**13** Click **Highlight** and then click **OK**.

The **Assign Macro** dialog box disappears. Clicking the **Highlight** button on the **Custom Macros** toolbar when the **Customize** dialog box is closed will now run the **Highlight** macro.

**14** In the **Customize** dialog box, click **Close**.

The **Customize** dialog box disappears.

**15** On the **Custom Macros** toolbar, click the **Highlight** button.

The **Highlight** macro runs. The contents of cells E6, E11, E18, F8, and F17 appear in bold type.

**16** Right-click the title bar of the **Custom Macros** toolbar, and then, from the shortcut menu that appears, click **Custom Macros**.

The **Custom Macros** toolbar disappears.

**17** On the **Tools** menu, click **Customize**.

The **Customize** dialog box appears.

**18** If necessary, click the **Toolbars** tab.

**19** In the **Toolbars** list, click **Custom Macros**, click **Delete**, and then click **OK** in the warning dialog box that appears.

The toolbar is deleted.

**20** Click **Close** to close the **Customize** dialog box.

**21** On the Standard toolbar, click the **Save** button to save your work.

CLOSE: Toolbar.

## Creating a Menu to Hold Macros

*Microsoft Office Specialist*

As with toolbars, you can create custom menus to hold your macros. To create a custom menu, you open the **Customize** dialog box to the **Commands** page and then, in the **Categories** list, click **New Menu**. The **New Menu** option appears in the **Commands** list.

To add the new menu to an existing menu bar or toolbar, you drag the **New Menu** command from the **Customize** dialog box to the desired spot.

**Note** When your menu is over a place where it can be dropped, the indicator at the lower right of your mouse pointer changes to a plus sign.

Once the menu is in place, you can rename it and add items to it. You can rename a menu by right-clicking the menu head and choosing **Name** from the shortcut menu that appears. The shortcut menu will stay open, and the menu's name will be high-lighted. Just type the new name and press [Enter] to rename your menu.

To add a macro to a menu, click the **Macros** item in the **Categories** list of the **Customize** dialog box to display the macros available in the current workbook. When you add a macro to a menu, you need to create a new menu item and then assign the macro to the new item. You can add a new menu item to a menu by clicking the **Macros** item in the **Categories** list and then, from the **Commands** list, dragging **Custom Menu Item** to your menu.

When you get **Custom Menu Item** to the menu, hold the mouse pointer over the menu head until a small gray box appears below the menu head.

Drag the mouse pointer to that gray box to add the item to the menu. Once you have added the item to the menu, you can rename it by right-clicking it, choosing **Name** from the shortcut menu that appears, and then typing the name in the space provided. To assign a macro to the menu item, right-click the menu item, choose **Assign**

**Macro** from the shortcut menu that appears, and then choose the macro in the **Assign Macro** dialog box.

Whether you create a toolbar or a menu is entirely up to you because there is no functional difference between running a macro by clicking a toolbar button and clicking a menu item. Remember, clicking the **Save** button on the Standard toolbar and clicking **Save** on the **File** menu perform the same task!

If you remove the macros you've created from your workbook, or if you don't want to make the macros available on a menu, you can delete the menu while the **Customize** dialog box is open. To do so, right-click the menu head and then, from the shortcut menu that appears, click **Delete.** If you want to delete a menu item, but not the entire menu, right-click the item and click **Delete.**

**Warning** Be careful! You can delete any Excel menu. If you accidentally delete a menu from the default set, you will have to reinstall Excel to restore it.

In this exercise, you create and name a menu, add an item to that menu and name the item, and then assign a macro to be run when the menu item is clicked. You then delete the custom menu.

OPEN: Menu from the *SBS\Excel\Macros* folder.

1 If a warning dialog box appears, click **Enable Macros.**

2 On the **Tools** menu, click **Customize.**

The **Customize** dialog box appears.

3 If necessary, click the **Commands** tab to display the **Commands** tab page.

4 In the **Categories** list, click **New Menu.**

**New Menu** appears in the **Commands** list.

5 Drag **New Menu** to the end of the main menu bar.

An insertion point appears at the position on the main menu bar where the new menu will be inserted. When you release the mouse button, the new menu appears on the main menu bar.

6 Right-click the **New Menu** heading, and then, from the shortcut menu that appears, click **Name.**

The shortcut menu stays open, with the new menu's name highlighted on the shortcut menu.

7 Type **Custom Macros,** and then press [Enter].

The new menu's name changes to Custom Macros.

**8**   In the **Categories** list of the **Customize** dialog box, click **Macros**.

The contents of the **Commands** list change to reflect your choice.

**9**   In the **Commands** list, drag the **Custom Menu Item** command to the **Custom Macros** menu head. When a box appears under the **Custom Macros** menu head, drag **Custom Menu Item** onto it.

The **Custom Menu Item** command appears on the **Custom Macros** menu.

**10**  On the **Custom Macros** menu, right-click **Custom Menu Item** and then, from the shortcut menu that appears, click **Name**.

The shortcut menu stays open, with the menu item's name highlighted on the shortcut menu.

**11**  Type Highlight, and then press ⟨Enter⟩.

The name of the menu item changes to Highlight.

**12**  On the **Custom Macros** menu, right-click **Highlight** and then, from the shortcut menu that appears, click **Assign Macro**.

The **Assign Macro** dialog box appears.

**13**  In the **Macro name** box, click **Highlight** and then click **OK**.

Excel assigns the **Highlight** macro to the selected menu item and closes the **Assign Macro** dialog box.

**14**  Click **Close** to close the **Customize** dialog box.

**15**  On the **Custom Macros** menu, click **Highlight**.

The **Highlight** macro runs. The contents of cells E6, E11, E18, F8, and F17 appear in bold type.

**16**  On the **Tools** menu, click **Customize**.

The **Customize** dialog box appears.

**17**  Right-click the **Custom Macros** menu head, and then, from the shortcut menu that appears, click **Delete**.

The **Custom Macros** menu is deleted.

**18** In the **Customize** dialog box, click **Close**.

The **Customize** dialog box disappears.

**19** On the Standard toolbar, click the **Save** button to save your work.

CLOSE: Menu.

# Running a Macro When a Workbook Is Opened

*Microsoft*
*Office*
*Specialist*

One advantage of writing Excel macros in VBA is that you can have Excel run a macro whenever a workbook is opened. For example, if you use a worksheet for presentations, you can create macros that render the contents of selected cells in bold type, italics, or different typefaces to set the data apart from data in neighboring cells. If you should close a workbook without removing that formatting, however, the contents of your workbook will have highlights when you open it. While this is not a catastrophe, returning the workbook to its original formatting will take only a few seconds to accomplish.

Rather than run a macro by hand, or even from a toolbar button or a menu, you can have Excel run a macro whenever a workbook is opened. The trick to making that happen is in the name you give the macro. Whenever Excel finds a macro with a name starting with *Auto_* (*Auto* followed by an underscore), it runs the macro when the workbook to which it is attached is opened.

In this exercise, you create a macro that will run whenever someone opens the workbook to which it is attached.

OPEN: RunOnOpen from the *SBS\Excel\Macros* folder.

**1** If a warning dialog box appears, click **Enable Macros**.

RunOnOpen.xls opens. Notice that the contents of cells E6, E11, E18, F8, and F17 appear in bold.

**2** On the **Tools** menu, point to **Macro** and then click **Record New Macro**.

The **Record Macro** dialog box appears.

**3** In the **Macro name** box, type Auto_Open and then click **OK**.

The **Record Macro** dialog box disappears, and the **Stop Recording** toolbar appears.

**4** Select the cell range D6:O36, and then, on the **Format** menu, click **Cells**.

The **Format Cells** dialog box appears.

**5** If necessary, click the **Font** tab.

**6** In the **Font style** box, click **Regular** and then click **OK**.

The **Format Cells** dialog box disappears, and the contents of cells E6, E11, E18, F8, and F17 appear in regular type.

Stop Recording

Save

Close

**7** On the **Stop Recording** toolbar, click the **Stop Recording** button.

Excel stops recording your macro, and the **Stop Recording** toolbar disappears.

**8** On the **Tools** menu, point to **Macro** and then click **Macros**.

The **Macro** dialog box appears.

**9** Click **Highlight**, and then click **Run**.

The contents of cells E6, E11, E18, F8, and F17 appear in bold type.

**10** On the Standard toolbar, click the **Save** button to save your work.

**11** Click the **Close** button to close RunOnOpen.xls.

**12** Open the **File** menu, and then click **RunOnOpen.xls**. If a warning dialog box appears, click **Enable Macros**.

RunOnOpen.xls opens, with the contents of cells E6, E11, E18, F8, and F17 appearing in regular type.

**13** On the Standard toolbar, click the **Save** button to save your work.

**14** Click the **Close** button to close RunOnOpen.xls.

# Key Points

- Macros are handy tools you can use to perform repetitive tasks quickly, such as inserting blocks of text.

- You don't have to be a programmer to use macros; you can record your actions and have Excel save them as a macro.

- Always keep control over whether you want to enable macros in a particular workbook by setting your security level to *Medium* or *High*.

- If you're curious about what a macro looks like, you can display it in the Visual Basic Editor. If you know a little VBA, or if you just want to experiment, feel free to modify the macro code and see what happens.

- You can create toolbar buttons or menu items that, when clicked, will run a macro.

- Starting a macro name with *Auto_* tells Excel to run the macro when it opens the workbook to which the macro is attached.

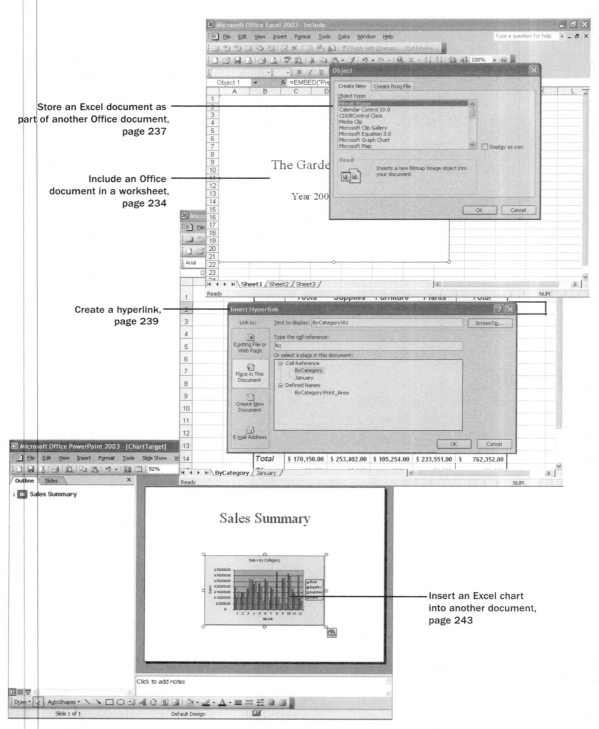

Store an Excel document as part of another Office document, page 237

Include an Office document in a worksheet, page 234

Create a hyperlink, page 239

Insert an Excel chart into another document, page 243

*Chapter 13 at a Glance*

# 13 Working with Other Microsoft Office Programs

**In this chapter you will learn to:**

✔ Include an Office document in a worksheet.

✔ Store an Excel document as part of another Office document.

✔ Create a hyperlink.

✔ Paste an Excel chart into another document.

By itself, Microsoft Excel is a powerful program that gives you a broad range of tools so that you can store, present, and summarize your financial data. Other Microsoft Office programs extend your capabilities even further, letting you create databases, presentations, written reports, and custom Web pages through which you can organize and communicate your data in print and over networks.

A tremendous benefit of Excel being part of the Office 2003 suite is that the programs can interact in many useful ways. For example, you can include a file created with another Office program in an Excel worksheet. If you use Microsoft Word to write a quick note on why tool sales increased significantly in January, you can include the report in your workbook. Similarly, you can include your Excel workbooks in documents created with other Office programs. If you want to copy only part of a workbook, such as a chart, to another Office document, you can do that as well.

One of the hallmarks of the World Wide Web is the *hyperlink*, or connection from a document to a place in the same file or to another file anywhere on a network the user's computer can reach. You can create hyperlinks in Excel documents, connecting to other cells or worksheets in the active workbook, to other Office files anywhere on your computer, or to files anywhere else on your company's intranet or the Internet.

In this chapter, you'll learn how to include an Office document in a worksheet, store an Excel workbook as part of another Office document, create hyperlinks, and paste an Excel chart into another document.

---

**See Also**  Do you need a quick refresher on the topics in this chapter? See the quick reference entries on pages lvii–lviii.

---

**233**

**Important** Before you can use the practice files in this chapter, be sure you install them from the book's companion CD-ROM to their default location. See "Using the Book's CD-ROM" on page xi for more information.

# Including an Office Document in an Excel Worksheet

A benefit of working with Excel is that, because Excel is part of the Microsoft Office program suite, it is possible to combine data from Excel and other Office programs to create informative presentations. Just like combining data from more than one Excel document, combining information from other Office files with an Excel workbook entails either pasting another Office document into an Excel workbook or creating a link between a workbook and the other document.

There are two advantages to creating a link between your Excel workbook and another file. The first benefit is that linking to the other file, as opposed to copying the entire file into your workbook, keeps your Excel workbook small. If the workbook is copied to another drive or computer, you can maintain the link by copying the linked file along with the Excel workbook, re-creating the link if the linked file is on the same network as the Excel workbook. It is also possible to use the workbook without the linked file. The second benefit of linking to another file is that any changes in the file to which you link will be reflected in your Excel workbook.

**Tip** Usually, you must close and reopen your Excel workbook for any changes in the linked document to appear in your workbook. The exception to this rule occurs when you open the file for editing from within your Excel workbook (as discussed later in this chapter).

You create a link between an Excel workbook and another Office document by clicking **Object** on the **Insert** menu to display the **Object** dialog box. Once the **Object** dialog box appears, click the **Create from File** tab.

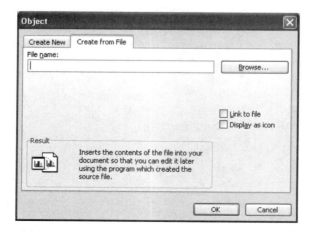

The **Create from File** tab page appears. Clicking the **Browse** button opens the **Browse** dialog box, from which you can navigate to the folder with the file you want to link to Excel. Once you locate the file, double-clicking it closes the **Browse** dialog box and adds the file's name and path to the **File name** box of the **Object** dialog box. To create a link to the file, select the **Link to file** check box and click **OK**. The file appears in your workbook.

If you want to link a file to your workbook but don't want the file's image to take up much space on the screen, you can also select the **Display as icon** check box. After you select the file and click **OK**, the file will be represented by the same icon used to represent it in **My Computer**.

Once you have linked a file to your Excel workbook, you can edit the file by right-clicking its image in your workbook and then, from the shortcut menu that appears, pointing to **Presentation Object** and clicking **Edit**. The file will open in its native application (in this case, Microsoft PowerPoint). When you're done editing the file, your changes will be reflected in your workbook.

**Note**   The specific menu item you point to changes to reflect the program used to create the file to which you want to link. For a Word document, for example, the menu item you point to is **Document Object**.

In this exercise, you link a PowerPoint presentation showing a yearly business summary to an Excel workbook and then edit the presentation from within Excel.

**Important**   You must have PowerPoint installed on your computer to complete this exercise.

OPEN: Include from the *SBS\Excel\OtherPrograms* folder.

1   On the **Insert** menu, click **Object**.

The **Object** dialog box appears.

2   Click the **Create from File** tab to display the **Create from File** tab page.

3   Click **Browse**.

The **Browse** dialog box appears.

4   Navigate to the OtherPrograms folder, and double-click **YearEndSummary.ppt**.

The **Browse** dialog box closes, and the **Object** dialog box reappears.

**5** Select the **Link to file** check box, and then click **OK**.

Excel creates a link to the external file, and the file appears in the workbook.

**Tip** Adding the link means that changes in the external file will be reflected in the worksheet.

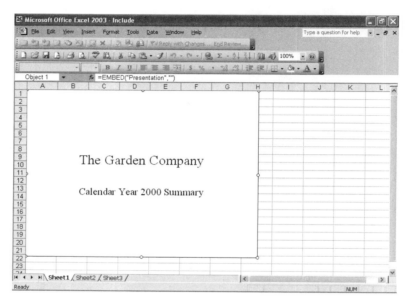

**6** Right-click the presentation, and then, from the shortcut menu that appears, point to **Presentation Object** and then click **Edit**.

The presentation opens in a PowerPoint window.

**7** Click **Year 2000 Summary**.

The text box containing *Year 2000 Summary* is activated.

**8** Click to the left of the text in the box, and type Calendar.

**9** On the Standard toolbar, click the **Save** button.

Save

PowerPoint saves your changes.

**10** Click the **Close** button.

Close

PowerPoint closes, and your change is reflected in Include.xls.

**11** On the Standard toolbar, click the **Save** button to save your work.

CLOSE: Include.

# Storing an Excel Document
# as Part of Another Office Document

In the preceding section of this chapter, you learned how to link to another file from within your Excel workbook. The advantages of linking to another file are that the size of your workbook is kept small and that any changes in the document to which you link will be reflected in your workbook. The disadvantage is that the linked document must be copied along with the workbook, or at least be on a network-accessible computer. If Excel can't find or access the file where the link says it is located, Excel won't be able to display it.

If file size isn't an issue and you want to ensure that the other document will always be available, you can *embed* the file in your workbook. Embedding another file in an Excel workbook means that the entirety of the other file is saved as part of your workbook. Wherever your workbook goes, the embedded file goes along with it. Of course, this file is no longer connected to the original file, so changes in one aren't reflected in the other.

**Important** To view the embedded file, you will need to have the program used to create it installed on the computer where you open the workbook.

You can embed a file in an Excel workbook by following the procedure described in the preceding section, with the exception that the **Link to file** check box should not be selected.

It is also possible to embed your Excel workbooks in other Office documents. In PowerPoint, for example, you can embed an Excel file in a presentation by clicking **Object** on the PowerPoint **Insert** menu to display the **Insert Object** dialog box.

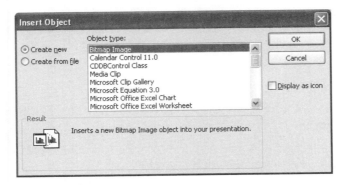

When the **Insert Object** dialog box appears, select the **Create from file** option button. To identify the file you want to embed, click the **Browse** button and then, in the **Browse** dialog box that appears, navigate to the folder where the file is stored and double-click it. The **Browse** dialog box disappears, and the file appears in the **File name** box. Click **OK** to embed your workbook in the presentation.

If you want to embed a workbook in a file created with another program but don't want the worksheet to take up much space on the screen, you can select the **Display as icon** check box. After you select the file to embed and click **OK**, the file will be represented by the same icon used to represent it in **My Computer**. Double-clicking the icon opens the embedded document in its original application.

To edit the embedded Excel workbook, right-click the workbook (or the icon representing it) and then, from the shortcut menu that appears, point to **Worksheet Object** and click **Edit**. The workbook opens for editing. When you are done making your changes, you can click anywhere outside the workbook to return to the presentation.

In this exercise, you embed an Excel workbook containing sales data in a PowerPoint presentation and then change the formatting of the workbook from within PowerPoint.

**Important**    You must have PowerPoint installed on your computer to complete this exercise.

1    Double-click **My Computer,** and navigate to the *C:\SBS\Excel\OtherPrograms* directory.

The contents of the *C:\SBS\Excel\OtherPrograms* directory appear.

2    Double-click **Worksheet.ppt**.

Worksheet.ppt opens.

3    On the **Insert** menu, click **Object**.

The **Insert Object** dialog box appears.

4    Select the **Create from file** option button.

The **Insert Object** dialog box changes to reflect your choice.

5    Click the **Browse** button.

The **Browse** dialog box appears.

6    Navigate to the *C:\SBS\Excel\OtherPrograms* directory, and then double-click **SalesByCategory.xls**.

The **Browse** dialog box closes, and C:\SBS\Excel\OtherPrograms\ SalesByCategory.xls appears in the **File** box.

7    Click **OK**.

The worksheet that was active when SalesByCategory.xls was last closed appears in the presentation.

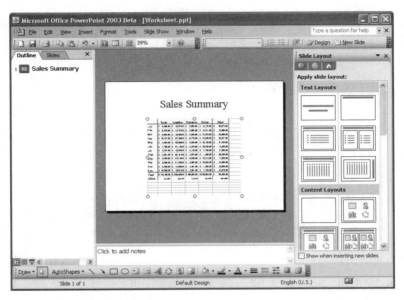

8      Right-click the worksheet, and then, from the shortcut menu that appears, point to **Worksheet Object** and then click **Edit**.

The workbook opens for editing.

9      Select cells D15:H15, and then, on the Formatting toolbar, click the **Bold** button.

The contents of cells D15:H15 appear without bold formatting.

10    Click any blank spot on the presentation to deactivate the included workbook.

11    On the Standard toolbar, click the **Save** button to save your work.

CLOSE: Worksheet.ppt and PowerPoint.

# Creating a Hyperlink

*Microsoft Office Specialist*

One of the hallmarks of the World Wide Web is that documents published on the Web can have references, or hyperlinks, to points in the same document or to other Web documents. A hyperlink functions much like a link between two cells or between two files, but hyperlinks can reach any computer on the Web, not just those on a corporate network. Hyperlinks that haven't been clicked usually appear as underlined blue text, and followed hyperlinks appear as underlined purple text, but those settings can be changed.

| | | |
|---|---|---|
| Nov | $ 18,208.00 | $ 14,408.00 |
| Dec | $ 30,805.00 | $ 10,031.00 |
| *Total* | $ 170,150.00 | $ 253,402.00 |
| *Share* | 22.32% | 33.24% |
| | Followed | Unfollowed |

To create a hyperlink, right-click the cell in which you want to insert the hyperlink and then, from the shortcut menu that appears, click **Hyperlink**. The **Insert Hyperlink** dialog box appears.

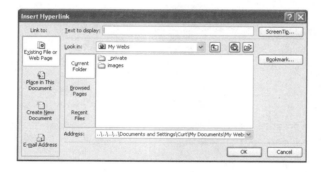

**Tip**    You can also open the **Insert Hyperlink** dialog box by pressing Ctrl+K.

You can choose one of four types of targets for your hyperlink: an existing file or Web page, a place in the current document, a new document you create on the spot, or an e-mail address.

**Tip**    The default target for the **Insert Hyperlink** dialog box is an existing file or Web page.

To create a hyperlink to another file or Web page, you can use the **Look in** box's navigation tool to locate the file. If you recently opened the file or Web page to which you want to link, you can click either the **Browsed Pages** or the **Recent Files** button to display the Web pages or files in your History list.

If you want to create a hyperlink to another place in the current Excel workbook, you click the **Place in This Document** button to display a list of available targets in the current workbook.

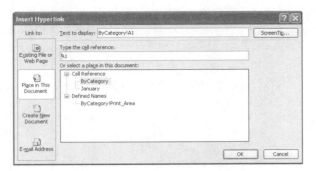

To select the worksheet to which you want to refer, you click the worksheet name in the **Or select a place in this document** box. When you do, a 3-D reference with the name of the worksheet and cell A1 on that worksheet appears in the **Text to display** box.

If you want to refer to a specific cell on a worksheet, click the worksheet's name in the **Or select a place in this document** box, and then change the cell reference in the **Type the cell reference** box.

You can also create hyperlinks that generate e-mail messages to an address of your choice. To create this type of hyperlink, which is called a *mailto* hyperlink, click the **E-mail Address** button.

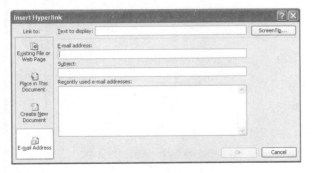

In the dialog box that appears, you can type the recipient's e-mail address in the **E-mail address** box and the subject line for messages sent via this hyperlink in the **Subject** box.

**Tip** If you use Outlook or Outlook Express as your e-mail program, a list of recently used addresses will appear in the **Recently used e-mail addresses** box. You can insert any of those addresses in the **E-mail address** box by clicking the address.

When the hyperlink is clicked, the user's default e-mail program will open and a new e-mail message will be created. The e-mail will be addressed to the address you entered in the **E-mail address** box and the subject will be set to the text you typed in the **Subject** box.

Regardless of the type of hyperlink you create, you can specify the text you want to represent the hyperlink in your worksheet. You type that text in the **Text to display** box. When you click **OK**, the text you type there will appear in your worksheet, formatted as a hyperlink.

**Tip**   If you leave the **Text to display** box empty, the actual link will appear in your worksheet.

You can edit an existing hyperlink by clicking the cell containing the hyperlink and then, from the shortcut menu that appears, clicking **Edit Hyperlink**. You can also click **Open Hyperlink** to go to the target document or create a new e-mail message, or click **Remove Hyperlink** to delete the hyperlink.

**Tip**   If you delete a hyperlink from a cell, the text from the **Text to display** box remains in the cell, but it no longer functions as a hyperlink.

In this exercise, you create a hyperlink to another document and then a second hyperlink to a different location in the current workbook.

OPEN: Hyperlink from the *SBS\Excel\OtherPrograms* folder.

**1**   Right-click cell D17, and then, from the shortcut menu that appears, click **Hyperlink**.

The **Insert Hyperlink** dialog box appears.

**2**   If necessary, click the **Existing File or Web Page** button.

**3**   Navigate to the *C:\SBS\Excel\OtherPrograms* folder.

**4**   Click **ProductList.xls**.

**5**   In the **Text to display** box, type Product List and then click **OK**.

A hyperlink with the text *Product List* appears in cell D17.

| Oct | $ 5,689.00 | $ 31,763.00 |
|------|------------|-------------|
| Nov | $ 18,208.00 | $ 14,408.00 |
| Dec | $ 30,805.00 | $ 10,031.00 |
| Total | $ 170,150.00 | $ 253,402.00 |
| Share | 22.32% | 33.24% |
|  | Product List |  |

**6** Right-click cell I2, and then, from the shortcut menu that appears, click **Hyperlink**.

The **Insert Hyperlink** dialog box appears.

**7** Click the **Place in This Document** button.

The **Insert Hyperlink** dialog box changes to reflect your choice.

**8** In the **Or select a place in this document** box, click **January**.

**9** In the **Text to display box**, type January details and then click **OK**.

A hyperlink with the text *January details* appears in cell I2.

**10** Right-click cell I2, and click **Edit Hyperlink**.

The **Edit Hyperlink** dialog box appears.

**11** In the **Text to display box**, type January sales and then click **OK**.

The text displayed in cell I2 changes to *January sales*.

**12** Click the hyperlink in cell I2.

The **January** worksheet appears.

**13** On the Standard toolbar, click the **Save** button to save your work.

CLOSE: Hyperlink.

# Pasting a Chart into Another Document

A final way to include objects from one workbook in another workbook is to copy the object you want to share and then paste it into its new location. One object type for which this ability is particularly handy is chart images. You could copy the worksheet with the data used for a chart and then re-create the chart in its new location, but if you just want to copy the image of the chart in its current form to another document, simply right-click the chart image, click **Copy** from the shortcut menu that appears, and then paste the image into the other document.

In this exercise, you copy a chart image containing sales information to the Clipboard and paste the image into a PowerPoint presentation.

**OPEN: PasteChart** from the *SBS\Excel\OtherPrograms* folder.

**1** Right-click a blank spot on the chart, and then, from the shortcut menu that appears, click **Copy** to copy the chart image to the Clipboard.

**2** On the Windows desktop, double-click **My Computer**, navigate to the *C:\SBS\Excel\OtherPrograms* directory, and then double-click **ChartTarget.ppt**.

ChartTarget.ppt opens in PowerPoint.

**3** Right-click a blank spot on the active slide, and from the shortcut menu that appears, click **Paste**.

The chart appears on the slide.

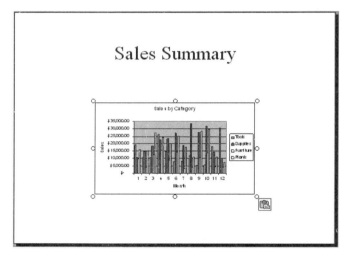

**4** On the Standard toolbar, click the **Save** button to save the presentation.

**5** In PowerPoint, open the **File** menu and click **Exit**.

PowerPoint closes.

**6** In PasteChart.xls, on the Standard toolbar, click the **Save** button to save any changes.

**CLOSE: PasteChart.**

# Key Points

- Excel is a versatile program. You can exchange data between Excel and quite a few other programs in just a few steps.

- One benefit of Excel being part of the Office program suite is that you can embed Excel worksheets in other Office documents, and embed other Office documents (such as PowerPoint presentations) in Excel workbooks.

- Excel works smoothly with the Web; adding hyperlinks to Web pages, other documents, or specific locations in the current workbook is possible through the **Insert Hyperlink** dialog box.

- Once you've created a hyperlink, you can change any part of it.

- Excel is probably the easiest Office program in which to create charts. Once you've created a chart in Excel, you can paste it directly into another Office document.

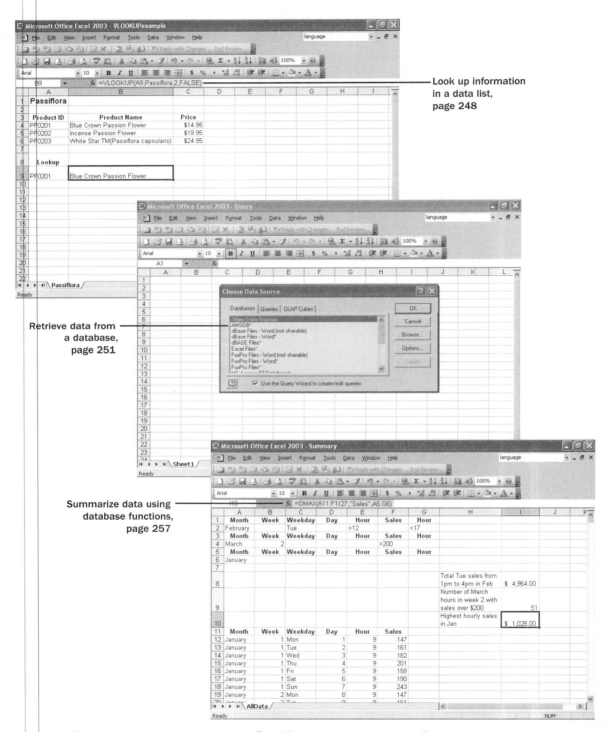

Look up information in a data list, page 248

Retrieve data from a database, page 251

Summarize data using database functions, page 257

*Chapter 14 at a Glance*

# 14 Working with Database Data

**In this chapter you will learn to:**

✔ Look up information in a data list.

✔ Retrieve data from a database.

✔ Summarize data using database functions.

All of the programs in the Microsoft Office 2003 suite work well together, but two programs that have a particularly strong synergy are Microsoft Excel and Microsoft Access. Access, which lets you create and manage databases, and Excel both work with lists of data. In Excel, that data is often stored in complex lists such as PivotTables, but the data used to create PivotTables and other data lists can be represented as a series of rows in a worksheet.

Excel does have a capability you might expect to find only in a database program—the ability to have a user type a value in a cell and have Excel look in a named range to find a corresponding value. For instance, you can have a two-column named range with one column displaying the ISBN of a book and the second column displaying the title of the same book. By using a VLOOKUP formula that references the named range, you can let colleagues using your workbook type an ISBN in a cell and have the name of the book with that ISBN appear in the cell with the formula.

If you have data in a database that you'd like to bring into Excel, you can create a *query*, or statement that locates database records that meet specific criteria, to locate the desired data. Similarly, if you have a data list in a worksheet that is structured in the same way as a database table, you can use the database functions built into Excel to query the data list and summarize the data it contains.

In this chapter, you'll learn how to look up information in a data list, retrieve data from a database, and summarize information in an Excel list using database functions.

---

**See Also**   Do you need a quick refresher on the topics in this chapter? See the quick reference entries on pages lviii–lx.

---

 **Important**   Before you can use the practice files in this chapter, be sure you install them from the book's companion CD-ROM to their default location. See "Using the Book's CD-ROM" on page xi for more information.

# Looking Up Information in a Data List

Whenever you create a worksheet that holds information about a list of distinct items, such as products offered for sale by a company, you should ensure that at least one column in the list contains a unique value that distinguishes that row (and the item the row represents) from every other row in the list. Assigning each row a column with a unique value means that you can associate data in one worksheet with data in another worksheet. For example, if every customer is assigned a unique identification number, you can store a customer's contact information in one worksheet and all of that customer's orders in another worksheet, and be able to associate the customer's orders and contact information without writing the contact information in a worksheet every time the customer places an order.

In the case of products sold by The Garden Company, the column with those unique values, or *primary key* column, is the Product ID column.

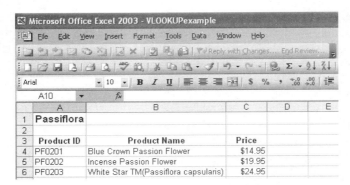

If you know a product's Product ID, it's no trouble to look through a list of 20 or 30 products to find the product represented by a particular ID. If, however, you have a list of several hundred products, looking through the list to find a product would take quite a bit of time. Instead, you can use the VLOOKUP function to let your colleagues type a Product ID in a cell and have the corresponding product information appear in another cell.

The VLOOKUP function finds a value in the leftmost column of a named range and then returns the value from the specified cell to the right of the cell with the found value. A properly formed VLOOKUP function has four arguments (data that is passed to the function), as shown in the following definition: *=VLOOKUP(lookup_value, table_array, col_index_num, range_lookup)*. The following table summarizes the values Excel expects for each of these arguments.

| Argument | Expected Value |
|---|---|
| lookup_value | The value to be found in the first column of the named range specified by the table_array argument. The lookup_value argument can be a value, a cell reference, or a text string. |
| table_array | The multicolumn range or name of the range to be searched. |
| col_index_num | The number of the column in the named range with the value to be returned. |
| range_lookup | A TRUE or FALSE value, indicating whether the function should find an approximate match (TRUE) or an exact match (FALSE) for the lookup_value. If left blank, the default value for this argument is TRUE. |

**Important**   When range_lookup is left blank or set to TRUE, for VLOOKUP to work properly the rows in the named range specified in the table_array argument must be sorted in ascending order based on the values in the leftmost column of the named range.

The VLOOKUP function works a bit differently depending on whether the range_lookup argument is set to TRUE or FALSE. The following list summarizes how the function works based on the value of range_lookup.

- If the *range_lookup* argument is left blank or set to TRUE and VLOOKUP doesn't find an exact match for *lookup_value*, the function returns the largest value that is less than *lookup_value*.

- If the *range_lookup* argument is left blank or set to TRUE and *lookup_value* is smaller than the smallest value in the named range, an *#N/A* error is returned.

- If the *range_lookup* argument is left blank or set to TRUE and *lookup_value* is larger than all values in the named range, the largest value in the named range is returned.

- If the *range_lookup* argument is set to FALSE and VLOOKUP doesn't find an exact match for *lookup_value*, the function returns an *#N/A* error.

As an example of a VLOOKUP function, consider the following worksheet and the accompanying VLOOKUP formula.

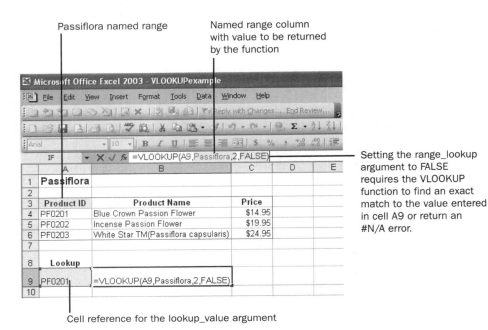

Passiflora named range

Named range column with value to be returned by the function

Setting the range_lookup argument to FALSE requires the VLOOKUP function to find an exact match to the value entered in cell A9 or return an #N/A error.

Cell reference for the lookup_value argument

When you type **PF0202** in cell A9 and press [Enter], the VLOOKUP function searches the first column of the Passiflora named range, finds an exact match, and returns the value *Incense Passion Flower* to cell B9.

**Tip** A related function is HLOOKUP, which matches a value in a column of the first row of a table and returns the value in the specified row number of the same column. For more information on using the HLOOKUP function, type **HLOOKUP** in the **Ask A Question** box.

In this exercise, you create a VLOOKUP function to return the names of products with Product IDs typed in a specific cell.

OPEN: Lookup from the *SBS\Excel\Database* folder.

**1** Select the cell range A4:C18.

**2** Click in the Name box, type ToolList, and then press [Enter].

Excel creates a range, named ToolList, that is made up of cells A4:C18.

**3** In cell E6, type =VLOOKUP(E4, ToolList, 2, FALSE) and press [Enter].

Excel adds the VLOOKUP function to your worksheet. Because there is no value in cell E4, the *#N/A* error code appears in cell E6.

**4** In cell E4, type TL0038 and press [Enter].

*Nutcracker* appears in cell E6.

**5**    In cell E4, type TL3001.

*Pruners, Left-handed* appears in cell E6.

**6**    On the Standard toolbar, click the **Save** button to save your work.

CLOSE: Lookup.

# Retrieving Data from a Database

Just as you can save an Excel workbook as a tab-delimited text file and then open it in other spreadsheet programs, you can also save data lists, or *tables*, that you've created in other database and spreadsheet programs and then import those tables into an Excel worksheet. Excel lets you go one step further, however. In Excel, you can reach directly into an Access, dBASE, Microsoft FoxPro, or Microsoft Visual FoxPro database and retrieve data from that database's tables.

Three steps are required to bring data from a database into Excel: defining a data source, building a query to create a link to that data source, and, if desired, creating a filter to limit the rows that appear in your Excel worksheet.

To define a data source, on the **Data** menu, point to **Import External Data** and then click **New Database Query**. In the **Choose Data Source** dialog box that appears, you click the **<New Data Source>** item and then click **OK** to move to the **Create New Data Source** dialog box. You use the first two controls in the **Create New Data Source** dialog box to name the data source and then pick the *driver* (a program that controls access to a file or device) Excel should use to connect with and open the target database.

Once you have identified the type of database you want to connect with, you click the **Connect** button to open the dialog box from which you select the target database.

**Note**    The name of the dialog box that appears after you click the **Connect** button depends on the database driver you chose earlier.

When you choose Access as the database type to which you want to connect, the **ODBC Microsoft Access Setup** dialog box appears. *ODBC*, which is short for *Open DataBase Connectivity*, is a protocol that facilitates data transfer among databases and related programs (such as spreadsheet programs). Clicking the **Select** button opens a navigation dialog box you can use to pick the database from which you want to import table data. Once you have chosen the target database, you can close the navigation dialog box and click **OK** in the **ODBC Microsoft Access Setup** dialog box to return to the **Create New Data Source** dialog box, where the database's path appears next to the **Connect** button. You can then pick the default table to use in the selected database. Clicking **OK** creates the source, which now appears on the **Databases** tab of the **Choose Data Source** dialog box.

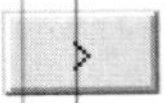

To create a query to pull information from a data source, click the source and then click **OK** to launch the **Query Wizard**. On the **Choose Columns** page of the **Query Wizard**, you can add a column to the data brought into Excel by clicking the column name in the left box and then clicking the **Add** button. The column name appears in the **Columns in your query** box.

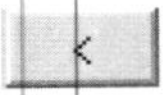

Add

You can remove a specific column by clicking the column name in the **Columns in your query** box and then clicking the **Remove** button, or you can reset your selection completely by clicking the **Remove All** button. When you've selected the columns you want included in your query, click **Next** to move to the **Filter Data** wizard page.

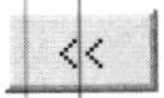

<

Remove

If you want to import the entire table to which you have linked, just click **Next** to move to the next wizard page. If you want to limit the data returned by the query, especially if the table has hundreds of records or more, you can filter the table based on the contents of one or more columns. To filter the query results, click the first column by which you want to filter, click the down arrow in the first box, and click the comparison operator (for example, **is less than or equal to**) for the filter. Then, in the second box, type the value to be used in the comparison. If you select the **Price** column, select **is less than or equal to** in the first box, and then type **50** in the second box, your query will return only products that cost $50.00 or less.

<<

Remove All

**Tip**  You can filter based on more than one criterion. After you've created the first filter, the second field box will become active.

When you're done setting your criteria, click **Next** to move to the **Sort Order** page. On this page, you can specify a sort order to determine the order in which the table rows are imported into your worksheet. To set the criteria, click the **Sort by** down arrow, click the column by which you want to sort the imported rows, and then select the **Ascending** or **Descending** option button to determine the order in which the rows should be arranged. You can sort the imported rows by the contents of more than one column by entering additional criteria in the **Then by** boxes.

When you're done, click **Next** to move to the **Finish** page of the **Query Wizard**, where you can save your query so that you don't have to re-create it every time you want to run it. Product prices change, for instance, so if The Garden Company published a monthly flyer featuring all products that cost less than $30, an employee could save the query that locates those items in the Products database and rerun it every month. To save your query, click the **Save Query** button and then, in the dialog box that appears, type the name of the query in the **File name** box and click **Save**.

To run an existing query, on the **Data** menu, point to **Import External Data** and then click **New Database Query** to open the **Choose Data Source** dialog box. Clicking the **Queries** tab will display all saved queries. To run a saved query, click its name and then click **Open**.

In this exercise, you define a table in an Access database as a data source and then create a query to import data from that source into Excel.

OPEN: Query from the *SBS\Excel\Database* folder.

**1** On the **Data** menu, point to **Import External Data** and then click **New Database Query**.

 Microsoft Query launches, and the **Choose Data Source** dialog box appears.

**2** If necessary, click the **Databases** tab.

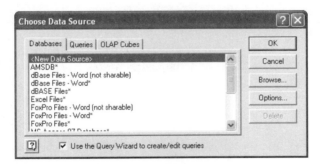

**3** Click **<New Data Source>**, and then click **OK**.

 The **Create New Data Source** dialog box appears.

**4** In the first box, type **Product Information** as the name of the source.

 The second box becomes active.

**5** In the second box, click the down arrow and then, from the list that appears, click **Microsoft Access Driver (\*.mdb)**.

 The **Connect** button becomes active.

**6** Click **Connect**.

The **ODBC Microsoft Access Setup** dialog box appears.

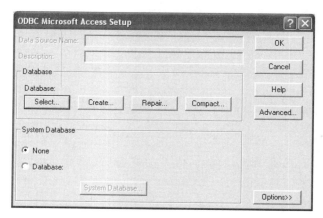

**7** Click **Select**.

The **Select Database** dialog box appears.

**8** Navigate to the *C:\SBS\Excel\Database* folder, click **Products.mdb**, and then click **OK**.

The **Select Database** dialog box disappears, and *C:\SBS\Excel\Database\Products.mdb* appears in the **ODBC Microsoft Access Setup** dialog box.

**9** Click **OK**.

The **ODBC Microsoft Access Setup** dialog box disappears, and the **Create New Data Source** dialog box reappears.

**10** In the fourth box, click the down arrow and then, from the list that appears, click **Products**.

Excel assigns **Products** as the default table for this data source.

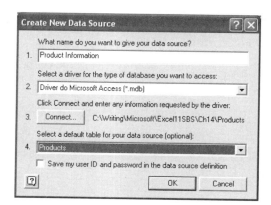

**11** Click **OK**.

*Product Information* is listed as a new data source in the **Choose Data Source** dialog box.

**12** Click **Product Information** if necessary, and then click **OK**.

The **Query Wizard** appears; the columns in the Products table appear in the **Available tables and columns** box.

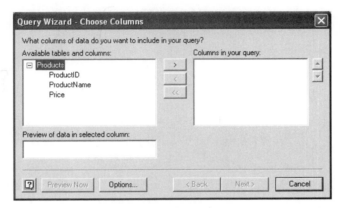

**13** Click the **ProductID** column name, and then click the **Add** button.

*ProductID* appears in the **Columns in your query** box, and **ProductName** is selected in the left box.

**14** Click the **Add** button.

*ProductName* appears in the **Columns in your query** box, and **Price** is selected in the left box.

**15** Click the **Add** button.

*Price* appears in the **Columns in your query** box.

**16** Click **Next**.

The **Filter Data** page of the **Query Wizard** appears.

**17** In the **Column to filter** list, click **Price**.

In the **Only include rows where** section, the first comparison operator box becomes active.

**18** In the first comparison operator box, click the down arrow and then, from the list that appears, click **is greater than or equal to**.

The words *is greater than or equal to* appear in the comparison operator box, and the first value box becomes active.

**19** In the first value box, type **50** and then click **Next**.

**Note** This filter limits the data brought into the workbook to products that cost $50 or more.

The **Sort Order** page of the **Query Wizard** appears.

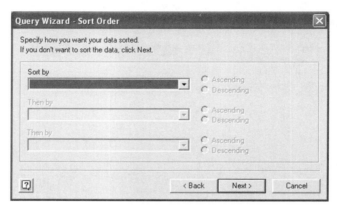

**20** In the **Sort by** box, click the down arrow and then, from the list that appears, click **ProductID**.

*ProductID* appears in the **Sort by** box, and the **Ascending** and **Descending** option buttons become active, with the **Ascending** option button selected. The **Then by** box also becomes active.

**21** Click **Next**.

The **Finish** page of the **Query Wizard** appears, with the **Return Data to Microsoft Excel** option button selected.

**22** Click **Save Query**.

The **Save As** dialog box appears.

**23** In the **File name** box, type **Products50AndOver** and then click **Save**.

Excel saves your query, and the **Save As** dialog box disappears.

**24** Click **Finish**.

The **Query Wizard** disappears, and Query.xls reappears with the **Import Data** dialog box open.

**25** In the **Import Data** dialog box, click **OK**.

**Note** Clicking **OK** accepts the active workbook cell as the upper left corner cell for the range to hold the query results.

The query results appear in the workbook.

| | A | B | C | D | E | F |
|---|---|---|---|---|---|---|
| 1 | ProductID | ProductName | Price | | | |
| 2 | FN0801 | Bench (4') | 52.95 | | | |
| 3 | FN0802 | Bench w/ 2 large pots | 149.95 | | | |
| 4 | FN0803 | Potting Bench/Barbeque Cart | 149.95 | | | |
| 5 | FN1402 | Bamboo Night Table | 95 | | | |
| 6 | FN1999 | Comfy Chair | 119.95 | | | |
| 7 | FN2002 | Cedar Planter Box | 59.95 | | | |
| 8 | FN2004 | Picnic Table w/ flip benches | 349.95 | | | |
| 9 | FN3402 | Northeastern Arbor | 199.95 | | | |
| 10 | SP0902 | Bamboo fencing 8' long x 6' tall | 54 | | | |
| 11 | SP1483 | English Fruit Cage | 149.95 | | | |
| 12 | TL0802 | Long-handled Loppers | 64.95 | | | |
| 13 | TL1549 | Overhead Loppers | 69.95 | | | |
| 14 | TL2538 | Grafting/Splicing Tool | 57.95 | | | |
| 15 | TL3001 | "Pruners, Left-handed" | 54 | | | |
| 16 | TL3002 | "Pruners, Right-handed" | 54 | | | |

**26** On the Standard toolbar, click the **Save** button to save your work.

CLOSE: Query.

# Summarizing List Data

*Microsoft Office Specialist*

A final, useful aspect of the relationship between spreadsheet programs and databases is that it is possible to build many of the data summary functions found in databases into spreadsheet programs, and vice versa. For example, Chapter 3 mentioned several functions you can use to create formulas that summarize the values in ranges of cells. The five functions mentioned in Chapter 3 were SUM, AVERAGE, COUNT, MAX, and MIN. Each of those functions examined every cell in the range named in the formula and used each cell's value to calculate the formula result.

Similar functions are available for use with Excel data lists: DSUM, DAVERAGE, DCOUNT, DMAX, and DMIN. Each function operates in the same way as the simpler version, but with an important difference: with the database functions, you can define criteria to limit the cells the function considers when it generates its result. Each database function follows this format (using DSUM as an example):

*=DSUM(values, "field", criteria)*

where *values* is the range of cells comprising the data list, *field* is the name of the field (not the letter of the worksheet column in which the data is stored), and *criteria* is the range of cells that contains the field names and criteria.

---

**See Also**   For more information on data lists and their properties, see "Creating Dynamic Lists with PivotTables" on page 152.

---

As an example, consider the following worksheet, which has a set of criteria defined above the data list.

| | A | B | C | D | E | F |
|---|---|---|---|---|---|---|
| 1 | Month | Week | Weekday | Day | Hour | Sales |
| 2 | March | | Wed | | >13 | |

The criteria defined in cells A1:F2 (which includes the field heads), when referenced in a database function, limit the function to cells that contain data relating to sales after 1:00 pm (hour 13 of the day) on Wednesdays in March. (In this example, the data is in the cell range A11:F1127.) A DSUM formula to find the total of sales using the criteria would look like this:

*=DSUM(A11:F1127,"Sales",A1:F2)*

**Important**   Your criteria must not overlap any part of the data list, nor should the criteria be placed below the data list (placing the criteria below the list would make it appear as if the criteria were additional rows in the list). The best places for your criteria are above the data list or to the side.

If you want to create complex criteria for a field, such as including sales from two days or within a range of hours, you can create a second field heading for the field with the multi-part criteria and use operators such as < and >, as in the examples in the following graphic.

| | A | B | C | D | E | F | G |
|---|---|---|---|---|---|---|---|
| 1 | Month | Week | Weekday | Day | Hour | Sales | Weekday |
| 2 | March | | Wed | | >13 | | Tue |

In this exercise, you create a series of database functions to summarize the values in an Excel data list.

OPEN: Summary from the *SBS\Excel\Database* folder.

**1**   In cell G1, type Hour.

**Note**   Creating a second **Hour** heading lets you place more than one constraint on values in the **Hour** field.

**2**   Select cells A1:G1, and then, on the Standard toolbar, click the **Copy** button.

**3**   Click cell A3, and then, on the Standard toolbar, click the **Paste** button.

The column headings from the copied cells are pasted in cells A3:G3.

**4** Click cell A5, and then, on the Standard toolbar, click the **Paste** button.

The column headings from the copied cells are pasted in cells A5:G5.

**5** In cell A2, type February; in cell C2, type Tue; in cell E2, type >12; and in cell G2, type <17.

**6** In cell A4, type March; in cell B4, type 2; and in cell F4, type >200.

**7** In cell A6, type January.

| | A | B | C | D | E | F | G |
|---|---|---|---|---|---|---|---|
| 1 | Month | Week | Weekday | Day | Hour | Sales | Hour |
| 2 | February | | Tue | | >12 | | <17 |
| 3 | Month | Week | Weekday | Day | Hour | Sales | Hour |
| 4 | March | 2 | | | | >200 | |
| 5 | Month | Week | Weekday | Day | Hour | Sales | Hour |
| 6 | January | | | | | | |

**8** In cell H8, type Total Tue sales from 1pm to 4pm in Feb.

**9** In cell H9, type Number of March hours in week 2 with sales over $200.

**10** In cell H10, type Highest hourly sales in Jan.

**11** In cell I8, type =DSUM(A11:F1127,"Sales",A1:G2) and press ⌈Enter⌋.

*$4,964.00 appears in cell I8.*

**12** In cell I9, type =DCOUNT(A11:F1127,"Hour",A3:G4) and press ⌈Enter⌋.

*51 appears in cell I9.*

**13** In cell I10, type =DMAX(A11:F1127,"Sales",A5:G6) and press ⌈Enter⌋.

*$1,028.00 appears in cell I10.*

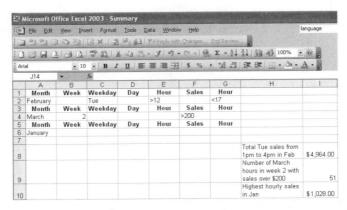

**14** On the Standard toolbar, click the **Save** button to save your work.

CLOSE: Summary.

# Key Points

- Use the VLOOKUP function to look up a value in one column of a data list and return a value from another column of the same row.

- You can create database queries to pull selected records from database tables into your Excel worksheets.

- Excel knows about many types of data sources, so there are few limits on what data you can bring into your worksheets.

- If you want to limit the data your database queries bring in, you can define filters to act on a query's results.

- By using database functions such as DSUM and DAVERAGE, you can summarize the data in an Excel data list.

- Just as with database queries, you can set criteria to limit the list rows considered by database functions.

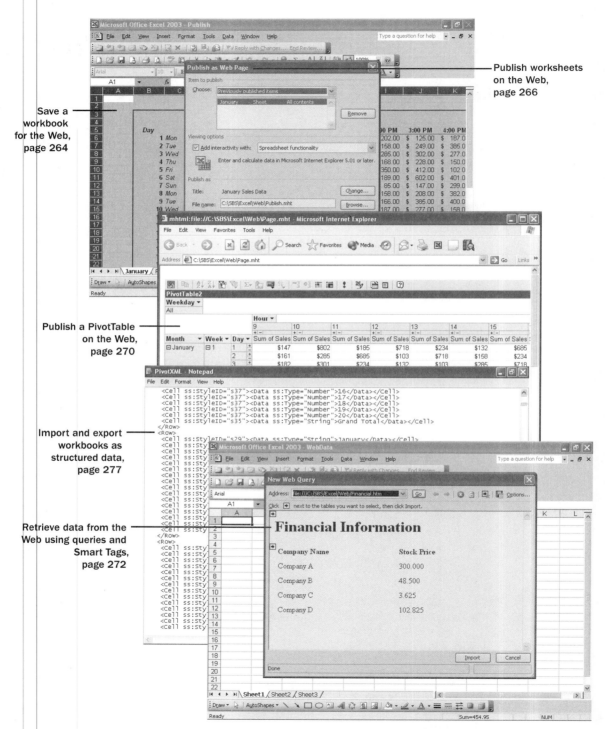

Save a
workbook
for the Web,
page 264

Publish worksheets
on the Web,
page 266

Publish a PivotTable
on the Web,
page 270

Import and export
workbooks as
structured data,
page 277

Retrieve data from the
Web using queries and
Smart Tags,
page 272

*Chapter 15 at a Glance*

# 15 Publishing Information on the Web

**In this chapter you will learn to:**

✔ Save a workbook for the Web.

✔ Publish worksheets on the Web.

✔ Publish a PivotTable on the Web.

✔ Retrieve data from the Web using queries and Smart Tags.

✔ Import and export workbooks as structured XML data.

✔ Create, apply, and modify custom XML data maps.

One of the hallmarks of Microsoft Excel has been that it lets you save your Excel workbooks and worksheets as files that can be accessed and interacted with via the World Wide Web. Previous versions of Excel also let you bring data from the Web into your workbooks by creating queries.

Excel 2003 extends those capabilities, adding entirely new functions and making existing capabilities easier to use. For example, previous versions of Excel created copies of workbooks or worksheets that had been saved for the Web and that were not connected to the original file, meaning that any updates in the original file would not be reflected in the file published on the Web. In Excel 2003, you can create stand-alone files or create a linked file that is updated whenever the original file is saved.

One of the hallmark technologies used in Excel 2003 is *Extensible Markup Language (XML)*. XML is a content markup language, meaning that an XML file has information about the data contained within it (as compared with Hypertext Markup Language (HTML), which tells a Web browser how to display a file's contents). Saving Excel workbooks as XML files means that your Excel data will be readable by a wide range of programs, not just those listed in the **Save As** dialog box's **Save as type** drop-down list. One application of XML is *Smart Tags*, a technology that recognizes certain types of information, such as stock symbols, and looks up related information on the Web. You can also create custom XML data arrangements, called *data maps*, that allow you fine-grained control over how data is brought into your worksheets.

In this chapter, you'll learn how to save a workbook for posting on the Web, publish worksheets and PivotTables on the Web, retrieve data from the Web, move data from one application to another, save Excel files as XML files, create XML data maps, and define XML options.

**See Also** Do you need a quick refresher on the topics in this chapter? See the quick reference entries on pages lx–lxiii.

**Important** Before you can use the practice files in this chapter, be sure you install them from the book's companion CD-ROM to their default location. See "Using the Book's CD-ROM" on page xi for more information.

# Saving a Workbook for the Web

*Microsoft Office Specialist*

One of the strengths of Excel 2003 is that you can save Excel workbooks as Web documents, allowing you and your colleagues to view workbooks over the Internet or a corporate intranet. For a document to be viewed via the World Wide Web, the document must be saved as a *Hypertext Markup Language (HTML)* file. HTML files, which end with either the .htm or the .html extension, include *tags* that tell a Web *browser* such as Microsoft Internet Explorer how to display the contents of the file.

For example, you might want to set the data labels in a workbook apart from the rest of the data by having the labels displayed with bold text. The HTML tag pair that indicates text to be displayed as bold text is *<B>...</B>*, where the ellipsis points between the tags are replaced by the text to be displayed. So the HTML fragment

```
<B>Excel</B>
```

would be displayed as **Excel**.

You can create HTML files with Microsoft FrontPage, but you can also create a file in Excel and then click **Save as Web Page** on the **File** menu to open the **Save As** dialog box.

To save a workbook as an HTML file, verify that the **Entire Workbook** option button is selected, type a name for the file in the **File name** box, and then click **Save** to have Excel create an HTML document for each sheet in the workbook.

Once you have saved an Excel workbook as a series of HTML documents, you can open it in Internet Explorer 4.01 or later. To open the Excel file, start Internet Explorer, open the **File** menu, and then click **Open** to display the **Open** dialog box. In the **Open** dialog box, clicking the **Browse** button opens the **Microsoft Internet Explorer** dialog box. Use the controls in that box to identify the file you want to open.

**Note** Excel represents the HTML files as a single Microsoft HTML 5 file in the **Microsoft Internet Explorer** dialog box.

When you double-click the file to open, the **Microsoft Internet Explorer** dialog box disappears and the file's name and path appear in the **Open** box. To display the Excel workbook, click **OK**, and the workbook appears in Internet Explorer. You can move between pages in the workbook by clicking the HTML representation of the sheet tabs in the lower left corner of the workbook.

**Note** When you move the mouse pointer over a sheet tab, the address of the HTML page representing that worksheet appears on the status bar.

In this exercise, you save an Excel workbook as a series of HTML files and then view the files in Internet Explorer.

OPEN: Saving from the *SBS\Excel\Web* folder.

**1** On the **File** menu, click **Save as Web Page**.

The **Save As** dialog box appears.

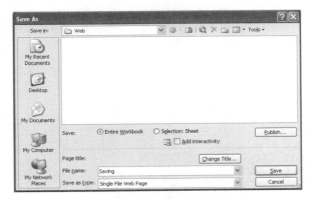

**2** If necessary, in the **Save** section, select the **Entire Workbook** option button.

**3** Verify that Saving.mht appears in the **File name** box, and then click **Save**.

Excel saves the workbook as a set of HTML documents.

**4** Click the **Close** button to close Saving.htm.

Close

**5** Start Internet Explorer.

**6** In Internet Explorer, on the **File** menu, click **Open**.

The **Open** dialog box appears.

**7** Click **Browse**.

The **Browse** dialog box appears.

**8** Navigate to the C:\SBS\Excel\Web folder, and then double-click **Saving.mht**.

The **Browse** dialog box disappears, and *C:\SBS\Excel\Web\Saving.mht* appears in the **Open** box.

9    Click **OK**.

Saving.mht appears in Internet Explorer.

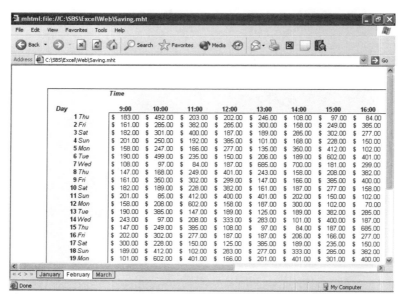

10   Click the **March** sheet tab.

The March worksheet appears.

CLOSE: Internet Explorer.

# Publishing Worksheets on the Web

*Microsoft Office Specialist*

In addition to the ability to save an Excel workbook as an HTML file, you also have the option of choosing to save individual worksheets as HTML documents. To save a single worksheet as an HTML document, on the **File** menu, click **Save as Web Page** to open the **Save As** dialog box.

Selecting the **Selection: Sheet** option button tells Excel to save the active worksheet as an HTML document. You can also change the title that appears on the title bar of the file when it is opened in a Web browser, allow viewers to interact with the file after it is published on the Web, and have Excel update the Web file whenever the file on which it is based is updated.

If you like, you can store any HTML files in a separate folder. To create a folder in Excel, on the **File** menu, click **Open**. In the **Open** dialog box, click the **Create New Folder** button to create a new folder within the current folder. You can rename the new folder by right-clicking its icon, choosing **Rename** from the shortcut menu that appears, and then typing the folder's new name.

When you open an HTML document in a Web browser, a title appears on the document's title bar. You can set the document's title with an HTML tag; if you don't, the file's name appears on the title bar. In Excel, you can set a title for a workbook or worksheet you save to the Web by clicking the **Publish** button to display the **Publish as Web Page** dialog box. Clicking the **Change** button in the **Publish as** section of the dialog box opens another dialog box, in which you can type a title for the Excel document.

There are several other options you can set in the **Publish as Web Page** dialog box. For example, you can let colleagues interact with a workbook or worksheet you save as an HTML document. To allow interaction, select the **Add interactivity with** check box, select **Spreadsheet functionality** from the adjoining drop-down list, verify that the **Open published web page in browser** check box is selected, and then click **Publish**.

By default, your Web page will be published to your hard disk in the same folder as your Excel file. However, if you have access to an intranet or a Web site, you can enter the address of the site and the name of the Web page you are publishing in the **File name** box, such as *http://www.microsoft.com/publish.mht*. You'll be prompted for a user name and password for the site, then the page will be uploaded immediately (if you have an active Internet connection.) Then when you work with the original file in the future and save changes, the changed file will be republished to the same Web site.

Commands
and Options

You and your colleagues can now interact with the worksheet by editing cell values, sorting, filtering, or calculating values with formulas. It's also possible to change cell formatting; to get access to the formatting tools when you view an Excel worksheet via the Web, click the **Commands and Options** button to display the **Commands and Options** dialog box.

*AutoRepublish*, a feature introduced in Excel 2002, tells Excel to retain a link to the Web file you create and to update the Web version of that file whenever the original document is saved. You turn on AutoRepublish by opening the **Publish as Web Page** dialog box and selecting the **AutoRepublish every time this workbook is saved** check box.

In this exercise, you publish a worksheet to the Web, set a title for the worksheet, make the worksheet interactive, change the format of worksheet elements in a Web browser, and turn on AutoRepublish so that any changes in the original document will be reflected in the Web document created from it.

**OPEN: Publish from the *SBS\Excel\Web* folder.**

1   If necessary, on the tab bar, click the **January** sheet tab to display the January worksheet.

2   On the **File** menu, click **Save as Web Page**.

The **Save As** dialog box appears.

**3** In the **File name** box, type **Publish**.

**4** In the **Save** section of the dialog box, select the **Selection: Sheet** option button to publish the active worksheet on the Web.

**5** In the **Save** section of the dialog box, select the **Add interactivity** check box, and then click **Publish**.

The **Publish as Web Page** dialog box appears.

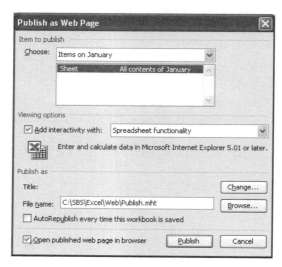

**6** In the **Publish as** section of the dialog box, click the **Change** button.

The **Set Title** dialog box appears.

**7** In the **Title** box, type January Sales Data and then click **OK**.

The **Set Title** dialog box disappears, and *January Sales Data* appears as the title of the Web page.

**8** Select the **AutoRepublish every time this workbook is saved** check box.

**9** Select the **Open published web page in browser** check box, and then click **Publish**.

The workbook appears in Internet Explorer.

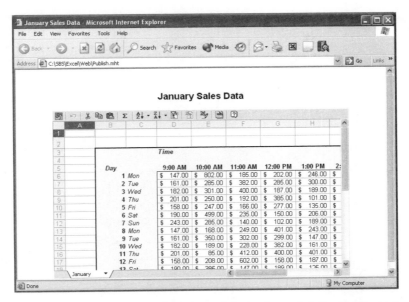

**10** Click cell B5, and then, on the **Interactivity** toolbar, click the **Commands and Options** button.

The **Commands and Options** dialog box appears.

**11** If necessary, click the **Format** tab.

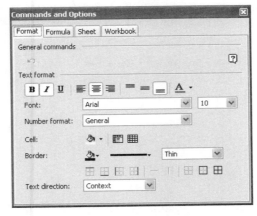

Align Left

**12** In the **Text format** section of the dialog box, click the **Align Left** button.

The contents of cell B5 are aligned with the left edge of the cell.

**13** In the **Commands and Options** dialog box, click the **Close** button.

The **Commands and Options** dialog box closes.

CLOSE: Internet Explorer.

# Publishing a PivotTable on the Web

When you publish an Excel workbook on the Web, you can allow users to interact with the worksheets. The preceding section of this chapter described how to let you and your colleagues interact with an Excel document over the Web. This section continues that theme by demonstrating how to export a PivotTable to the Web. If Catherine Turner, The Garden Company's owner, were on vacation but wanted to participate in a meeting, she could still use her laptop to connect to the company's Web site and use a PivotTable published there to view any updated information.

Once you have created a PivotTable, you can publish it on the Web by clicking any cell in the PivotTable and clicking **Save as Web Page** on the **File** menu to open the **Save As** dialog box. To publish just the worksheet with the PivotTable, select the **Selection: Sheet** option button, select the **Add interactivity** check box, and then click **Publish** to open the **Publish as Web Page** dialog box.

The **Publish as Web Page** dialog box shows the name of the worksheet containing the PivotTable in the **Choose** box, with the items on that worksheet in the lower pane of the box. In the lower pane of the **Choose** box, click the entry beginning with *Pivot-Table*. The contents of the **Add interactivity with** box in the **Viewing options** section of the dialog box will change to reflect that you are publishing a PivotTable.

**Important**    If you publish an entire worksheet, rather than just the PivotTable, viewers will not be able to interact with the PivotTable.

To finish publishing the PivotTable on the Web, select the **Open published web page in browser** check box, and then click **Publish** to save the PivotTable as a Web document and to show the PivotTable in Internet Explorer.

Show Details

You and your colleagues can now interact with the PivotTable by reorganizing and filtering the PivotTable's contents with Internet Explorer 4.01 or later. To expand the PivotTable so that it shows every cell, and not just the totals and grand totals, click the **Show Details** button.

In this exercise, you publish a PivotTable on your hard disk and then filter the Pivot-Table's contents using Internet Explorer.

OPEN: Pivot from the *SBS\Excel\Web* folder.

1    If necessary, on the tab bar, click the **Pivot** sheet tab and then click any cell in the PivotTable.

2    On the **File** menu, click **Save as Web Page**.

     The **Save As** dialog box appears.

3    In the **File name** box, type Pivot.

**4** In the **Save** section of the dialog box, select the **Selection: Sheet** option button.

**5** In the **Save** section of the dialog box, select the **Add interactivity** check box and then click **Publish**.

The **Publish as Web Page** dialog box appears.

**6** If **Items on Pivot** does not appear in the **Choose** box, click the **Choose** down arrow and then, from the list that appears, click **Items on Pivot**.

*Items on Pivot* appears in the **Choose** box, and the items in the Pivot worksheet appear in the list below the **Choose** box.

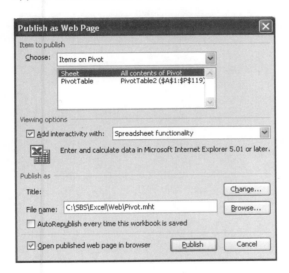

**7** In the list below the **Choose** box, click the item beginning with *PivotTable*.

In the **Viewing options** section of the dialog box, select the **Add interactivity with** check box and select **PivotTable functionality** in the drop-down list.

**8** If necessary, in the bottom section of the dialog box, select the **Open published web page in browser** check box.

**Note** If you have access to your own Web site, you can enter a location on your site in the **File name** box, in a form like *http://www.microsoft.com/subfolder/pivot.mht*.

**9** Click **Publish**.

The PivotTable is saved as a Web page and appears in Internet Explorer.

**Important** If you're publishing to an intranet or Web site, Excel will prompt you for a valid user name and password.

**10** Click the **Show Details** button.

The PivotTable expands to show every cell.

**11** In the **Page Area** of the PivotTable, click the **Weekday** down arrow and then, from the list that appears, clear the **Mon**, **Tue**, **Wed**, **Thu**, and **Fri** check boxes.

**12** Click **OK**.

The PivotTable is filtered so that only sales for Saturdays and Sundays are shown.

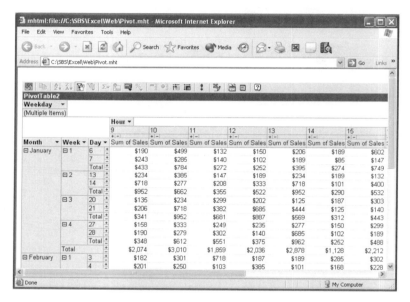

**13** In the **Page Area** of the PivotTable, click the **Weekday** down arrow and then, from the list that appears, select the **All** check box and click **OK**.

The filter is removed.

**14** Click the **Close** button to close Internet Explorer.

**15** In Excel, on the Standard toolbar, click the **Save** button to save your work.

CLOSE: Pivot.

# Retrieving Data from the Web

*Microsoft Office Specialist*

The World Wide Web is a great source of information. From stock quotes to product descriptions, many companies publish useful information on their Web sites. The most common HTML structure used to present financial information is the table, which, like a spreadsheet, organizes the data into rows and columns, as in the following graphic.

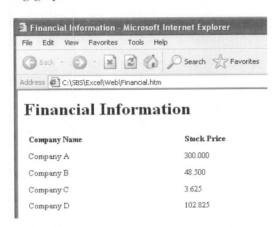

Excel 2003 makes creating a Web query easy by letting you copy data directly from a Web page into Excel and then create a query to retrieve data from the HTML table you copied. To create a Copy Paste Web Query, open the target Web page in Internet Explorer, copy the data to the Clipboard, click a cell in the Excel workbook, and then paste the data into the workbook. The data will appear in the workbook, with a **Paste Options** button next to it.

Paste Options

Clicking the **Paste Options** button and then clicking **Create Refreshable Web Query** from the list that appears opens the **New Web Query** dialog box, which contains the data you copied from the Web page.

To select a table to import into Excel, click the table icon next to it. The icon will change to a selected table icon, and the table will be outlined and highlighted to identify it as having been selected. After you select the table, click **Import** to create the query.

**Tip**  You can select an entire Web page by clicking the top table icon in the display pane.

To refresh query data, right-click any cell in the query and then, from the shortcut menu that appears, click **Refresh Data**. The new data will appear in your workbook.

In this exercise, you create a Web query to retrieve data using the new Copy Paste Web Query method.

**OPEN: WebData from the *SBS\Excel\Web* folder.**

**1**  Start Internet Explorer, and then, on the **File** menu, click **Open**.

The **Open** dialog box appears.

**2** Click **Browse**.

The **Microsoft Internet Explorer** dialog box appears.

**3** Navigate to the C:\SBS\Excel\Web directory, and then double-click **Financial.htm**.

The **Microsoft Internet Explorer** dialog box disappears, and *C:\SBS\Excel\Web\Financial.htm* appears in the **Open** box.

**4** Click **OK**.

Financial.htm appears in Internet Explorer.

**5** Select the table data, and then press Ctrl+C to copy the data to the Clipboard.

Paste

**6** In Microsoft Excel, click cell A1, and then, on the Standard toolbar, click the **Paste** button.

The HTML table data is pasted into the worksheet, and the **Paste Options** button appears next to the data.

**7** Click the **Paste Options** button, and then, from the list that appears, click **Create Refreshable Web Query**.

The **New Web Query** dialog box appears, with Financial.htm displayed.

Table icon

**8** Click the table icon next to *Company Name* (it changes to a check mark), and then click **Import**.

The HTML table data appears in the worksheet, with its original HTML formatting.

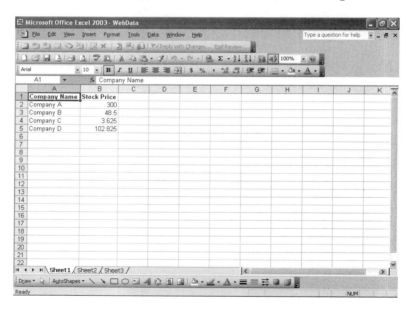

**9**    On the Standard toolbar, click the **Save** button to save your work.

CLOSE: WebData.

# Acquiring Web Data with Smart Tags

Another useful capability in Excel 2003 is that of bringing information from the Web that is related to the contents of a worksheet cell. The technology that accomplishes this is called Smart Tags.

The clearest example of how Smart Tags work is with stock symbols, the abbreviations of company names on stock market tickers. You can turn on Smart Tags and have Excel look for known stock symbols (such as Microsoft's stock symbol, *MSFT*) and connect to a Web site that has information related to that symbol.

To turn on Smart Tags, on the **Tools** menu, click **AutoCorrect Options** to display the **AutoCorrect** dialog box. In the **AutoCorrect** dialog box, click the **Smart Tags** tab to display the **Smart Tags** tab page.

Select the **Label data with smart tags** check box to activate Smart Tags, and then, in the **Recognizers** box, select the check boxes next to the sets of Smart Tags you want Excel to use. You can also determine how Excel indicates that a cell has a value recognized by Smart Tags by opening the **Show smart tags as** drop-down list and choosing whether the cell will have an indicator in the lower right corner of the cell, a button that appears beside the cell when the mouse pointer is over it, or both. Selecting the **Embed smart tags in this workbook** check box means that Excel will save the reference to any cells with values recognized by Smart Tags and copy the list of Smart Tags into the body of the workbook.

To check the workbook for cell values recognized as Smart Tags, click the **Check Workbook** button. The **AutoCorrect** dialog box will disappear, and cells with recognized values will have an indicator in the lower right corner.

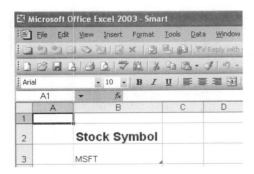

Smart Tag
Actions

Moving the mouse pointer over the cell will display an indicator button. Click the indicator button, and then choose the type of information you want from the list that appears. If you click **Stock Quote on MSN MoneyCentral**, for example, Internet Explorer will launch and find the MSN MoneyCentral page for Microsoft.

To delete an individual Smart Tag, click the indicator button next to the cell with the Smart Tag and then click **Remove this Smart Tag**. To turn off Smart Tags entirely, open the **AutoCorrect** dialog box, display the **Smart Tags** tab page, clear the **Label data with smart tags** check box, and then click **OK**.

In this exercise, you turn on Smart Tags, check a worksheet for Smart Tags, and then use the Smart Tag you find to get stock information about the company represented by a stock symbol.

OPEN: Smart from the *SBS\Excel\Web* folder.

**1** On the **Tools** menu, click **AutoCorrect Options**.

The **AutoCorrect** dialog box appears.

**2** Click the **Smart Tags** tab to display the **Smart Tags** tab page.

**3** Select the **Label data with smart tags** check box.

The **Recognizers** box becomes active.

**4** Verify that all five check boxes in the **Recognizers** pane are selected.

**5** Select the **Embed smart tags in this workbook** check box.

Smart Tags will now be saved as part of the workbook file.

**6** Click **Check Workbook**.

The **AutoCorrect** dialog box disappears, and a Smart Tag indicator appears in cell B3.

**7** Move the mouse pointer over cell B3.

A **Smart Tag Actions** button appears next to the cell.

**8** Click the **Smart Tag Actions** button, point to **Financial Symbol**, and click **Insert refreshable stock price**.

The **Insert Stock Price** dialog box appears.

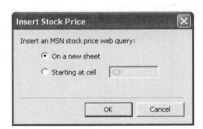

**9** Select the **Starting at cell** option button, verify that C3 appears in the **Starting at cell** box, and then click **OK**.

The stock quote appears in the workbook.

**10** On the Standard toolbar, click the **Save** button to save your work.

CLOSE: Smart.

# Working with Structured Data

HTML lets you determine how a document will be displayed in a Web browser, such as by telling Internet Explorer to display certain text in bold type or to start a new paragraph. However, HTML doesn't tell you anything about the meaning of data in a document. Internet Explorer might "know" it should display a set of data in a table, but it wouldn't "know" that the data represented an Excel spreadsheet.

You can add *metadata*, or data about data, to Web documents using Extensible Markup Language (XML). While a full discussion of XML is beyond the scope of this book, the following bit of XML code shows how to identify an Excel workbook in XML:

```
<?xml version="1.0"?>
<Workbook xmlns="urn:schemas-microsoft-com:office:spreadsheet"
xmlns:o="urn:schemas-microsoft-com:office:office"
xmlns:x="urn:schemas-microsoft-com:office:excel"
xmlns:ss="urn:schemas-microsoft-com:office:spreadsheet"
xmlns:html="http://www.w3.org/TR/REC-html40">
```

Also, XML can identify rows and cells within the spreadsheet, as in the following example:

```
<Row>
    <Cell><Data ss:Type="String">January</Data></Cell>
    <Cell><Data ss:Type="Number">1</Data></Cell>
    <Cell><Data ss:Type="String">Tue</Data></Cell>
    <Cell><Data ss:Type="Number">2</Data></Cell>
    <Cell><Data ss:Type="Number">9</Data></Cell>
    <Cell><Data ss:Type="Number">161</Data></Cell>
</Row>
```

This represents the following worksheet row.

The goal of XML is to be a universal language, allowing data to move freely from one application to another. In this case, that means that saving an Excel workbook as an XML document would allow another spreadsheet program to read the XML file, separate out the cell data, and use the metadata to decide how to structure a worksheet to contain that data.

To save an Excel document as an XML file, click **Save As** on the **File** menu to open the **Save As** dialog box. In the **Save As** dialog box, click the **Save as type** down arrow, click **XML Spreadsheet (*.xml)** from the list that appears, and then click **Save**. You can open Excel spreadsheets saved as XML documents by clicking the **Open** button, displaying all Excel files, and then clicking **Open**.

In this exercise, you save an Excel workbook as an XML document and then import an XML document into Excel.

OPEN: Structured from the *SBS\Excel\Web* folder.

**1**  On the **File** menu, click **Save As**.

The **Save As** dialog box appears.

**2**  Click the **Save as type** down arrow, and then, from the list that appears, click **XML Spreadsheet (*.xml)**.

The file type changes to XML.

**3**  Click **Save**.

A message box appears, indicating that any Microsoft Visual Basic projects or header or footer image associated with the workbook will not be saved.

**4**  Click **Yes** to clear the message box and save the workbook as an XML spreadsheet.

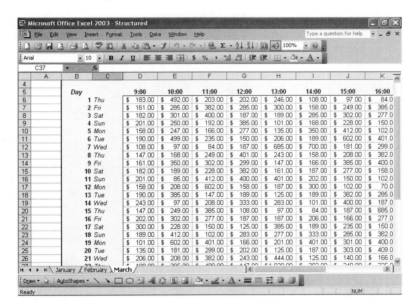

**5**  Click the **Close** button to close Structured.xml.

Close

**6**  On the Standard toolbar, click the **Open** button.

The **Open** dialog box appears.

**7**  Navigate to the C:\SBS\Excel\Web folder, and double-click **Structured.xml**.

Structured.xml opens.

CLOSE: Structured.xml.

# Use Professional XML Data Capabilities

XML Data
Structuring

**New in
Office 2003**

Support for XML, including the ability to save files as XML documents, was introduced in Microsoft Office XP, but the technology is one of the focal points of Office 2003. If you work in an enterprise that exchanges data with other organizations in the form of purchase orders, parts data, financial data, or product catalogs, you can use XML to transfer the data regardless of the program used to create the data.

At the heart of XML-based data interchange is the *schema*, which is a document that defines the structure of a set of XML files. Creating a schema, which in Excel is stored in a .xsd file, is beyond the scope of this book, but it's helpful to know what one looks like. The following code listing shows the schema used in the exercise at the end of this section.

```
<?xml version="1.0" encoding="utf-8" ?>
<xs:schema targetNamespace="http://schemas.thegardencompany.com/product"
elementFormDefault="qualified"
xmlns="http://schemas.thegardencompany.com/product"
xmlns:xs="http://www.w3.org/2001/XMLSchema">
    <xs:annotation>
        <xs:documentation>Defines a product with a "product" root
        element.</xs:documentation>
    </xs:annotation>
    <xs:complexType name="productType">
        <xs:sequence>
            <xs:element name="productId" type="xs:string" />
            <xs:element name="productName" type="xs:string" />
            <xs:element name="priceEach" type="xs:decimal" />
        </xs:sequence>
    </xs:complexType>
<xs:element name="product" type="productType"></xs:element>
</xs:schema>
```

The top part of the file (down to the annotation), contains technical information about the schema, such as the XML version used to create it (1.0), the URL of the document against which the structure of the schema can be verified (*http://www.w3.org/2001/XMLSchema*), and a comment about the schema (the annotation).

The data definition found in the `<xs:complexType name="productType">` statement tells Excel to expect a single instance of a product with three attributes, which will appear in the named order: *productId*, *productName*, and *priceEach*.

XML Source
Task Pane

New in
Office 2003

Once you have created an XML schema, the next step in bringing associated XML data into your worksheet is to add the structure of the schema to the worksheet. To do so, you establish a *data map*, or pattern of data represented in a file, in your worksheet. The first step in the process is to open the **Data** menu, point to **XML**, and click **XML Source** to display the **XML Source** task pane.

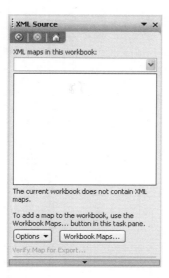

**Important** The XML Source menu item is only available if the active worksheet is blank.

Click **Workbook Maps** to display the **XML Maps** dialog box, and click **Add**. You then use the controls in the **XML Source** dialog box to locate the schema to add, and click **Open** to add the schema to the **XML Maps** dialog box. Click **OK** to make the structure in the selected XML map appear in the **XML Source** task pane.

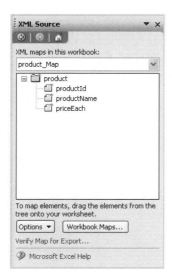

You can now drag the elements from the map to the worksheet cells where you want the data to appear. After you drag an element to the worksheet, an icon will appear next to the cell. Click the icon, and select where you want the element label (the element's name, such as *productId*) to appear.

**Note** The names of elements you have mapped to a cell in a worksheet appear in bold type.

After you've added the desired elements to your workbook, you can delete them as you would delete any other workbook contents. You can also remove an element from a worksheet by right-clicking the element in the **XML Source** task pane and clicking **Remove Element** on the shortcut menu.

If you want to change how the XML data is inserted into your worksheet, click the **Options** button in the **XML Source** task pane. You can use the options to preview your data in the task pane, hide help messages in the task pane, and let Excel know you have already added data labels so that it won't ask every time you insert a field.

You can also change how Excel imports XML data by opening the **Data** menu, pointing to **XML**, and clicking **XML Map Properties**. You can use the controls in the **XML Map Properties** dialog box to change whether Excel resizes the columns to reflect the size of the data, preserves number formatting, and validates XML data against the associated schema before importing or exporting that data.

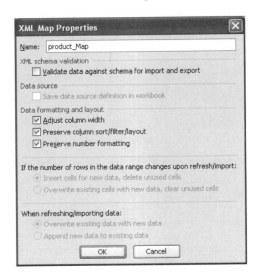

Once you have assigned the schema elements to worksheet cells, you can import data into the worksheet from an XML data file that matches the structure of the schema. Here is a data file that matches the schema shown earlier:

```
<?xml version="1.0" encoding="UTF-8" standalone="no"?>
<product xmlns="http://schemas.thegardencompany.com/product">
    <productId>TL2539</productId>
    <productName>Grafting Knife</productName>
    <priceEach>18.95</priceEach>
</product>
```

Note that the data file refers to the schema defined earlier (*http://schemas.thegarden-company.com/product*) and then lists the data for each field. To import the data from this file into your worksheet, open the **Data** menu, point to **XML**, and click **Import**. In the **Import XML** dialog box, click the data file and click **Import**.

**START: Microsoft Excel.**

**1**    On the **Data** menu, point to **XML**, and then click **XML Source**.

The **XML Source** task pane appears.

**Important**    Remember, the XML Source menu item is only available if the active worksheet is blank.

**2**    Click **XML Maps**.

The **XML Maps** dialog box appears.

**3**    Click **Add**.

The **Select XML Source** dialog box appears.

**4**    Navigate to the SBS\Excel\Web folder, click **Product.xsd.xml**, and click **Open**.

An entry representing Product.xsd.xml appears in the **XML Maps** dialog box.

**5**    Click **OK**.

An outline of the Product schema appears in the **XML Source** task pane.

**6**    Drag the **productId** element from the task pane to B2. Click the icon that appears next to the cell, and click **Place XML Heading to the Left**.

The name of the element, *productId*, appears in cell A2.

**7**    Drag the **productName** element from the task pane to B3. Click the icon that appears next to the cell, and click **Place XML Heading to the Left**.

The name of the element, *productName*, appears in cell A3.

**8** Drag the **priceEach** element from the task pane to B4. Click the icon that appears next to the cell, and click **Place XML Heading to the Left**.

The name of the element, *priceEach*, appears in cell A4.

|   | A | B | C |
|---|---|---|---|
| 1 |   |   |   |
| 2 | productId |   |   |
| 3 | productName |   |   |
| 4 | priceEach |   |   |
| 5 |   |   |   |

**9** On the **Data** menu, point to **XML**, and click **Import**.

The **Import XML** dialog box appears.

**10** Click **Product.xml**, and then click **Import**.

The data from Product.xml appears in cells B2:B4.

**11** In the **XML Source** task pane, click **Options**, and then click **Hide Border of Inactive Lists**.

**12** Click any cell that is not in the list.

The border around the list disappears.

**13** In the **XML Source** task pane, right-click the **productName** element, and click **Remove Element**. Click **OK** to acknowledge that the deletion will cause data to be lost.

Excel removes the XML field in cell B3 and the data that was read into it, but the field's label remains in cell A3.

**14** Click **XML Maps** in the **XML Source** task pane.

The **XML Maps** dialog box appears with the entry representing Product.xsd highlighted.

**15** Click **Delete**, and then click **OK** to clear the message box that appears. Click **OK** again to close the **XML Maps** dialog box.

Excel removes the association between Product.xsd and your workbook, but the data remains in place.

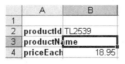

|   | A | B |
|---|---|---|
| 1 |   |   |
| 2 | productId | TL2539 |
| 3 | productName |   |
| 4 | priceEach | 18.95 |

**16** On the **File** menu, click **Save**.

**17** The **Save As** dialog box appears.

**18** Type XMLExample in the **File name** box and click **Save**.

**19** Excel saves XMLExample.

CLOSE: XMLExample.

# Key Points

- Saving a workbook as a Web-accessible HTML document is as easy as saving it as a regular Excel file, and opening a workbook saved for the Web is just as easy as opening any other Web page.

- Excel lets you add interactivity to workbooks and worksheets saved for the Web. You can even publish PivotTables!

- Use the AutoRepublish facility to update Excel files on the Web. Whenever the original workbook is changed, the edits will be written to the HTML version of the file.

- Web pages often contain useful data such as stock prices and sales figures. You can create a Web Query to download that data into an Excel worksheet.

- Smart Tags extend the basic capabilities of Excel, making it easy to create links to external data.

- XML is a terrific tool for making Excel data readable in many other programs, and for reading in data created in other programs.

- You can create custom XML data maps to facilitate electronic data interchange between you and your clients.

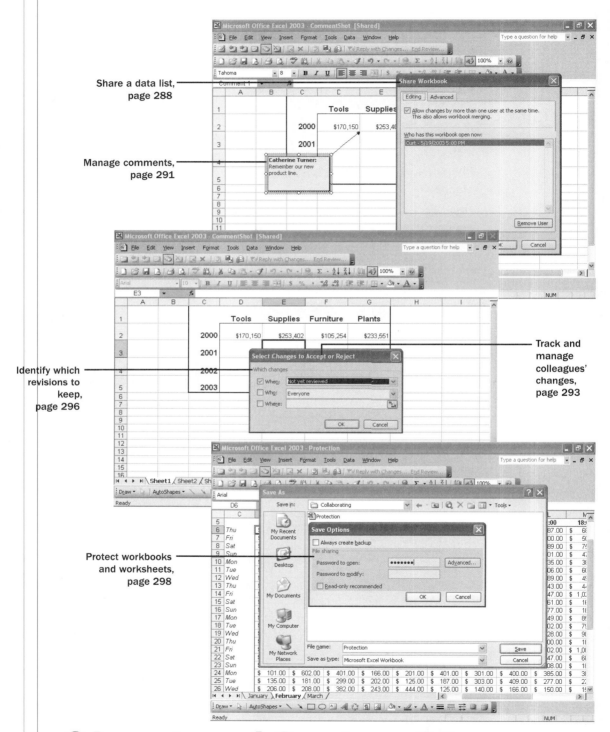

Share a data list, page 288

Manage comments, page 291

Identify which revisions to keep, page 296

Track and manage colleagues' changes, page 293

Protect workbooks and worksheets, page 298

*Chapter 16 at a Glance*

# 16 Collaborating with Colleagues

**In this chapter you will learn to:**

✔  Share a data list.

✔  Manage comments.

✔  Track and manage colleagues' changes.

✔  Identify which revisions to keep.

✔  Protect workbooks and worksheets.

✔  Sign a workbook using a digital signature.

Even though a single individual might be tasked with managing a company's financial data and related information, there is also usually a group of individuals who either enter data into workbooks themselves or have input into future sales or growth projections. You and your colleagues can also enhance workbook data by adding comments that offer insight into why sales were so good on a particular day or whether a product might be discontinued. If the workbook in which those projections and comments will be stored is available on a local area network (LAN) or intranet, you can allow more than one user to access the workbook at a time by turning on workbook *sharing*.

Once a workbook has been shared with your colleagues, you can mark and record any changes made to the workbook. Once all changes have been made, the workbook's administrator can decide which changes to keep and which to reject. If several individuals need to make changes to a workbook and they can't access it via a network, you can create several copies of the original file and distribute them via e-mail to your colleagues. After you receive all of the changed files, you can merge the changes into the original file and choose which changes to keep.

If you would prefer to limit which of your colleagues is able to view and edit your workbooks, you can add password protection to a workbook, worksheet, or cell range (including an individual cell). Adding password protection lets you prevent changes to critical elements of your workbooks and, if you like, hide formulas used to calculate values.

Finally, if you work in an environment where you and your colleagues exchange files frequently, including exchanges with individuals from outside your organization, you can use a digital signature to help verify that your workbooks, and any macros they contain, are from a trusted source.

In this chapter, you'll learn how to share a data list, manage comments to workbook cells, track and manage changes made by colleagues, identify which changes to a workbook you'll keep, protect workbooks and worksheets, and digitally sign your workbooks.

---

**See Also**   Do you need a quick refresher on the topics in this chapter? See the quick reference entries on pages lxiv–lxvii.

---

**Important**   Before you can use the practice files in this chapter, be sure you install them from the book's companion CD-ROM to their default location. See "Using the Book's CD-ROM" on page xi for more information.

# Sharing a Data List

*Microsoft Office Specialist*

The first step in making a workbook available to your colleagues is to turn on workbook sharing. When you turn on workbook sharing, you let more than one user edit a workbook simultaneously, which is perfect for a fair-sized business such as The Garden Company, where employees need to look up customer, sales, and product data frequently.

To turn on workbook sharing, on the **Tools** menu, click **Share Workbook**. In the **Share Workbook** dialog box that appears, you turn on workbook sharing by selecting the **Allow changes by more than one user at the same time** check box. You can then set the sharing options for the active workbook by clicking the **Advanced** tab.

There are several settings you can change on the **Advanced** tab page of the **Share Workbook** dialog box, but two settings are of greater interest than the others. The first setting has to do with whether Microsoft Excel should maintain a history of changes made to the workbook and, if so, for how many days Excel should keep the changes. The default setting is to retain a record of all changes made in the past 30 days, but you can enter any number of days you like. Unless it's critical that you keep all changes made to a workbook, you should probably stay with the default setting of 30 days.

The other important setting on this tab page deals with how Excel will decide which of two conflicting changes in a cell should be applied. For example, a product's price might change, and two of your colleagues could type in what they think is the new price. Selecting the **Ask me which changes win** option button lets you decide which price to keep.

Attach

Another way to share a workbook is to send a copy of it to your colleagues via e-mail. If, for example, The Garden Company's owner, Catherine Turner, were on a business trip visiting a supplier, she could receive a copy of a workbook as an e-mail attachment.

While the specific command to attach a file to an e-mail message will be different in every program, the most common method of attaching a file is to create a new e-mail message and then click the **Attach** button, as in Microsoft Outlook Express.

In this exercise, you turn on workbook sharing and then attach the file to an Outlook Express e-mail message.

**Important**   You will need Outlook Express to complete this exercise.

OPEN: Sharing from the *SBS\Excel\Collaborating* folder.

**1**   On the **Tools** menu, click **Share Workbook**.

The **Share Workbook** dialog box appears with a list of every user who is accessing the workbook.

**2**   Select the **Allow changes by more than one user at the same time** check box, and then click the **Advanced** tab.

The **Advanced** tab page appears.

**3**   Click **OK** to accept the default settings.

**4**   If a message box appears, click **OK** to close it, and then save the workbook.

**5**   Click the document's **Close** button to close Sharing.xls.

Close

**6**   On the Microsoft Windows taskbar, open the **Start** menu, and open **Outlook Express**.

The Outlook Express window opens.

Create Mail

New Mail

**7** Click the **New Mail** button.

A new e-mail message appears.

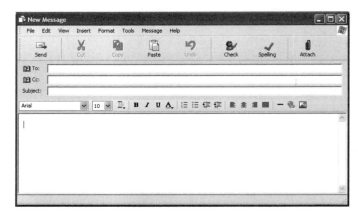

**8** Click the **Attach** button.

The **Insert Attachment** dialog box appears.

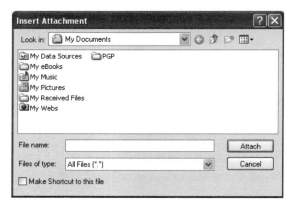

**9** Navigate to the C:\SBS\Excel\Collaborating directory, and then double-click **Sharing.xls**.

The **Insert Attachment** dialog box disappears, and *Sharing.xls* appears in the header in the **Attach** field.

**10** Click the **Close** button to close the message, and then click **No** in the message box that appears, to close the message without saving it.

**Note** There is no e-mail address in the **To** box, so clicking the **Send** button would have no effect.

CLOSE: Outlook Express.

# Managing Comments

Excel makes it easy for you and your colleagues to insert comments in workbook cells, adding insights that go beyond the cell data. For example, if sales were exceptionally high for an hour of a particular day, the manager on duty could add a comment to the cell in which she records the sales for that hour, noting that two exceptionally large purchases accounted for the disparity.

When you add a comment to a cell, a flag appears in the upper right corner of the cell. When the mouse pointer hovers over a cell with a comment, the comment can appear in a box next to the cell, along with the name of the user logged on to the computer at the time.

**Important** Note that the name attributed to a comment might not be the same as the person who actually created it. Enforcing access controls, such as requiring users to enter account names and passwords when they access a computer, can help track who made what comment or change.

You can add a comment to a cell by clicking the cell and clicking **Comment** on the **Insert** menu. When you do, the comment flag appears in the cell and a comment box appears next to the cell. You can type the comment in the box and, when you're done, click another cell to close the box for editing. When you move the mouse pointer over the cell with the comment, the comment will appear next to the cell.

If you want the comment to be shown the entire time the workbook is open, right-click the cell with the comment and then click **Show Comment** from the shortcut menu that appears. You can hide the comment by clicking **Hide Comment** from the same menu, delete the comment by clicking **Delete Comment**, or open the comment for editing by clicking **Edit Comment**.

**Note** When someone other than the original user edits a comment, that person's input is marked with the new user's name and is added to the original comment.

If you want to select every cell with a comment, you can do so using the **Go To** dialog box. To display the **Go To** dialog box, open the **Edit** menu and click **Go To**. In the **Go To** dialog box, click **Special** to display the **Go To Special** dialog box, which has the controls to select cells with comments (or formulas, or constants, or other special types of contents). When you select the **Comments** option button and click **OK**, Excel will select every cell that contains a comment.

In this exercise, you add comments to two cells. You then highlight the cells with comments, review a comment, and delete that comment.

OPEN: Comments from the *SBS\Excel\Collaborating* folder.

**1**  Click cell D3.

**2**  On the **Insert** menu, click **Comment**.

A comment field appears.

| C | D | E | F | G |
|---|---|---|---|---|
| | **Tools** | **Supplies** | **Furniture** | **Plants** |
| 2003 | $170,150 | Curt: | ,254 | $233,551 |
| 2004 | | | | |
| 2005 | | | | |
| 2006 | | | | |

**3**  In the comment field, type **Remember to figure in our two new lines** and then click cell F5.

A red comment flag appears in the upper right corner of cell D3.

**4**  Move the mouse pointer over cell D3.

The comment in cell D3 appears.

**5**  On the **Insert** menu, click **Comment**.

A comment field appears for cell F5.

**6**  In the comment field, type **Hope to build our own furniture by 2006**. Click on another field to close the comment.

**7**  On the **Edit** menu, click **Go To**.

The **Go To** dialog box appears.

**8**  Click **Special**.

The **Go To Special** dialog box appears.

**9**  If necessary, select the **Comments** option button, and click **OK**.

Cells D3 and F5, which contain comments, are selected.

**10**  Click any cell other than D3 or F5 to clear the selection.

**11**  Right-click cell D3, and then, from the shortcut menu that appears, click **Delete Comment**.

The comment is deleted from cell D3.

Save

**12**   On the Standard toolbar, click the **Save** button to save your work.

CLOSE: Comments.

# Tracking and Managing Colleagues' Changes

*Microsoft Office Specialist*

Whenever you collaborate with a number of your colleagues in producing or editing a document, you should consider tracking the changes each user makes. When you turn on change tracking, any changes made to the workbook are highlighted in a color assigned to the user who made the changes. One benefit of tracking changes is that if you have a question about a change, you can quickly identify who made the change and verify that it is correct. In Excel, you can turn on change tracking in a workbook by pointing to **Track Changes** on the **Tools** menu and then clicking **Highlight Changes**.

In the **Highlight Changes** dialog box that appears, you select the **Track changes while editing** check box. Selecting this check box saves your workbook, turns on change tracking, and also shares your workbook, allowing more than one user to access the workbook simultaneously. You can use the controls in the **Highlight Changes** dialog box to choose which changes to track, but clearing the **When**, **Who**, and **Where** check boxes will have Excel track all changes. Now whenever anyone makes a change to the workbook, the change will be attributed to the user logged in to the computer from which the change was made. Each user's changes will be displayed in a unique color. As with a comment, when you move the mouse pointer over a change, the date and time the change was made and the name of the user who made it appear as a ScreenTip.

Once you and your colleagues are finished modifying a workbook, you can decide which changes to accept and which changes to reject. To start the process, on the **Tools** menu, point to **Track Changes**, and then click **Accept or Reject Changes**. After you clear the message box indicating that Excel will save your workbook, the **Select Changes to Accept or Reject** dialog box appears.

You can use the **When** down arrow to choose which changes to review. The default choice is **Not yet reviewed**, but you can also click **Since date** to open a dialog box into which you can enter the starting date of changes you want to review. To review all changes in your workbook, clear the **When**, **Who**, and **Where** check boxes.

When you are ready to accept or reject changes, click **OK**. The **Accept or Reject Changes** dialog box appears, with the first change described in the body of the dialog box. Clicking the **Accept** button lets the change take effect, while clicking the **Reject** button removes the change, restores the cell to its previous value, and erases any record of the change. Clicking **Accept All** or **Reject All** will implement all changes or restore all cells to their original values, but you should choose one of those options only if you are *absolutely certain* you are doing the right thing.

If you want an itemized record of all changes you have made since the last time you saved the workbook, you can add a History worksheet to your workbook. To add a History worksheet, open the **Highlight Changes** dialog box and select the **List changes on a new sheet** check box. When you click **OK**, a new worksheet, named *History*, appears in your workbook. The next time you save your workbook, the History worksheet is deleted.

In this exercise, you turn on change tracking in a workbook, accept or reject changes, and create a History worksheet.

OPEN: Tracking from the *SBS\Excel\Collaborating* folder.

1   On the **Tools** menu, point to **Track Changes** and then click **Highlight Changes**.

The **Highlight Changes** dialog box appears.

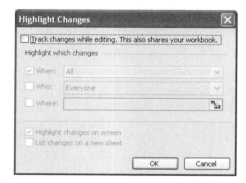

2   Select the **Track changes while editing** check box.

**Tip**   Selecting the **Track changes while editing** check box also turns on workbook sharing.

3   If necessary, clear the **When** check box.

4   If necessary, clear the **Who** check box.

5   If necessary, select the **Highlight changes on screen** check box.

6   Click **OK**.

The **Highlight Changes** dialog box disappears.

7   Click **OK** to save the workbook and clear the message box that appears.

8   In cell D3, type 235000 and press ⏎.

The value *$235,000* appears in cell D3, the cell is outlined in the color assigned to the current user, and a flag appears in the upper left corner of the cell.

9   In cell D4, type 300000 and press ⏎.

The value *$300,000* appears in cell D4, the cell is outlined in the color assigned to the current user, and a flag appears in the upper left corner of the cell.

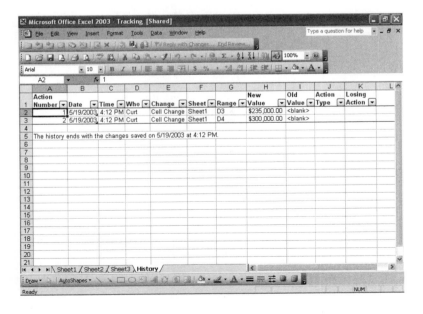

| | C | D | E | F | G |
|---|---|---|---|---|---|
| | | **Tools** | **Supplies** | **Furniture** | **Plants** |
| **2003** | | $170,150 | $253,402 | $105,254 | $233,551 |
| **2004** | | $235,000 | | | |
| **2005** | | $300,000 | | | |
| **2006** | | | | | |

Save

**10** On the Standard toolbar, click the **Save** button to save your work.

**11** On the **Tools** menu, point to **Track Changes** and then click **Highlight Changes**.

The **Highlight Changes** dialog box appears.

**12** Select the **List changes on a new sheet** check box, and then click **OK**.

**Tip** If the workbook had sharing turned on when you enabled change tracking, the **List changes on a new sheet** check box would have been available when you opened the **Highlight Changes** dialog box earlier.

A new worksheet named *History* appears in the workbook.

**13** If necessary, on the tab bar, click the **History** sheet tab.

The History worksheet appears.

**14** On the tab bar, click the **Sheet1** sheet tab.

The Sheet1 worksheet appears.

**15** Click cell A1.

**16** On the **Tools** menu, point to **Track Changes** and then click **Accept or Reject Changes**.

**17** Click **OK** to save the workbook and clear the message box that appears.

The **Select Changes to Accept or Reject** dialog box appears.

**18** Verify that the **When** check box is selected and that *Not yet reviewed* appears in the **When** box.

**19** Click **OK**.

The **Accept or Reject Changes** dialog box appears with the first change listed.

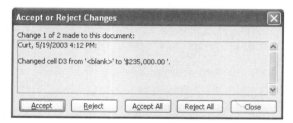

**20** Click **Accept** to accept the change.

The second change appears in the dialog box.

**21** Click **Reject**.

The value in cell D4 is removed, and the History worksheet is deleted.

**22** On the Standard toolbar, click the **Save** button to save your work.

CLOSE: Tracking.

# Identifying Which Revisions to Keep

*Microsoft*
*Office*
*Specialist*

Tracking changes lets you and your colleagues modify a document, maintain a record of the changes, and choose which changes to keep in the final version. When every individual with input into a document can't access the same copy of the workbook, such as if a senior manager is away on a business trip, you can still allow your colleagues input into the final version of a document by sending them duplicates of the original document and then merging the changes in their copies into the original document.

To distribute copies of a document and merge the changes into the original, the files involved must meet these criteria:

■ All distributed files must be copies of the same workbook, which must have had sharing, change tracking, and change history turned on when it was copied.

■ All files must have different file names.

■ All files must either have no password or have the same password.

■ All distributed files must have maintained a change history continuously since distribution (that is, never had sharing, change tracking, or change history turned off).

When all files meet these criteria, you can merge changes from the distributed copies of a file into the original file and then choose which changes to keep. To begin merging files, open the original file and then, on the **Tools** menu, click **Compare and Merge Workbooks**. When you do, the **Select Files to Merge Into Current Workbook** dialog box appears.

Hold down Ctrl while you click the files to merge into the active workbook, and then click **OK** to make the changes appear in the active workbook.

**Troubleshooting**   If the changed cells don't display with a flag in the upper left corner or with an outline around the cells, on the **Tools** menu, point to **Track Changes**, and then click **Highlight Changes** to open the **Highlight Changes** dialog box. In the **Highlight Changes** dialog box, clear the **When** check box and then click **OK**. The dialog box will disappear, and the changed cells will have change flags and outlines.

To pick which changes to keep, on the **Tools** menu, point to **Track Changes**, and then click **Accept or Reject Changes**. Click **OK** to clear the **Select Changes to Accept or Reject** dialog box and display the **Accept or Reject Changes** dialog box. You can then accept or reject individual changes. If there are conflicting changes for a cell, all changes for that cell will appear in the **Accept or Reject Changes** dialog box. You select which changes to keep by clicking the desired change and then clicking **Accept**.

In this exercise, you merge changes from two workbooks into a master workbook.

OPEN: MergeTarget from the *SBS\Excel\Collaborating* folder.

**1**   On the **Tools** menu, click **Compare and Merge Workbooks**.

The **Select Files to Merge Into Current Workbook** dialog box appears.

**2**   Hold down Ctrl while clicking **Buyer.xls** and **Owner.xls**, and then click **OK**.

The changes from the other files appear in MergeTarget.xls.

**Troubleshooting** If there are no flags in the corners of cells with changes, on the **Tools** menu, point to **Track Changes**, and then click **Highlight Changes**. In the **Highlight Changes** dialog box, clear the **When** check box and then click **OK**.

**Save**

**3** On the Standard toolbar, click the **Save** button to save your work.

**4** On the **Tools** menu, point to **Track Changes** and then click **Accept or Reject Changes**.

The **Select Changes to Accept or Reject** dialog box appears.

**5** Verify that the **When** check box is selected and that *Not yet reviewed* appears in the **When** box, that the **Who** check box is cleared, and that the **Where** check box is cleared.

**6** Click **OK**.

The **Select Changes to Accept or Reject** dialog box disappears, and the **Accept or Reject Changes** dialog box appears with a list of changes in the **Select a value** box.

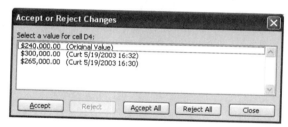

**7** Click the change starting with *$265,000.00*, and then click **Accept**.

The change you accepted takes effect, and the next change appears in the **Accept or Reject Changes** box.

**8** Click **Accept** to accept the change.

The value in cell F4 is *$175,000*, and the **Accept or Reject Changes** box disappears.

**Save**

**9** On the Standard toolbar, click the **Save** button to save your work.

CLOSE: MergeTarget.

# Protecting Workbooks and Worksheets

*Microsoft*
*Office*
*Specialist*

Excel gives you the ability to share your workbooks over the Web, via a corporate intranet, and by copying files for other users to take with them on business trips. An important part of sharing files, however, is ensuring that only those users you want to have access to the files can open or modify them. For example, The Garden Company might have a series of computers available on the sales floor so that sales associates can look up prices and inventory information. While those computers are vital tools in making sales, it wouldn't help the company to have customers, even those with good intentions, accessing critical workbooks.

You can limit access to your workbooks, or elements within a workbook, by setting passwords. Setting a password for an Excel workbook means that any users who want to access the protected workbook must enter the workbook's password in a dialog box that appears when they try to open the file. If the person doesn't know the password, he or she will be unable to open the workbook.

To set a password for a workbook, open the workbook to be protected, and on the **File** menu, click **Save As**. The **Save As** dialog box appears, with the name of the open workbook in the **File name** box.

On the toolbar, click the **Tools** menu head and then click **General Options** to open the **Save Options** dialog box. In the **Save Options** dialog box, you can require users to enter one password to open the workbook and another to modify it. After you click **OK**, a **Confirm Password** dialog box will appear so that you can verify the passwords required to access and modify the workbook. After you have confirmed the passwords, click **Save** in the **Save As** dialog box to finish adding password protection to the workbook. To later remove the passwords from a workbook, repeat these steps, but delete the passwords from the **Save Options** dialog box and save the file.

**Tip**   The best passwords are random strings of characters, but random characters are hard to remember. One good method of creating hard-to-guess passwords is to combine elements of two words with a number in between. For example, you might have a password *wbk16pro*, which could be read as "workbook, Chapter 16, protection." In any event, avoid dictionary words in English or any other language, as they can be found easily by password-guessing programs available on the Internet.

If you want to allow anyone to open a workbook but want to prevent unauthorized users from editing a worksheet, you can protect a worksheet by displaying that worksheet, pointing to **Protection** on the **Tools** menu, and then clicking **Protect Sheet** to open the **Protect Sheet** dialog box.

In the **Protect Sheet** dialog box, you select the **Protect worksheet and contents of locked cells** check box to protect the sheet. You can also set a password that a user must type in before protection can be turned off again and choose which elements of the worksheet a user can change while protection is turned on. To allow a user to change a worksheet element without entering the password, select the check box next to that element's name.

The check box at the top of the worksheet mentions *locked cells*. A locked cell is a cell that can't be changed when worksheet protection is turned on. You can lock or unlock a cell by right-clicking the cell and choosing **Format Cells** from the shortcut menu that appears. In the **Format Cells** dialog box, you click the **Protection** tab to display the **Protection** tab page and select the **Locked** check box.

When worksheet protection is turned on, selecting the **Locked** check box prevents unauthorized users from changing the contents or formatting of the locked cell, while selecting the **Hidden** check box hides the formulas in the cell. You might want to hide the formula in a cell if you draw sensitive data, such as customer contact information, from another workbook and don't want casual users to see the name of the work-book in a formula.

Finally, you can password-protect a cell range. For example, you might want to let users enter values in most worksheet cells but also want to protect the cells with for-mulas that perform calculations based on those values. To password-protect a range of cells, select the cells to protect, and then on the **Tools** menu, point to **Protection** and click **Allow Users to Edit Ranges**. The **Allow Users to Edit Ranges** dialog box appears.

To create a protected range, click the **New** button to display the **New Range** dialog box. Type a name for the range in the **Title** box, and then type a password in the **Range password** box. When you click **OK**, Excel will ask you to confirm the password; after you do, click **OK** in the **Confirm Password** dialog box and again in the **Allow Users to Edit Ranges** dialog box to protect the range. Now whenever a user tries to edit a cell in the protected range, he or she will be prompted for a password.

**Tip**   Remember that a range of cells can mean just one cell!

In this exercise, you password-protect a workbook, a worksheet, and a range of cells and then hide and unhide the formula in a cell.

OPEN: Protection from the *SBS\Excel\Collaborating* folder.

**1**   On the **File** menu, click **Save As**.

The **Save As** dialog box appears.

**2**   Click the **Tools** menu head, and then click **General Options**.

The **Save Options** dialog box appears.

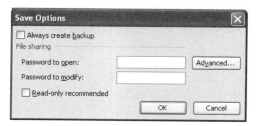

**3**   In the **Password to open** box, type wbk16pro and then click **OK**.

The **Confirm Password** dialog box appears.

**4**     In the **Reenter password to proceed** box, type wbk16pro and then click **OK**.

The **Confirm Password** dialog box disappears.

**5**     Click **Save**.

**6**     If a message box appears, click **Yes** to close it.

Excel saves the workbook, and the **Save As** dialog box disappears.

**7**     On the tab bar, click the **March** sheet tab to move to the March worksheet.

**8**     On the **Tools** menu, point to **Protection** and then click **Protect Sheet**.

The **Protect Sheet** dialog box appears.

**9**     In the **Password to unprotect sheet** box, type wbk16pro and then click **OK**.

The **Confirm Password** dialog box appears.

**10**    Type wbk16pro in the space provided, and then click **OK**.

The **Confirm Password** dialog box disappears.

**11**    On the **Tools** menu, point to **Protection** and then click **Unprotect Sheet**.

The **Unprotect Sheet** dialog box appears.

**12**    In the **Password** box, type wbk16pro and then click **OK**.

The **Unprotect Sheet** dialog box disappears, and the password is removed.

**13**    Select cells L36:O36.

**14**    On the **Tools** menu, point to **Protection** and then click **Allow Users to Edit Ranges**.

The **Allow Users to Edit Ranges** dialog box appears.

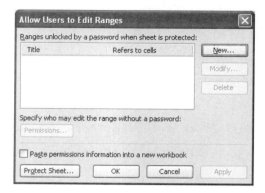

15   Click **New**.

The **New Range** dialog box appears, with =$L$36:$O$36 in the **Refers to cells** box.

16   In the **Title** box, type LastDay.

17   In the **Range password** box, type wbk16pro and then click **OK**.

The **Confirm Password** dialog box appears.

18   Type wbk16pro, and then click **OK**.

The **Confirm Password** dialog box disappears.

19   Click **OK**.

The **Allow Users to Edit Ranges** dialog box disappears.

20   On the **Tools** menu, point to **Protection** and then click **Allow Users to Edit Ranges**.

The **Allow Users to Edit Ranges** dialog box appears.

21   In the **Ranges** box, click **LastDay** and then click **Delete**.

The range disappears from the dialog box.

22   Click **OK** to close the **Allow Users to Edit Ranges** dialog box.

23   Right-click cell Q38, and then, from the shortcut menu that appears, click **Format Cells**.

The **Format Cells** dialog box appears.

24   Click the **Protection** tab to display the **Protection** tab page.

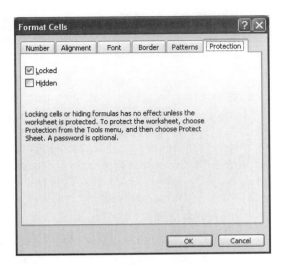

**25** Select the **Hidden** check box, and then click **OK**.

The **Format Cells** dialog box disappears.

**26** On the **Tools** menu, point to **Protection** and then click **Protect Sheet**.

The **Protect Sheet** dialog box appears.

**27** Click **OK** to close the **Protect Sheet** dialog box.

The **Protect Sheet** dialog box disappears. Cell Q38 still has the value calculated by its formula, but the formula doesn't appear in the formula bar.

**28** On the **Tools** menu, point to **Protection** and then click **Unprotect Sheet**.

The formula in cell Q38 appears in the formula bar.

**29** On the Standard toolbar, click the **Save** button to save your work.

Save

CLOSE: Protection.

# Authenticate Workbooks

*Microsoft*
*Office*
*Specialist*

The unfortunate reality of exchanging files over networks, especially over the Internet, is that you need to be sure you know where the files you're working with came from. One way an organization can guard against files with viruses or substitute data is to authenticate every workbook using a digital signature. A digital signature is a value, created by combining a user's unique secret digital signature file mathematically with the contents of the workbook, that programs such as Excel can recognize and use to verify the identity of the user who signed the file. A good analog for a digital signature is a wax seal, which was used for thousands of years to verify the integrity and origin of a document.

**Note** The technical details of and procedure for managing digital certificates are beyond the scope of this book, but your network administrator should be able to create a digital certificate for you. You can also directly purchase a digital signature from a third party, which can usually be renewed annually for a small fee. For the purposes of this book, you'll use the *selfcert.exe* Office accessory program to generate a certificate with which to perform the exercise at the end of the chapter. This type of certificate is useful for certifying a document on your own computer but is not a valid certificate to verify yourself to others across your network or on the Internet.

Read the information that explains the limitations of a self-signed digital certificate. Notice too that you can click the link **Click here for a list of commercial certificate authorities** if you want to purchase a digital certificate that can be used to verify your identity over a network or the Internet. To create a digital certificate you can use as a demonstration, you would open the **Start** menu and click **Run**. In the **Open** box, type **C:\Program Files\Microsoft Office\OFFICE11\Selfcert.exe** (or the directory where Office is installed, if not in the default directory) and press ⏎. In the **Create Digital Certificate** dialog box, type a name for your certificate and click **OK** to have the program create your trial certificate. Then, on the **Tools** menu, click **Options**. In the **Options** dialog box, click the **Security** tab, and click **Digital Signatures**. In the **Digital Signatures** dialog box, click **Add** to display the **Select Certificate** dialog box.

In the **Select Certificate** dialog box, click the certificate with which you want to sign the workbook and click **OK**. The **Select Certificate** dialog box will disappear, and the certificate with which you signed the workbook will be listed in the **The following have digitally signed this document** box. Click **OK** to close the **Digital Signatures** dialog box, and again to close the **Options** dialog box.

In this exercise, you create a digital certificate and digitally sign a workbook with the certificate.

OPEN: Signature from the *SBS\Excel\Collaborating* folder.

**1** On the **Start** menu, click **Run**.

The **Run** dialog box appears.

**2** Type **C:\Program Files\Microsoft Office\OFFICE11\Selfcert.exe** in the **Open** box, and press ⏎.

**Note** If Office 2003 is installed in a different location than indicated above, you will need to adjust the path accordingly.

The **Create Digital Certificate** dialog box appears.

**3**   In the **Your Certificate's Name** box, type **ExcelTrial,** and click **OK**.

Selfcert.exe creates your trial certificate.

**4**   Click **OK** to close the **SelfCert Success** message box.

**5**   On the **Tools** menu, click **Options**.

The **Options** dialog box appears.

**6**   Click the **Security** tab to display the **Security** tab page, and click **Digital Signatures**.

The **Digital Signatures** dialog box appears.

**7**   Click **Add**.

The **Select Certificate** dialog box appears and lists available certificates.

**8**   Click the **ExcelTrial** certificate and click **OK**.

The **Select Certificate** dialog box disappears, and the certificate with which you signed the workbook will be listed in the **The following have digitally signed this document** box.

**9**   Click **OK** to close the **Digital Signatures** dialog box, and again to close the **Options** dialog box.

**10**   On the Standard toolbar, click the **Save** button to save your work.

Save

**CLOSE: Collaborating.**

# Key Points

- Sharing a workbook lets more than one user view and edit the data at one time, which is useful in group projects where each member has a distinct area of responsibility.

- Sending files by e-mail is a very efficient means of collaborating with colleagues.

- Adding comments to cells is a quick way to let your colleagues know what you're thinking, without taking up valuable space in a cell.

- Use the **Go To** dialog box to find cells with special contents, such as comments, constants, or formulas.

- Tracking changes is vital when you share responsibility for a workbook with several other people.

- If your colleagues aren't in the office when you are, you can distribute copies of your workbook and later merge your colleagues' changes all at once.

- When your workbook's data is too important to leave lying around in the open, use passwords to protect all or part of the file!

- Authenticating workbooks with digital signatures helps to identify the source of your files, so you won't have to guess about the origins of that next attachment in your e-mail inbox.

# Glossary

**3-D reference**   A pattern for referring to the workbook, worksheet, and cell from which a value should be read

**active cell**   The cell that is currently selected and open for editing

**Add-In**   A supplemental program that can be used to extend Excel's functions

**alignment**   The manner in which a cell's contents are arranged within that cell (for example, centered)

**arguments**   Specific data a function requires to calculate a value

**aspect ratio**   The relationship between a graphic's height and width

**auditing**   The process of examining a worksheet for errors

**AutoComplete**   The ability to complete data entry for a cell based on similar values in other cells in the same column

**AutoFill**   The ability to extend a series of values based on the contents of a single cell

**AutoFilter**   A Microsoft Excel tool you can use to create filters

**AutoFormats**   Predefined formats that can be applied to a worksheet

**AutoRepublish**   An Excel technology that maintains a link between a Web document and the worksheet on which the Web document is based and updates the Web document whenever the original worksheet is saved

**browser**   A program that lets users view Web documents

**cell**   The box at the intersection of a row and a column

**cell range**   A group of cells

**cell reference**   The letter and number combination, such as C16, that identifies the row and column intersection of a cell

**charts**   Visual summaries of worksheet data, also called graphs

**columns**   Cells that are on the same vertical line in a worksheet

**conditional formats**   Formats that are applied only when cell contents meet certain criteria

**conditional formula**   A formula that calculates a value using one of two different expressions, depending on whether a third expression is true or false

**data consolidation**   Summarizing data from a set of similar cell ranges

**data list**   One or more columns of data depicting multiple instances of a single thing (such as an order)

**data map**   A pattern of data represented in an XML file

**dependents**   The cells with formulas that use the value from a particular cell

**driver**   A program that controls access to a file or device

**dynamic-link library**   A file with programming code that can be called by a worksheet function

**embed**   To save a file as part of another file, as opposed to linking one file to another

**error code**   A brief message that appears in a worksheet cell, describing a problem with a formula or a function

**Extensible Markup Language (XML)**   A content-marking system that lets you store data about the contents of a document in that document

**field**   A column in a data list

**fill handle**   The square at the lower right corner of a cell you drag to indicate other cells that should hold values in the series defined by the active cell

**Fill Series**   The ability to extend a series of values based on the contents of two cells, where the first cell has the starting value for the series and the second cell shows the increment

**filter**   A rule that Excel uses to determine which worksheet rows to display

**formats**   Predefined sets of characteristics that can be applied to cell contents

**formula**   An expression used to calculate a value

**freeze**   To assign cells that will remain at the top of a worksheet regardless of how far down the worksheet a user scrolls

**function**   A predefined formula

**Goal Seek**   An analysis tool that finds the value for a selected cell that would produce a given result from a calculation

**graphs**   Visual summaries of worksheet data, also called charts

**hyperlink**   A reference to a file on the World Wide Web

**Hypertext Markup Language (HTML)**   A document-formatting system that tells a Web browser such as Internet Explorer how to display the contents of a file

**landscape mode**   A display and printing mode whereby columns run parallel to the short edge of a sheet of paper

**link**  A formula that has a cell show the value from another cell

**locked cells**  Cells that cannot be modified if their worksheet is protected

**macro**  A series of recorded automated actions that can be replayed

**mailto**  A special type of hyperlink that lets a user create an e-mail message to a particular e-mail address

**Merge and Center**  An operation, initiated by clicking the **Merge and Center** toolbar button, that combines a contiguous group of cells into a single cell. Selecting a merged cell and clicking the **Merge and Center** toolbar button splits the merged cells into the original group of separate cells.

**metadata**  Data that describes the contents of a file

**named range**  A group of related cells defined by a single name

**Open DataBase Connectivity (ODBC)**  A protocol that facilitates data transfer between databases and related programs

**Paste Options**  A button, which appears after you paste an item from the Clipboard into your workbook, that lets you control how the item appears in the workbook

**Pick from List**  The ability to enter a value into a cell by choosing the value from the set of values already entered into cells in the same column

**pivot**  To reorganize the contents of a PivotTable

**PivotChart**  A chart that is linked to a PivotTable and that can be reorganized dynamically to emphasize different aspects of the underlying data

**PivotTable**  A dynamic worksheet that can be reorganized by a user

**portrait mode**  A display and printing mode whereby columns run parallel to the long edge of a sheet of paper

**precedents**  The cells that are used in a formula

**primary key**  A field or group of fields with values that distinguish a row in a data list from all other rows in the list

**property**  A file detail, such as an author name or project code, that helps identify the file

**query**  A statement that locates records in a database

**range**  A group of related cells

**refresh**  To update the contents of one document when the contents of another document are changed

**relative reference**   A cell reference in a formula, such as =B3, that refers to a cell that is a specific distance away from the cell that contains the formula. For example, if the formula =B3 were in cell C3, copying the formula to cell C4 would cause the formula to change to =B4.

**report**   A special document with links to one or more worksheets from the same workbook

**rows**   Cells that are on the same horizontal line in a worksheet

**scenarios**   Alternative data sets that let you view the impact of specific changes on your worksheet

**schema**   A document that defines the structure of a set of XML files

**sharing**   Making a workbook available for more than one user to open and modify simultaneously

**sheet tab**   The indicator for selecting a worksheet, located in the lower left corner of the workbook window

**smart tags**   A Microsoft Office technology that recognizes values in a spreadsheet and finds related information on the Web

**sort**   To reorder the contents of a worksheet based on a criterion

**split bar**   A line that defines which cells have been frozen at the top of a worksheet

**subtotals**   Partial totals for related data in a worksheet

**tables**   Data lists in a database

**tags**   Marks used to indicate display properties or to communicate data about the contents of a document

**template**   A workbook used as a pattern for creating other workbooks

**trend line**   A projection of future data (such as sales) based on past performance

**validation rule**   A test that data must pass to be entered into a cell without generating a warning message

**what-if analysis**   Analysis of the contents of a worksheet to determine the impact that specific changes have on your calculations

**workbook**   The basic Excel document, consisting of one or more worksheets

**worksheet**   A page in an Excel workbook

**workspace**   An Excel file type (.xlw) that allows you to open several files at once

# Index

NOTE: Items with roman numerals refer to the Quick Reference pages at the front of the book.

# X

# Z

# Curtis Frye

Curt Frye is a freelance writer from Portland, Oregon. He is the author of five books from Microsoft Press: *Microsoft Excel 2003 Step by Step, Microsoft Access 2002 Plain & Simple, Microsoft Excel 2002 Plain & Simple, Microsoft Excel 2002 Step by Step,* and *Faster Smarter Home Networking.* He contributed six chapters to *Microsoft Office v. X for Mac Inside Out.* He's also written several other books and online courses on Microsoft technologies, programming, and privacy-enhancing technologies.

Before beginning his writing career in June 1995, Curt spent four years with The MITRE Corporation as a defense trade analyst and one year as Director of Sales and Marketing for Digital Gateway Systems, an Internet service provider. Curt graduated from Syracuse University in 1990 with an honors degree in political science. When he's not writing, Curt is a professional improvisational comedian with ComedySportz.

# Acknowledgments

Creating a book is a time-consuming (sometimes all-consuming) process, but working within an established relationship makes everything go much more smoothly. In that light, I'd like to thank Alex Blanton, the acquisitions editor, for inviting me back for another tilt at the windmill. I've been lucky to work with Microsoft Press for the past three years, but this is my first time sharing a project with Aileen Wrothwell, the Step by Step series editor. She kept us all on track and moving forward while maintaining her sense of humor.

I'd also like to thank technical editor and production coordinator Curtis Philips of Publishing.com. Aileen touted his group as one of Microsoft's best packagers, and they all lived up to their reputation. Curt Philips did a great job with the technical edit, Teri Kieffer kept me on the straight and narrow with a thorough copy edit, Molly Sharp brought everything together as the book's compositor, and Andrea Fox completed the project with a careful proofread. I hope I get the chance to work with all of them again.

# Learning
## solutions for *every*
# software user

**Microsoft Press learning solutions are ideal for every software user—from business users to developers to IT professionals**

Microsoft Press® creates comprehensive learning solutions that empower everyone from business professionals and decision makers to software developers and IT professionals to work more productively with Microsoft® software. We design books for every business computer user, from beginners up to tech-savvy power users. We produce in-depth learning and reference titles to help developers work more productively with Microsoft programming tools and technologies. And we give IT professionals the training and technical resources they need to deploy, install, and support Microsoft products during all phases of the software adoption cycle. Whatever technology you're working with and no matter what your skill level, we have a learning tool to help you.

**The tools you need to put technology to work.**

**Microsoft**®
**microsoft.com/mspress**